AFRICAN FEMINIST POLITICS OF KNOWLEDGE

Tensions, Challenges, Possibilities

Edited by
Akosua Adomako Ampofo and Signe Arnfred

NORDISKA AFRIKAINSTITUTET 2009

Indexing terms:
Gender studies
Feminism
Women's rights
Academic freedom
Higher education
Research
Research workers
Women in development
Empowerment
Africa south of Sahara

Cover illustration:
Wangechi Mutu
Mask (Yoruba), 2006
6 1/2 x 4 3/4 inches
Contact paper and photo collage
Copyright Wangechi Mutu
Courtesy of the Sikemma Jenkins Gallery and the artist

Cover design: Rogue Four Design
Language checking: Peter Colenbrander
Index: Rohan Bolton
ISBN 978-91-7106-662-6
© The authors and Nordiska Afrikainstitutet 2010

Contents

Introduction: Feminist Politics of Knowledge
*Signe Arnfred and Akosua Adomako Ampofo,
Denmark/Ghana*... 5

Chapter 1 One Who has Truth – She has Strength:
The Feminist Activist Inside and Outside the Academy
in Ghana
Akosua Adomako Ampofo, Ghana................................... 28

Chapter 2 Connections to Research:
The Southern African Network of Higher Education
Institutions Challenging Sexual Harassment /Sexual
Violence, 1996-2001
Jane Bennett, South Africa... 52

Chapter 3 Reflections of a Feminist Scholar-Activist in Nigeria
Charmaine Pereira, Nigeria... 83

Chapter 4 Advocacy for Women's Reproductive and Sexual Health
and Rights in Africa:
Between the Devil and the Deep Blue Sea
Adetoun Ilumoka, Nigeria.. 111

Chapter 5 Critical Feminism in Mozambique:
Situated in the Context of our Experience as Women,
Academics and Activists
Isabel Maria Casimiro and Ximena Andrade, Mozambique 137

Chapter 6 Disappearing Dodos?
Reflections on Women and Academic Freedom Based on
Experiences in Ghana and the United States
Nancy Lundgren and Mansah Prah, Ghana...................... 157

Chapter 7 Doing Women's Studies:
Problems and Prospects for Researchers and Activists
in Nigeria
Nkoli N Ezumah, Nigeria.. 187

Chapter 8 Discursive Challenges for African Feminisms
          Desiree Lewis, South Africa.. 205
Contributors 222
Index   226

INTRODUCTION

Feminist Politics of Knowledge

Signe Arnfred and Akosua Adomako Ampofo

This book has two aims. First we seek to create a space in which feminist manoeuvrings in the diverse and often troubled waters of donor agencies, university institutions and governmental and non-governmental organisations are revealed and discussed. We expose the dilemmas and conflicts that feminist researcher-practitioners living and working in the Global South have to deal with on a daily basis. The chapters are written by feminist researchers and activists living and working in Africa. However, we believe that many of the challenges addressed will be recognised by feminist researchers living anywhere in the postcolonial world. The book does not seek to 'represent the entire continent', nor does it provide an exhaustive list of the kinds of challenges postcolonial feminist researchers and practitioners in Africa face. Second, we embark on some much needed analysis – disentangling the dilemmas, tensions, challenges and possibilities of feminist research and activism in the minefields of the cultures, practices and expectations of university bureaucracies, donor agencies and North-South collaboration. This kind of analysis is by its very nature 'bottom-up', taking as a point of departure the lived experiences, insights and context-specific reflections of the authors. The volume is innovative in this regard – building knowledge which we did not have before.

The field with which the book is concerned may thus be described as a series of interrelated dilemmas. A major dilemma of general relevance is that of funding. In a situation where much work on gender in Africa is commissioned by donor agencies, it is not always easy for the researchers involved to strike the delicate balance between autonomous research on the one hand and servicing the agendas of donors and/or governments on the other. As far as Africa-based researchers are concerned, the situation is often aggravated by the fact that many African countries and/or universities have not allocated independent funds for research, and that in general university teachers' salaries are not very high. Thus, in order to survive, or simply in order to have funds for academic research, many university employees in Africa take on consultancy work as a complementary activity. The dilemma in this context is the terms of reference for the research and consulting: who decides the research agenda, the focus of the study and the concepts to be used? Thus dilemmas of funding extend into conflicting politics and strategies of knowledge. The epistemic power of donor agencies is a fact to be reckoned with – as testified and discussed in several of the chapters in this volume.

A second dilemma, related to the first, is the extent to which feminist researchers can carve out a relationship between political activism on the one hand and donor-driven projects, programmes and agendas on the other. Sometimes, donor initiatives may be taken up and taken over by feminists, with donor money being used for autonomous, transformative agendas. At other times, donor agendas are allowed to absorb all efforts and energies. The questions that emerge from the chapters are how to take advantage of donor money while maintaining organisational autonomy, and how to deploy donor priorities to serve a feminist agenda.

A third dilemma is the double identity – felt and experienced by many feminists – as academic researchers on the one hand and as activists/advocates for women's issues on the other. On the face of it, there would appear to be no reason why these two identities should not coexist happily, or at least comfortably. In reality, however, praxis and theory are often positioned in opposition to each other. Activists often find theory empty and removed from reality because it fails to speak to women's (and men's) lived experiences, the "immediacy, messiness and raw brutality" (Nnameka 2003, 358) of their lives. Scholars, by contrast, find activists unwilling to engage with the centrality of theory as providing a roadmap for transformation. How are these dilemmas between academic and activist concerns being worked out and resolved in practice? Gender research rooted in activist work, informed by women's struggles on the ground, is often an ideal of politically oriented feminist research. But through which networks and institutions can this work in practice? These are questions the book seeks to answer.

Although the authors of the volume come from different geographical and professional places and positions, they also share many similarities. All are located in a few countries on the African continent: Nigeria, South Africa, Ghana and Mozambique. It was never the intention for the reflections and analyses in this book to 'cover the continent', and the book does not embark on comparisons between different countries in terms of conditions or possibilities.[1] Further, although the authors come from diverse professional

---

1. We recognise that South Africa has better conditions for research compared to most other African countries.

locations, all are researchers – some are, or have been located in the academy, others are independent researchers, while yet others work within the NGO world, in some cases in organisations they have set up. They theorise from their experiences as persons based in Africa, highlighting the dilemmas and conflicts posed by identities as academics and researchers on the one hand, and dependence on donor funding on the other. Somewhere in the mix are often also ideological commitments to activism and advocacy work that may be in conflict with the philosophies of particular funding agencies or the climate of their institutional bases. The authors present stories of joys and pains, alliances and betrayals, successes and failures. Most write from a first person perspective, not merely because this is a feminist mode of writing, but also because in so doing they are able to unearth the relationships between their personal reflections and feminist politics and epistemologies. Thus, they are compelled to engage with notions of, and commitment to, the social utility of their work.

Bennett and Pereira show how groups of researchers, in spite of consultancy work, through mutual support and organised networks have managed to maintain their own agendas and carry out work whose relevance is perceived along the journey as well as at the destination. Ilumoka's chapter reflects the absurdity as well as the insidious nature of globally problematised issues, while Adomako Ampofo shows that problems of African women, which have been defined in the global North while experienced in the global South, can actually be destabilised both methodologically and conceptually, using funding agencies' money. Adomako Ampofo, Ezumah and Casimiro/Andrade speak to the tensions within and across feminist spaces, but they also show that finding a common ground is possible. There are also more painful accounts, such as those of Lundgren/Prah, and also Peirera, of how the research environment, especially in the university, cannot only stifle imaginative endeavours, but also erode women's sense of competence as knowledge producers. Lewis's chapter is painful at a more general level, showing how feminist endeavours are being coopted and depoliticised through subtle changes in modes of speech: how cooption and compromise occur through language. Throughout the volume, painful accounts intersect with success stories, while the authors also chart the challenges ahead and share visions of (more) feminist futures.

Perhaps some of the authors could be accused of being polemical and providing insufficient 'empirical evidence'. But questions of what constitutes 'evidence', the ways in which what is considered 'knowledge' is gathered and what kinds of 'knowledge' are validated, are among the very issues that the book seeks to highlight. Perhaps it is time for African feminists to speak more forcefully for the liberation of feminist theory (and indeed all theory) from the personalisation and jargons that characterise Western scholarship? For example, Nnaemeka (2003) notes that those whose epistemological journeys are guided by orality are bound to theorise differently from those who come from a more literary tradition. Positionality is important. All the authors argue that what is generally considered mainstream, 'scientific' and 'objective' is usually only 'malestream'. Among the Akan of West Africa, when the community is totally stumped for ideas on an issue or when there is a deadlock over a decision, the community usually consults the *abrewa*, 'old lady'. The old lady's wisdom is received without question and the community can relax in the assurance that she will know what to do. No one requires that she produce 'empirical evidence' for her perspectives. Her perspectives are respected and validated because they have been built over a lifetime of experience, including the spiritual insight that comes with being an abrewa. In the same way, the feminist writers in this volume argue that their experiences and perspectives constitute knowledge that needs to be recognised, validated and included in the business of knowledge production and, ultimately, the transformation of their societies.

The Beginnings and Location of this Project

This project has a history that goes back several years. In 2001, the Nordic Africa Institute's research programme on Sexuality, Gender and Society in Africa, coordinated by Signe Arnfred, called for papers for a conference entitled Contexts of Gender in Africa: Dilemmas and Challenges of Feminist Research. The call was for papers in three sections: 1) Research, Activism, Consultancies: Dilemmas and Challenges; 2) Conceptualising Gender: Reflections on Concepts and Methods of Research; and 3) Thinking Sexualities in Contexts of Gender. However, despite Arnfred's expectation that several people would be anxious to write about the challenges they faced in straddling the multiple roles of researcher, activist and practitioner, the conference, which was held in Uppsala in February 2002, yielded only one paper that spoke directly to the dilemmas of doing feminist research, consulting and activism in Africa. This paper was written by Akosua Adomako Ampofo. Throughout the meeting, both overt discussions as well as less specific observations made it clear that tensions and contradictions exist between and among these spaces of feminist endeavour as they coalesce and collide. Several if not all of the participants had experienced the tensions flowing from the triple identity as researcher, consultant and activist/advocate. Some also spoke of family-related identities as wives and mothers, daughters, sisters, aunts and so forth, and how these impinged on abilities to operate within and across these spheres. Many spoke of the difficulties of simply being a woman and/or working on gender-related issues, and how this created additional tensions. It became clear that these tensions form an important basis for sharing, reflection and analysis. The comments and discussions that followed the presentation of the only paper in the section also called for greater introspection, as all of us work within a global world with the different and often contradictory interests of donor agencies, especially international ones, and local populations. This latter theme emerged as an important one for almost all the authors in the current volume.

At the close of the Uppsala meeting, we (Adomako Ampofo and Arnfred) felt it was important to give words to these tensions and dilemmas. Because these dilemmas, lived by so many but spoken about by so few, are rarely put into writing, we decided to plan a second meeting which would focus specifically on the ways in which research, activism/advocacy and consultancy work challenge and/or reinforce each other. A new call for papers was circulated, and the workshop entitled Research, Activism, Consultancies: Dilemmas and Challenges was held at the University of Ghana in October 2003. The majority of the papers in this volume were first presented at that workshop. As is so often the case with edited collections like this one, the final assemblage of papers is the outcome of several factors. There was the open call for papers, but there were also specific attempts on our part to cover certain aspects of the issues we felt the collection ought to address. We wanted a mixture of researcher/activist identities; we wanted authors located in universities and outside universities; we wanted to show the interrelationship between women/feminist researchers and different types of women's organisations. We also wanted the papers (some of them at least) to reflect aspects of the history of feminist thinking and organising in Africa. We did not succeed equally well in fulfilling all of these intentions. We tried hard to get a contribution on the history, strengths and weaknesses of one of the very first African women's research organisation, AAWORD (Association of African Women for Research and Development).[2] We didn't succeed on this count. We were also unsuccessful in getting a contribution reflecting the general problems in the field from the specific vantage points of gay/lesbian activist/feminist scholars. Of course, the book may be read by some

---

2. In French, AFARD.

as leaving important themes unexplored – and perhaps this is as it should be, since, as we noted at the beginning, the point was never to exhaust the field, but rather to initiate discussion.

Feminist Politics of Knowledge: Researcher/Activist Alliances

Feminist knowledge must be situated, and very often is rooted in experience. Right from the start of the New Women's Movement, the so called 'Second Wave', knowledge and experience have been closely connected. Women's discovery of the fact that what counted as 'knowledge' (for example, in the social sciences) was based on male experience, often explicitly discounting women, gave rise in part to the very earliest connections between 'women's studies' and the New Women's Movement in the Global North. When Arnfred started her career as a feminist in Scandinavia in the 1970s, students were activists and activists were students. Political activism against gender discrimination in the labour market and for free access to abortions went hand in hand with consciousness raising groups, in which, through the sharing of experiences, young students/activists discovered that the personal is political. In student study circles, we, the students/activists, tried to develop thinking about women's positions in society. We also struggled long and hard against university cultures and authorities in order to redesign disciplines so they would take women's perspectives into account, and in order for universities to give space and resources to special centres for Women's Studies. An aspect of this struggle was the push for taking women into consideration in the context of Development Studies – a field of study which had emerged to support the development aid paradigm that had taken over where colonialism had left off in Africa.

The story of the theoretical and paradigmatic shifts and turns from Women in Development (WID) to Women and Development (WAD), and finally Gender and Development (GAD) have been told and analysed by several authors (see among others Kabeer 1994, Arnfred 2001, Sen 2006) with different emphases. However, what they have in common is a focus on the crucial role of the researcher/activist alliance in the push for integration, first of 'women', then of the power aspects of male-female gender relations in the analysis of 'development' as well as in the practice of development assistance. The push for 'gender' as an analytical category was indeed a push for new agenda setting in 'development', questioning the mainstream/malestream notion of 'development' spearheaded by the Bretton Woods Institutions (primarily the World Bank and the International

Monetary Fund, IMF). The series of UN World conferences on Women, Human Rights and Population held in the 1980s and 1990s provided a space for further advancements in feminist agendas in the area of 'development'. This advancement was still rooted in researcher/activist cooperation and culminated in the Platform for Action accepted at the Fourth World Conference on Women held in Beijing in 1995. In Africa, feminist scholarship and activism began to gain a foothold in women and development debates in the 1970s and 1980s. Both scholars and activists were involved in the establishment of the Association of African Women for Research and Development (AAWORD/AFARD) in Dakar in 1977. AAWORD envisioned an agenda for African feminism through research and activism (Adomako Ampofo et al. 2004).

Since then, however, the specific character of researcher/activist cooperation has changed from a situation where, as in Scandinavia in the 1970s, the researcher and the activist was more or less the same person, to one in which activism tends to be more local and specific (and often localised in the South), while research is perceived as more global, generalised and rooted in Northern perspectives. During this same period, many things have changed both in the women's movement and in the 'development' industry. Feminist theorising in the North, as noted by Lewis in this volume has lost the close contact with activism, becoming increasingly professionalised in an academic sense, transformed into a means for individual academic merit and career.[3] And in the field of 'development', to an increasing extent 'development discourse' has assumed a life of its own. Here the point of 'theory' is frequently to justify and legitimise practice, rather than to act as a guide for practice in a process of transformation. Development discourse may be seen, as Vincent Tucker argues, as "part of an imperial process whereby other peoples are appropriated and turned into objects" (Tucker 1999:1).

Nevertheless, at the same time other trends may also be discerned. The picture of Women/Gender in/and Development is rarely black and white. Many trends and good intentions are active simultaneously and issues of power and strategy are important in this context (see Arnfred 2001). Presumably, the fact that so many African academics depend on donor funding for their research, including funding from international NGOs, has meant that scholarship has had to have a relationship of some sort, even if a makeshift or tenuous one, with activist work. The challenge is to take advantage

---

3. An important exception to this generalisation is among women of colour in the Global North.

of this demand and to turn it into something useful from a feminist perspective (see Pereira's and Bennett's chapters).

Adomako Ampofo shows how the classroom, which is viewed as the theoretical space par excellence, can itself become an activist space with a conscious transformative agenda. Adomako Ampofo recounts a satisfying experience co-teaching a gender course on Culture and Gender in African Societies, with a focus on Men and Masculinities. She explains how a careful mix of course materials and pedagogic styles had the students (incidentally all male in this case) engaging in reflection and self-analysis, and in some cases led to a willingness to reconsider their own positions. As part of a carefully strategised political move in 2003, just such a transformative feminist agenda for teaching was institutionalised in the Gender and Women's Studies curriculum initiative of the African Gender Institute at the University of Cape Town. The programme brought together teachers of Gender and Women's Studies from across the continent to share, develop and refine resources and pedagogies for teaching that would transform gender relations. Workshops were held, curricula developed and a website and list serve established to facilitate sharing.

Struggling in the Discursive Field

One might assume that the point of carrying out research and creating knowledge would be for such knowledge to become a guide for practice, but this is not necessarily the case. Certainly the knowledge industry attached to development aid has grown. According to some analysts, however, the functions of this particular cooperation between knowledge and development aid has been more about the legitimisation of what already takes place than about the genuine transformation of practice. Guttal asserts, "Development now has entire armies of experts in every possible field at its disposal, ready and waiting to carry out its bidding. While these actors benefit greatly from grants and contracts through development aid budgets, equally important, they contribute to and hold up the massive corpus of knowledge that legitimizes development's existence and justifies its expansion" (Guttal 2006:27). Development buzzwords such as 'participation', 'empowerment', 'poverty reduction' and 'capacity building' – all frequently used in gender-and-development contexts – "lend development activities the normative basis they require, swathing development agencies with the mantle of rightness, and conferring on them the legitimacy to intervene on behalf of 'the poor' and needy" (Cornwall and Brock 2006:67).

These kind of dynamics are also behind the cooption into development discourse of initially radical feminist conceptualisations, from the notion of 'gender' over 'empowerment' to 'women's human rights'. As has been noted by some commentators, the shift in language from WID to GAD has not necessarily been paradigmatic, and for many people 'gender' has merely replaced 'women' (Kabeer 1994). Furthermore, like its earlier predecessor WID, in reality GAD has often restricted itself to dealing with women's practical needs and shown less concern for tackling politics – the unequal gender relations that feed and sustain the subordinate positions of women in many communities. The general picture today is one of radical concepts and ideas being coopted by powerful institutions and being transformed and depoliticised in the process. In her chapter, Lewis shows how processes very similar to those that have taken place in the general field of 'development discourse' have also been played out in the field of national South African politics. According to her analysis, "the emphasis in public discourse of gender transformation ... shifted dramatically from a bottom-up articulation of the interests of women's organizations, to the top-down codification of negotiated rights and entitlements that are believed to have national relevance" (Lewis, this volume).

Feminist reactions to this kind of analysis are diverse. Gita Sen offers an encouraging take on the situation, seeing the cooption of feminist conceptualisations by powerful states and development institutions not as a defeat, but rather as (partial) victory for the women's movement. Sen (2006) analyses the feminist agendas for and struggles during some of the important UN world conferences during the 1990s (particularly the International Conference on Human Rights held in Vienna in 1993 and the International Conference on Population and Development that took place in Cairo in 1994), during which critical research supported by activism waged major struggles to change old concepts and frameworks and introduce new ones. Based on this analysis, she cautions that "such a struggle is not a once-and-for-all-event. Winning the struggle over discourse (as happened at Vienna or Cairo) is only the first step. The greater the victory, the greater the likelihood that others will attempt to take over the discourse and subvert its meaning. The battle is not over, it has just begun" (Sen 2006:139).

The important insight here is that the battle over discourse is a battlefield in itself. Concepts change meaning depending on who uses them, for what purposes they are used and in which contexts they appear. If concepts like 'participation', 'empowerment' and 'poverty reduction' appear in a text along with 'ownership', 'accountability' and 'governance', they are brought to mean something different from what they might mean in a possible alternative 'chain of equivalence' with words like 'social justice', 'redistribution' and 'solidarity' (Cornwall and Brock 2006:71). The idea of a 'chain of equivalence' – meaning "words that work together to evoke a particular set of meanings" – is adopted from Ernesto Laclau. The idea is useful for making clear the extent to which the meaning of certain concepts depends on context and thus on continued struggle. Cornwall and Brock explain that "as a word comes to be included in a 'chain of equivalence', those meanings that are consistent with other words in the chain come to take precedence over other, more dissonant, meanings" (2006:48). The struggle in the field of discourse is not just about the words and concepts in isolation, but is also about how, and in which contexts, they are put to use. According to Gita Sen, feminists must continue struggling in order to maintain the feminist, transformative, agenda-setting meanings and implications of words such as 'empowerment' and 'women's human rights' (Sen 2006).

Deconstructing the Rights Discourse

The discursive victories pointed out by Gita Sen have typically been formulated in a language of rights. This was explicitly the case at the UN international conferences in Vienna and Cairo respectively ('Women's Human Rights' and 'Sexual and Reproductive Health and Rights'). Viewed from African perspectives there are, however, pitfalls embedded in this rights discourse. The battle for meaning must be rooted in men's and women's own experiences. Lewis points out that "transnational instruments set in place a language of rights which targets universal and transhistorical subjects as clients and beneficiaries who 'receive' what has been conceptualised as just mainly by others" (Lewis, this volume). Lewis's focus is on official state-level discourse in South Africa, but it is striking how South African state discourse on women (and gender) runs parallel to international development discourse. Ilumoka's chapter also discusses and deconstructs development discourse. From her point of view as a Nigerian participant in the NGO forum of the UN International Conference on Population and Development in Cairo in 1994, the framing of demands in terms of 'rights' was a Northern feminist agenda. The concept of 'reproductive rights' has come to be accepted almost unquestioningly today: however, in her chapter Ilumoka shows how, during the Cairo conference, pressure was put on African women to conform to the rights discourse "silencing dissent and further exploration into precisely what was meant by reproductive rights, and what might be differing perspectives on them" (Ilumoka, this volume). According to Ilumoka, based on her long experience of work with women's health issues as felt and experienced by Nigerian women, the health priorities of low income urban and rural women are related to means of livelihood, food, clean water, shelter, education and access to health services. They simply don't conceive of reproductive health as separate from other aspects of health that daily confront them. In Ilumoka's view then, to frame these things as rights and to re-prioritise them in terms of what is perceived to be specifically reproductive health issues is to impose a different framework and to redefine local women's roles and identities in a colonial manner.

In this optic, the dominance of the Global North over the South is ever present, a dominance which is also present within the women's movement, silencing dissent and stifling alternative views and perspectives. According to Ilumoka, these North-South as well as regional lobby efforts have done much to weaken national and regional level advocacy in Africa. The pressure is to speak in the accepted language, with no space allowed for conversations about ambivalences or for the voicing of discomfort, for example regarding advocacy of rights to abortion. Hence Ilumoka (this volume) notes that the "magic words – 'reproductive rights' – brought forth donor funding for projects professing to be focused on promoting women's reproductive rights, whilst any critique and reservation was viewed with suspicion". Similarly, Southern NGOs are seen as implementing partners, their task being not to conceptualise local issues and needs nor to define the agenda for action, but simply to implement predefined agendas. Based on this analysis, Ilumoka calls for resistance to the 'rights fundamentalism' imposed from the North. Her point is not that there is no basis for North/South alliances, but that such alliances must include a space for partners in the Global South to develop their own concepts and ideas.

According to this critique of the rights discourse, the struggles in the discursive field are even more complex: they cannot simply be about destabilising the established terminology regarding 'reproductive and sexual health and rights' against threats and onslaughts from conservative forces such as the New Right, some elements within the Catholic Church and/or fundamentalist Christianity and Islam, such as has been the case at the UN conferences. They must also be open to local critique, including the need for meaningful interpretation and reformulation in local contexts. Indeed, as Adomako Ampofo suggests in her chapter, religious spaces can be potent sites for activism, and a feminist (read: secular)/fundamentalist (read: religious) dichotomy may frequently be more theorised than real. Using the examples of an organisation that works on issues of violence against women and children, as well as the work of a coalition pushing for the passage of domestic violence legislation in Ghana, she shows how deeply religious individuals are frequently at the forefront of struggles for women's rights. Unfortunately, all too often the concept of 'rights', especially as conceptualised in discourse framed in the Global North, is pitted against religion as a taken-for-granted enemy or obstructionist force, thereby creating unnecessary cleavages in feminist spaces. Completely overlooked is the distinction between a personal faith in a God or higher power and the major religious institutions (overwhelmingly established by men). A personal faith does not need a religious institution to abide, while a religion and its religious leaders are both defunct without a collective of adherents. Thus, like any human institution, the people who run the religious shows and enterprises may sometimes do so in ways that are at odds with (and may even subvert) the ways in which the 'faithful' understand their relationship to God and her/his tenets.

Hegemonic Notions of 'Sexuality'

Knowledge hegemonies are not only constructed between the North and the South but also internally between feminists. In her chapter, Ezumah makes a similar argument to the one posed by Ilumoka. She recounts an encounter in South Africa during which she was criticised for (over) prioritising Nigerian women's 'reproductive health' concerns and not paying any attention to the seemingly more important question of their sexuality and pleasure. Perhaps the critic saw this as a prioritising of practical over strategic needs. In any case, it reveals that feminists on the continent do not share a common definition of feminist concerns. Implicit in the critique that issues of sexual pleasure have been ignored is a notion, also conveyed by McFadden (2003), that sexual pleasure and power are intrinsic to feminist empowerment and that the silences around them reflect a lack of feminist agency and determination:

> For the majority of black women, the connection between power and pleasure is often not recognised, and remains a largely unembraced and undefined heritage ... In often obscure or hidden ways, it lies at the heart of female freedom and power; and when it is harnessed and 'deployed', it has the capacity to infuse every woman's personal experience of living and being with a liberating political force (McFadden 2003:50).

Here McFadden is arguing in favour of a discourse that enables women to step beyond the "bounded, limited notions of sexuality as being tied to reproduction or to the avoidance of disease or violation". Nevertheless, it is also important to realise that many African feminists do not see the need to privilege sexual pleasure. They see issues of protection from HIV infection and abuse as very important and, from a historical perspective, they see silences around sexuality as legitimate. Charmaine Pereira's response to McFadden captures this aptly: "Why should these silences [about African women's sexualities] simply be *condemned*, given the historical conditions of imperial expansion and racist fascination with the hypersexuality projected onto Africans by Europeans ... Rather than condemning the silences, would it not be more productive to map them with a view to their future exploration and understanding?" (2003:62). It is to such a debate on sexuality that Ezumah returns, revealing the importance of paying attention to context and underscoring the need to avoid designing a universal feminist agenda.

Activism as Feminist Research

Several of the chapters show that close connections between activism and research have remained a characteristic of feminist research in Africa (see chapters by Adomako Ampofo, Bennett, Casimiro and Andrade, Lewis and Peirera). Thought provoking, cutting edge research carried out by African feminists has often been inspired by the researchers' involvement in feminist activism and/or networking. Bennett makes a case for moving beyond research-being-inspired-by-activism to a genuine redefinition of (feminist) research, "moving the term [research] from primary reference to a dynamic between researcher and subject participants, towards a mesh of interaction (textual, communicative, organizational, and individual), which gradually uncovers 'new' information and facilitates fresh, unexpected inquiry" (Bennett, this volume). Based on her own experience over a decisive five-year period of work as a member of the coordination committee of NETSH (Network of Southern African Higher Education Institutions Challenging Sexual Harassment/Sexual Violence), Bennett has developed an argument defining theoretically oriented feminist research as quintessentially disunterested in the polarisation of 'author'/'subject', 'theory'/'experience' and 'intellectual'/'activist'. In the context of NETSH, new insights emerged through discussions and debates at workshops and conferences that brought together network members from diverse professional backgrounds, different universities and a variety of countries throughout the Southern Africa region. Furthermore, within the context of NETSH, new insights also emerged from the difficulties and resistances encountered in the processes of carrying out the committee's work. The difficulties were practical as well as epistemological. In contexts where "academic knowledge was conceptualised as the encyclopaedic alphabet of patriarchal class interests, designed as a code for the exclusion of women and deeply implicated in the material effects of sexism", the institutional culture and authority would almost a *priori* exclude the incompatible authority of the subjective narratives of rape survivors. Bennett describes the evolution of feminist thinking during a series of NETSH conferences between 1994 and 2000. At the first conference (1994), subjective narratives were not given space on the official agenda: even the feminists themselves could not (yet) bridge the gap between 'academic rigour' and 'subjective narrative'. By the second conference (1997), this had changed, and rape survivors' narratives were now taken as a point of departure for further analysis. By the time of the third conference (2000), the focus had moved on to discussions of masculinities and investigations of forces perpetuating institutional cultures of sexual violence. Bennett's chapter gives a detailed and unique description and analysis of how new approaches emerge through discussion and debate between feminists with very different backgrounds. In Bennett's optic, this development of new approaches is in itself a process of research: during these processes boundaries between 'researcher' and 'activist' are blurred and new knowledge is developed through new channels in new institutions.

Building Networks and Institutions: Autonomy is Paramount

Networks such as NETSH are obviously not alternatives to universities, but they are important supplementary sources of knowledge production. This is also Pereira's position in her account of the history of another network, the Network for Women's Studies in Nigeria, NWSN. Pereira argues that the interdependence of universities and other organisations as devices for creating and sustaining knowledge through teaching and research requires recognition, and she posits that the need for scholars to create additional knowledge environments through networks is even more critical for researchers working in the field of gender and women's studies. The need for networks that maintain relations between feminist researchers scattered across different universities and research institutions, which are not infrequently hostile to feminist research and activism, should not be difficult to appreciate. Such networks are also important outside Africa, where feminist academics perpetually find themselves (ourselves) engaged in uphill epistemological struggles with mainstream academia, where 'man' and 'human' are perpetually conflated. According to Pereira, based on her experience of holding NWSN together for a number of years with no funding whatsoever, networks need autonomy and institutionalisation – autonomy in order to be able to set agendas determined solely by discussion among members. Such agenda setting has been the aim of NWSN from the very beginning, "to set up a process through which we will indeed be able to set our own agenda for the future development of gender and women's studies locally, but also with some awareness of the regional and international contexts" (Pereira quoting from Amina Mama's report from the network's inaugural workshop in 1996). Autonomy means autonomy in relation to universities, but also autonomy in relation to donors. Autonomy in relation to universities means minimising struggles with hostile environments. This aspect of the struggle played a major role in discussions during the first NETSH workshop in 1996, where the contradictory problematic of first having to fight for administrative acknowledgement and cooperation, and secondly – in order to maintain that autonomy – having to fight for political disengagement from this same administration was noted. Mama explains "concern was expressed over the difficulty of maintaining political and academic integrity, if we have to depend on administration. Relationships with administration represent a major challenge to all concerned with advancing women's studies" (Mama 1996:65).

Autonomy in relation to donors is a no less thorny issue since networks typically need at least some additional funding over and above what they can generate from members in order to keep them updated, and in order to arrange occasional workshops to share experiences and develop ideas. Membership fees are not enough for this. Personal commitment and collective engagement from members are necessary in any case, but sustainability and institutionalisation are the real challenges, and for this a great deal of funding is needed. Adomako Ampofo describes a network of feminist researchers both within and outside the academy that was born in an institutional (university) space in 1990 and eventually gained official blessing and support in 2005 when it was transformed into a centre at that same university. She shows how DAWS (the Development and Women's Studies Programme) successfully sourced funding from the British Council which enabled it to build a respectable collection of books and films for teaching and research, as well as research grants for its members to spend time at UK institutions. Today, CEGENSA, the Centre for Gender Studies and Advocacy, is officially mandated to carry out advocacy and build links with governmental and civil society organisations in addition to its research and curriculum-development mandates.

Casimiro and Andrade document another important network of feminist gender researchers, the Women and Law in Southern Africa research trust (WLSA). This network was initiated in 1990, partly as a follow up to discussions at the Nairobi UN World Conference for Women in 1985. In the early years, this research network was able to get funding from Danida (Danish International Development Agency) to carry out research combined with lobbying work and legal activism. This was possible because of the close collaboration between the African project managers and a few Danish researchers who had the confidence of Danida, and who acted as intermediaries between the donor agency and the African researchers. However, there have been constant struggles along the way. One problem, from the donor's point of view, has been that the researchers from the seven Southern African countries (including Mozambique) were not sufficiently poor and needy, nor were they rural women – i.e., they did not fit the victim-image, which is often so important in the development aid arena. Another problem has been that the immediate and short term impact of the donor money being spent could not be readily 'measured': donors often measure 'impact' in terms of visibly improved, immediate, quantifiable living conditions for a given target group. The impact of a series of research projects with a feminist inclination needs to be registered and legitimised in different ways. Thus, in terms of funding, the life of the WLSA network has not been smooth. On the other hand, the WLSA experience also provides lessons on the possibilities, through struggles and alliances, for securing funding for feminist research and for developing feminist approaches. According to Casimiro and Andrade:

> We in the Mozambican WLSA team learnt a lot through the regional collaboration, and meetings with feminist researchers in neighbouring countries were of great importance ... It was as part of the research conducted under this project that we acquired our information, our knowledge and our experience of feminist theory. It was in this project that we became feminists, learning that knowledge and the feminist position is recreated and developed day by day. (Casimiro and Andrade, this volume)

As was the case with the DAWS network in Ghana, the Mozambican WLSA was initially located within university space, the Centre of African Studies at the Eduardo Mondlane University. Later, when conditions at the Eduardo Mondlane University grew harsher politically, it moved out and established itself as a research NGO.

All these networks discuss bridging the gap between researchers and activists, although in different ways. NETSH could be characterised as a researcher/activist network, where the sharing of knowledge between 'researchers' and 'activists' is important, so important in fact that the very distinction between 'researchers' and 'activists' may be erased or is at least blurred, with new creative thinking emerging from the meeting between different types of knowledge and experience. CEGENSA, WLSA and NWSN are researchers' networks, where the importance of the network lies in the contact and communication between researchers who share experiences and draw inspiration from each other, for example regarding relevant conceptualisations and research methodologies, curricula for the teaching of gender studies, new literature and so forth. As funding becomes available, actual research projects may also be developed within these networks – as has indeed been the case in all three organisations. All these networks, however, also have an activist agenda, the researchers seeing themselves as activists and advocates, taking an active part in the gender politics of their countries, or – as in the case of NWSN – designing their research as 'action research'. Such action research at NWSN is developed in collaboration with activist agendas, and feeds back into political activism, calling attention to, and fighting against, sexual harassment on those university campuses where the NWSN work takes place.

Dilemmas of Funding

An incipient danger for feminist work in Africa is 'the consultancy syndrome', named thus in the report of the first meeting of the NWSN network in 1996 (Mama 1996:31). 'The consultancy syndrome' encapsulates the interlocking dangers of, on the one hand, low salaries and bad conditions for research in terms of "poor infrastructure, frequent power cuts, lack of communication and computing facilities, no running water, and abominable toilets – and whatever else characterises the daily realities of African university life (though to a lesser extent in most South African institutions than on the rest of the continent)", and on the other hand the "money, prestige and useful-for-the-future donor contacts" (Arnfred 2004:88, 94), which are embedded in consultancy work. Being able to survive as a researcher in poorly equipped university settings often necessitates generation of funds besides one's salary. An obvious and relatively well-paid way to achieve this is, of course, through consultancy work. Consultancies will also often be the only way for the social scientist to actually get a chance to conduct some fieldwork. We acknowledge that scholars in the Global North also engage in consultancy work, for prestige, status and monetary compensation. However, the exigencies for this are less present than for scholars in the South. The material conditions of African academics favour accepting consultancy work. The ethical and methodological dilemmas inherent in accepting being a 'consultant' are highlighted by most of the authors in this volume: they recognise that consultancies are not necessarily beneficial to their work as academics and/or activists. The saying "he who pays the piper calls the tune" summarises the dilemmas inherent in this phenomenon. In the chapter co-authored by Lundgren and Prah, Prah writes about the attractions of consultancy work: for instance, being paid US$ 1,000 for introducing a 'gender perspective' into a road impact assessment report in a matter of 12 days. She doesn't ask many questions, only to discover that the bulk of the report is very superficially done and that she herself will also not be able to do anything that she considers appropriate. "I felt very guilty", she writes. "What kind of research had I done? I thought I had as good as prostituted myself, allowing myself to be used. I had not helped the women in any way, for sure". The story says nothing about the donor being dissatisfied. The Ghanaian colleague who had asked Prah to help with the 'gender perspective' for this assignment was a 'professional consultant', nevertheless doing less than professional work, according to Prah's standards. One aspect of the dilemmas of funding, or at least the dilemma of consultancies, is that demands of consultancy work are very different from those of academic work, without the distinction always being drawn very clearly. Lundgren and Prah relate how consultancy styles of work can creep into university contexts. Lundgren reports from her experience reviewing files for promotion at her university in Ghana, noting that much of the work submitted turns out to be output from donor-related (consultancy) research. She asks: "What does it mean, for example, that out of 23 publications, ten are technical reports, out of the remaining 13, nine are commissioned reports from outside funds and two are training-oriented?"

The issue here is the quality of research, and also concepts, methods and autonomy. These are in fact interconnected. Good scholarly research must be open to questions regarding concepts, theory and methodological approaches. It must have the freedom to be critical and to pose unpopular questions. This, however, is not the style of mainstream donor-commissioned 'research'. As stated in a report from the second NWSN workshop held in 1996, "the incompatibility between some donor agencies and researchers was referred to. Whilst researchers needed the donor's funds (in the absence of domestic sources of funding), donors wanted short, sharp, project research that did not leave room for theory, or researchers setting their own agenda or for the intellectual development of academics" (Pereira1997:51).

In addition to being 'short and sharp', donor-funded project reports must also apply a certain language, in the style of 'development buzzwords'. Thus, donor organisations command not only economic power but also epistemic power. In much research in Africa and elsewhere in the global South, donors set the agenda, either explicitly or implicitly. The World Bank, for example, is a major, indeed a decisive, producer of knowledge (Guttal 2006). The World Bank is staffed by clever academics, who pick up trends, sometimes controversial trends, and reissue them as development blueprints. Such powerful organisations determine what is worth knowing, and also, in some cases, who is deemed worthy as a knower (see Pereira, this volume). What is not worth knowing, in this episteme, will be labelled ignorance. As less powerful or well-known donors follow the powerful ones, an implicit and often unrecognised politics of knowledge is embedded in the dilemmas of funding. On the surface, and in its own self-representation, the World Bank is pursuing 'rightness' and 'goodness' (see examples provided by Cornwall and Brock 2006). However, as pointed out by Pereira "one of the unfortunate consequences of the convergence of epistemic and economic power wielded by funders is that their practice (like that of dictators) is rarely subject to critique". Those who would be able to provide this critique are all too often those who receive the funding – and who bites the hand that feeds her? This is where the comparison with dictatorships becomes relevant: "The willingness to engage with dissenting views is a precondition not only for knowledge building, but also for democratisation. Yet, how many agencies, particularly those that champion both knowledge building and democratisation, are themselves able to engage with dissent or critique?" Pereira asks in this volume. Although most powerful organisations are loathe to give up any of their knowledge-creating clout, shifts in the World Bank's position on poverty eradication over the last decade and a half give room for muted hope. While the Bank's shift in paradigm can by no means be read as feminist, the responses to the Jubilee 2000 movement show that concerted pressure can be effective.[4]

Autonomy and Agenda Setting

Thus, despite the economic and epistemic power of donors, some of the chapters in this volume reflect local resistance and show that despite the minefield it is possible, sometimes, to direct both a theoretical process as well as the methodology of one's work. Getting funding for goals determined by oneself and not by the donor is a field of expertise – and maybe even an art – in its own right.

It is interesting that both DAWS *within* a university in Ghana, and NWSN *outside* the university in Nigeria were able to become institutionalised with UK development assistance funding through British Council Higher Education Links. Both CEGENSA (the Centre for Women's Studies and Advocacy, which developed out of DAWS) and NWSN (now IWSN) determine their own programmes and activities, suggesting that working with particular funders can open up space for autonomous work. This is not to suggest that the British Council does not have a framework (indeed, one currently has to link programmes to one or more of the Millennium Development Goals – MDGs). However, the framework is sufficiently broad to allow for local agenda setting. The funding provided support to run workshops, purchase equipment and other resources such as books and for members to travel to the UK, where they could enjoy much needed space

---

4. *Jubilee 2000* was an international coalition movement in over 40 countries based on the Biblical principle of a 'Jubilee year' quoted in Leviticus (every 50th year), in which inequalities were levelled, as people enslaved because of debts were to be freed and lands lost because of debt were returned. *Jubilee 2000* called for cancellation of Third World debt by the year 2000. Famous supporters of the movement were Bono, Muhammad Ali and Youssou N'dour. Since 1996, in response to *Jubilee 2000* and other civil society and governmental pressures, the IMF and World Bank HIPC (Highly Indebted Poor Countries) programmes have been modified in several ways to include some debt cancellation as well as other reliefs that recognise a stronger link between debt relief and poverty reduction. Gender also formed an important component of the drafting of Poverty Reduction Strategy papers to qualify for HIPC (and hence debt relief) status. Gender also formed an important component of the drafting of Poverty Reduction Strategy papers to qualify for HIPC (and hence debt relief) status. Although the HIPC initiatives that grew out of a response, in part, to *Jubilee 2000* are not about outright debt cancellation they do provide some debt relief and restructuring, and a stronger link between debt relief and poverty reduction, and thus represent a paradigm shift, albeit a rather small one.

to research and write. Although DAWS has now received formal university approval with an ambitious mandate as the Centre for Gender Studies and Advocacy, it is doubtful that either NWSN or DAWS could have survived without the external funding support they received.

Adomako Ampofo describes work in which she carries out research that critiques a dominant concept in population studies with funding received from the Population Council itself. Pereira – who as NWSN coordinator has a great deal of experience in fund raising – suggests that actual research into donor agendas may be needed. One has to study the funding sources and understand them on their own terms. What are their priorities, what programmes do they run, what language do they use? And what are the ideological assumptions underlying the issues as they present them and the determination of their funding priorities? "It seems to me", Pereira says, "that the pursuit of self-determined organizational agendas in the course of fund raising requires an engagement with the donor's own agenda as well as an understanding of, and healthy resistance to, the epistemic power wielded by the donor". Ultimately, the task of raising funds should be seen not as one of carrying out activities for which donor funds are available, but as one of deploying funders' priorities to serve the agenda of one's own projects. This is only partly an intellectual task – writing proposals with an extensive literature review, incisive research questions, appropriate methodology and so on. The covert features of this task have more to do with the internal politics of the funding agency: who runs which programmes?; how much power does 'the boss' wield?; who is willing to defend your proposal if the boss is not enthusiastic?; and the (lack of) internal democracy within funding agencies, including, perhaps even those that ostensibly strengthen 'democracy', 'transparency' and 'accountability'.

Feminism Survives on Visions

Feminist activism and scholarship are ultimately about transformation. Visions and hope for a better future are necessary ingredients of feminist knowledge production. Elsewhere, Pereira puts it like this:

> There is no way of creating knowledge that is not circumscribed by the oppressions of our times if we cannot imagine a better future, if we cannot dream of a way of life that does away with the domination that is part of our everyday realities, if we cannot envision other ways of being. Without imagination, we cannot search for the kind of knowledge that allows us to fully understand our divided realities in order to transcend them. (Pereira 2002)

As argued by several authors in this volume, feminist knowledge must connect to experience, activism and advocacy. In this context, Ilumoka (this volume) notes, "in the face of the onslaught of global capital, growing patriarchal power and the universalising tendencies of powerful Northern women's groups, two processes are indispensable: a) developing clear visions and agendas, and b) organising and institution building to actualise those visions". Activism and knowledge production go hand in hand. As noted by so many feminist scholars over the ages, charting new paths for gender and women's studies is a continuing political, institutional and intellectual struggle. We have tried in this introductory chapter to set out the political, epistemological and financial terrain on which feminist scholarship and activism on the continent is carried out. We hope we have been able to convey not only the challenges that litter the landscape, but also the dynamism of those voyaging across it.

References

Adomako Ampofo, Akosua and Josephine Beoku-Betts, Mary Osirim, and Wairimu Njambi, 2004, "Women's and Gender Studies in English Speaking Sub-Saharan Africa: A Review of Research in the Social Sciences", *Gender and Society* Vol. 18(6):685–714.

Arnfred, Signe, 2001, "Questions of Power: Feminist Theory and Development Aid", in N. Kabeer et al., *Discussions of Women's Empowerment*. Stockholm: Sida Studies No. 3.

—, 2004, "Gender Research in Africa: Dilemmas and Challenges as Seen by an Outsider", in S. Arnfred et al. (eds), *African Gender Scholarship: Concepts, Methods and Paradigms*. Dakar: CODESRIA Gender Series.

Cornwall, Andrea and Karen Brock, 2006, "The New Buzzwords", in Peter Utting (ed.), *Reclaiming Development Agendas*. New York: Palgrave/UNRISD

Guttal, Shalmali, 2006, "Challenging the Knowledge Business", in Peter Utting (ed.), *Reclaiming Development Agendas*. New York: Palgrave/UNRISD

Kabeer, Naila, 1994, *Reversed Realities: Gender, Hierarchies in Development Thought*. London: Verso.

Mama, Amina (ed.), 1996, *Setting an Agenda for Gender and Women's Studies in Nigeria*. Zaria: Tamaza Publishing Company.

McFadden, Patricia, 2003, "Sexual Pleasure as Feminist Choice", *Feminist Africa* (2):50–60.

Nnaemeka, Obioma, 2003, "NegoFeminsim: Theorising, Practicing, and Pruning Africa's Way", *Signs: Journal of Women in Culture and Society* 29(2):358–385.

Pereira, Charmaine (ed.), 1997, *Concepts and Methods for Gender and Women's Studies in Nigeria*. Zaria: Tamaza Publishing Company.

—, 2002, "Between knowing and imagining – What Space for Feminism in Scholarship on Africa", Feminist Africa (1):pp?.

—, 2003, "'Where Angels Fear to Tread?" Some Thoughts on Patricia McFadden's 'Sexual Pleasure as Feminist Choice'", *Feminist Africa* (2):61–65.

Salo, Elaine, 2005, "Multiple Targets, Mixing Strategies: Complicating Feminist Analysis of Contemporary South African Women's Movements", *Feminist Africa* (4):64–71.

Sen, Gita, 2006, "The Quest for Gender Equality", in Peter Utting (ed.), *Reclaiming Development Agendas*. New York: Palgrave/UNRISD

Tucker, Vincent, 1999, "The Myth of Development: A Critique of Eurocentric Discourse", in R. Munck and D. O'Hearn (eds), *Critical Development Theory*. London: Zed Books: 1–26.

CHAPTER ONE

One Who has Truth – She has Strength
The Feminist Activist Inside and Outside the Academy in Ghana[1]

Akosua Adomako Ampofo[2]

Introduction

The title of this chapter speaks to a conviction that maintaining commitment to core feminist goals in one's scholarship and praxis provides the strength needed to carry on scholarship and praxis in a context where the exigencies of life so often threaten to crowd out these goals. These 'exigencies' include, but are not limited to, the need to publish and progress in the academy, as well as the need to earn a living in a developing economy. The context is complicated by the fact that feminist scholarship is still viewed as being on the fringes by many in the academy in Africa. In other words, the threat of having apparently laudable (feminist) goals side-tracked by the material realities of life is very real and ever present. This may lead one to carry out research on subjects, or for organisations, that are at odds with one's (feminist) goals. It may also lead to the unquestioning adoption of the latest epistemological or methodological fads. Furthermore, in the pursuit of one's goals it is easy to fall into the trap of validating the product, for example an increase in the number of courses on women or gender, while paying less attention to the outcome, such as whether these courses are transformative in agenda and content. I contend that ultimately it is only possible to maintain one's strength as a feminist scholar and activist through constant reflection, both personal and communal.

The reflections and proposals in this chapter were first presented at a meeting on Contexts of Gender in Africa held in Uppsala, Sweden, in Feb-

---

1. A reversal and appropriation of a Mamprussi proverb, "One who has strength has the truth".
2. My sincere thanks to the external reviewers, to my sister colleagues Josephine Beoku-Betts and Mary Osirim and co-editor Signe Arnfred, who provided critical comments on earlier versions of this chapter.

ruary 2002. That meeting had three broad themes, one on Research, Activism, Consultancies: Dilemmas and Challenges, for which I wrote the earlier version of this paper, and two others, Conceptualising Gender: Reflections on Concepts and Methods of Research, for which I wrote another paper, "Whose 'Unmet Need' and Issues of 'Agreement' in Reproductive Decision Making" and Thinking Sexualities in Contexts of Gender.[3] As I shuttled between the writing of both papers, I found myself surprised that the one which has evolved into this chapter proved more difficult to write than the more technical theoretical/methodological paper. I had anticipated that this autobiographical narrative would simply flow from my inner being, as it were. This was not to be the case and there were several reasons for this. First, the process of personal reflection and self-analysis as it relates to so-called scientific enquiry remains something many academics, even feminist academics, do very little of, probably because the process does not seem to be a particularly intellectual exercise. After all, most scientific disciplines still train you to remove yourself, and the 'personal' from so-called objective scientific enquiry.[4] Secondly, and related to the first point, even where introspection occurs, it does not usually form part of the so-called intellectual discourse, except, perhaps, as an anecdote to support or expatiate on a finding.[5] Thirdly, African women academics who are also activists are frequently so overwhelmed by the constraints imposed by multi-tasking that we rarely find the opportunity to go behind the scenes of our ideological or theoretical positions to examine and re-examine them, to ask ourselves, "How do I really feel about this perspective? Do I really support this position or have I been compelled to?" Such an examination is important for the simple reason that it provides a barometer that can guide us to re-evaluate

---

3. Incidentally, only one paper was presented under the theme 'Research, Activism, Consultancies: Dilemmas and Challenges' – mine. Most of the remaining papers were published in a book that emerged out of that meeting, *Rethinking African Sexualities* edited by Signe Arnfred (2004).
4. There are a few exceptions to this trend and some notable exceptions are the co-authored pieces "Dialoguing Women" by Nwando Achebe and Bridget Teboh (2007) that appeared in *Africa after Gender* and Josephine Beoku-Betts's and Wairimū Njambi's "African Feminist Scholars in Women's Studies: Negotiating Spaces of Dislocation and Transformation in the Study of Women" that appeared in *Meridians* (2005). The journal *Feminist Africa* also routinely provides personal narratives and interviews with scholar-activists.
5. It is true that feminist work and writing has long engaged with the question of 'subjectivity'. However, this is typically limited to a personalised contextualisation apropos the topic of enquiry and autobiographical accounts per se are less common.

our positions, or even quit particular enterprises that we suddenly discover are at odds with our convictions. As feminist activists, we sometimes run with an issue that we hope will work for the well being of women, or that will promote greater gender equity. Then we develop a political commitment to an agenda that will, we hope, ensure that the issue receives attention. Often we seem to remain glued to this position, seemingly unable to concede that there might be nuances and perspectives that we may have ignored. Ilumoka's chapter in this volume illustrates this from the perspective of reproductive health and the concept of 'rights' and 'bodily integrity'. In our quest to ensure that women have control over their bodies, we run the danger of failing to acknowledge that the concept of rights over one's body is highly political, is viewed differently by women in different contexts (for example, there is frequently a conflict between individual rights, collective rights and individual responsibility) and that women have the right to differ from the perceived 'correct' feminist perspective. As scholars who need to publish, in order to have our intellectual efforts legitimised we work within particular paradigms and theoretical frameworks. Often these paradigms and frameworks are constructed in Western or Eurocentric contexts, either because these are the ones we have been trained in and are familiar with because they are (re)produced in the accepted international journals, or because we feel that failure to work within them reduces the value of our own work. Too often, we remain content to collect data for our colleagues from Europe of North America while they drive the theoretical directions of the intellectual enterprise. Yet in a world that remains divided along geopolitical lines and with conflicting geopolitical interests that determine how knowledge is produced and used, the African researcher cannot afford to provide a mere echo of thoughts emanating from the Global North, nor do we have the luxury, as Mkandawire argued (1997), of being mere empiricists. Happily, emerging feminist scholarship on the continent not only criticises Western forms of knowing and knowledge, it has also engaged in theory building that is impacting global feminist scholarship. I believe that African scholars have to be advocates for the survival of our continent and its people. To understand and appreciate our positions as African feminists located in Africa – positions of privilege and power in some contexts as well as positions of disadvantage and on the margins in others – requires a great deal of personal reflection. Reflections on the challenges and possibilities of these positions are the issues this chapter turns to.

I begin the chapter by providing a brief background of my academic training. I then go on to discuss my experiences as and perspectives on being a researcher/teacher/ consultant and an activist. This is an autobiographical account of the challenges, implications, as well as the responses that these multiple 'roles', responsibilities and allegiances have meant for me.[6] Nonetheless, while I make no claim that this account represents or describes general trends among African feminists, I dare say that my experiences are not unique, and have a broad relevance. On occasion, I have felt contradictions among these 'roles' that I have not always been able to resolve to my satisfaction. At the same time, I also believe the opportunity I have had to straddle these 'roles' has made me more skilful in the performance of each of them, as I have come into contact, made friends and shared experiences with, as well as learned from a variety of people, including many strong, wise, sensitive and intellectually stalwart women. The narrative also addresses my struggles with questions of doing 'academic' versus 'contract' research work, and the construction and dissemination of knowledge. Ultimately, I believe that it is only by being truthful to the principles of a feminist activism that we can be part of, and draw on the strength that emanates from being part of the collective enterprise that gender transformation requires.

My Academic Trajectory

Since the 1980s, African states have undergone much change and upheaval. While some continue to struggle with authoritarian and military regimes, almost all, whether multiparty democracies or dictatorships, whether 'free market'[7] or socialist, have experienced what Mikell refers to as "the failure of male-dominated" politics (1997:1). Our countries have suffered the imposition of Western-designed, neoliberal structural reforms. The economic dependence of our states has encouraged them to neglect the needs of women, who are invariably perceived as having an inelastic supply of emotional and physical energy to deal with the increasing demands placed on many of us. Women's studies and gender analyses within this context have come to be viewed by many feminists, myself included, as a project that will contribute to the desired end of greater equality. As feminists, many of us also feel compelled to become engaged in advocacy that will lead to immediate changes,

---

6. I parenthesise 'roles' because the word suggests that they carry with them comparable responsibilities, which is not necessarily the case.
7. I prefer to parenthesise 'free market' since, for many retailers and buyers in Africa the market has been anything but 'free', its character being determined to a large extent by people from outside the continent both physically and culturally.

such as law reforms. Therefore, as background to the accounts that follow, I present a brief sketch of my feminist journey.

By the time I arrived in my late teens, I had discovered that I was a feminist, as I found a synergy between my convictions and those of feminist scholars such as Mohanty and writers such as Ama Atta Aidoo.[8] Nonetheless, although I self-identified as a feminist, it was not until I was in my 30s that I was able to use the term unself-consciously. As a young student (of architecture), I had little exposure to feminist literature and my early misgivings, given my social context and this limited exposure, were evoked by images of bra-burning, man-hating women who rejected men, marriage, motherhood and family. I certainly enjoyed male company and anticipated marriage and motherhood. My second difficulty with stating my position at the time was with the oft-proposed contradiction between (my new-found) feminism and (my equally new-found) Christian conviction. However, as my knowledge of scripture deepened, and as I became more familiar with liberation theology and different feminisms (including the work of Christian feminists), the tensions eased. I begun to recognise that much of what is presented as "the place of women" by religious leaders did not reflect the life and teachings of Christ. Indeed, for me Christ emerged as someone who would identify strongly with the feminist cause.[9] This 'revelation' was an important part of the personal history that has shaped my philosophies, passions and practice of a feminist existence. For with the biblical Christ as

---

8. For me, a feminist is a person who believes in the equal personhood and humanity of the sexes, and advocates for equal treatment of, and opportunities for, females and males. The difference between people who are merely 'good' human beings who try to treat everyone fairly, and feminists, is that the latter actively promote and privilege the welfare of women (see Mohanty, Russo and Torres 1991).

9. There are several examples of Christ's counter-culture behaviour when it comes to his relationship with women. Jesus associated with women (Luke 23:49) at a time when Jewish tradition frowned on women studying with rabbis. According to Jewish thinking at the time, women were generally viewed as the cause of men's sexual sins, and so to prevent Jewish men from yielding to temptation they were instructed not to speak in public to women, including their own wives. Not only did Jesus speak to a woman in public (John 4:27), he dared to touch women in public (Mark 5:41). He also allowed a 'sinful' woman to shed tears over his feet and to dry them with her hair in a most intimate manner (Luke 8:2). He encouraged a woman who desired to follow him to do so, even when this conflicted with her domestic duties (Like 10:42). While not replete with them, the Old Testament does provide examples of women in prominent leadership positions (see, for example, the story of Deborah, Book of Judges), as do the New Testament letters of Paul.

an example, the feminist project could not be about change by any means possible, nor could it be about condemning those who differed: it meant one could be "Jew or Greek, female or male, slave or free".[10]

My university training in architecture, spatial planning, geography, development planning and finally sociology left a more ambivalent impression, even though the multidisciplinary accumulation helped me escape the restrictiveness of disciplinary correctness, something feminist scholarship seeks to do. Being in male-dominated undergraduate (architecture) and graduate (planning) programmes, my female colleagues and I learned to negotiate, and often struggle, for our space as equal partners. I also picked up a few lessons on how to strategise and lobby potential antagonists. Nonetheless, although at least two of my lecturers revealed sensitivity to gender in the design of buildings, until I entered a PhD programme there was certainly no reference to specific gender frameworks, let alone feminist work, in the rest of my academic training. Indeed, the undertones (and often overtones) of my training frequently encouraged a paternalistic, problem-solving approach to the 'woman question'. The so-called population problem, which became one of my early interests when I joined the University of Ghana as a Research Fellow, should suffice to illustrate first my ignorance and then my journey towards becoming critical.

In 1987, Momsen and Townsend identified fertility issues as one of the most significant aspects of 'women's worlds' in Third World countries. Whether true or not, I dare say that for women in sub-Saharan Africa concerns about our fertility and reproductive health have been among the most studied, discussed and contested of issues. The diverse representations speak volumes about the interpretations of women from the Global South in knowledge production and development efforts, but I will return to the issue of appropriation and representation shortly. During my early years at the Institute of African Studies in the late 1980s and early 1990s, I was attracted by the discourse on women's 'control over their fertility' and the focus on their 'reproductive health'. Constructions of women around childbearing and motherhood seemed logical to me, given my training in development and later in social demography. I was also influenced by the fact that both my father-in-law and husband worked in obstetrics and stories of women's fertility and infertility, childbearing and maternal mortality were daily fare. So while I may have approached the subject with a certain level of righteous indignation and missionary zeal, a critical (feminist) ap-

---

10. See Book of Galatians 3:28.

proach came belatedly and more slowly. There was something seductive in the development and demographic literature, supported by findings from large-scale surveys that pointed to the need to enhance women's uptake of modern family planning services for their physical and even emotional well being. Not to be ignored were the benefits that would accrue to countries of the Global South if women had fewer children. The methodological process based on quantitative analyses also made it possible to see the women (and men) as mere numbers. I am not proud to acknowledge that if I ran statistical analyses that suggested women had an 'unmet need' for contraception, I would get excited.[11] However, slowly an intuitive and intellectual transformation occurred: I became uncomfortable with the instrumental approach to issues of women's reproductive health and behaviour. Slowly, I began to reject much of what I was reading and sought alternative paradigms, for there was something wrong with the binary picture that essentially represented African women as not intelligent enough to be able to determine their fertility, or as completely dominated by and obedient to men. One day, I discovered that there were feminist demographers, and once I began to examine reproductive issues with a more critical eye informed by a feminist perspective, well-established and taken-for-granted concepts such as the notion of women's 'unmet need' for family planning began to crumble. The anecdotes of my father-in-law and husband took on a more nuanced character, involving partners, ex-partners, parents, in-laws as well as the political economy of the country.

The African Feminist Scholar Inside and Outside the Academy: Research

When I first started working as a Research Fellow at the Institute of African Studies, University of Ghana in 1989, I discovered that if I intended to undertake any research or attend conferences, I would have to seek external funding.

Additionally, like many of my colleagues, I began to rely on consulting work to make up for the deficient salary I earned at the time as a university researcher and teacher.[12] This had several implications. First, teaching

---

11. My critique of that demographic concept formed the basis of the second paper I presented at the 2002 conference and which appeared in the book *Rethinking African Sexualities* edited by Signe Arnfred (2004).
12. While salaries are still not adequate, they have improved considerably since those early adjustment years.

and research and consulting are each full time jobs and require significant investments of time if they are to be carried out properly. Further, while contract work paid some of the bills, it generally did little to further my academic career or significantly address issues of transformation. The local or international contractor rarely required one to have a deep or particularly critical engagement with the literature, although I often challenged myself to undertake this task. However, the outcomes have not always been negative. Doing work for international or local agencies has also opened doors to a number of domains which have benefited my work as an advocate by way of the networks I have built, and also because I have been privy to information that has supported lobbying and advocacy, sometimes in relation to the same agencies that have provided financial support. I have also tried to develop innovative ways of inserting the questions I consider important in the research. Finally, new opportunities for mentoring younger scholars have emerged that have been enriching for me both as mentee and mentor. In the next sections, I look at each of these three areas – researcher, consultant and advocate – in a little more detail.

The Feminist Scholar in the Academy

There are many useful articles on the role of African universities in shaping development and political trends in Africa (see, for example, Court 1982; Mkandawire 1997; Sawyerr 1994; Tettey and Pupulampu 2000). There is also a growing body of work on gender issues in the academy (for example Manuh, Gariba and Budu's, and Peirera's volumes in the 2007 Ford Foundation series, as well as two recent issues of *Feminist Africa*).[13] Here I do not repeat those debates, rather I try to link the issue of being a feminist scholar within the academy with one's role as an activist who also, from time to time, engages in contract research. Research, whatever form it takes, is important for the progress of societies, to the extent that it helps us to better understand them. Policies, issues, theories, plans and existing ways of doing things can be clarified and improved on the basis of research, so that research serves as the link between ideas, information and practice. For those of us in the academy, demands are placed on us by national governments, international institutions and our fellow citizens to provide information about particular aspects of society that serve as a basis

---

13. See *Feminist Africa*, issues 8 & 9, 2007 – Rethinking Universities II (http://www.feministafrica.org/index.php/issue_nine)

for planning and decision-making (Atteh 1996; Mkandawire 1997; Tettey and Pupulampu 2000).

The research and teaching terrain for an African woman in Africa is bedevilled by a host of challenges. First, the relations in academia are distorted both in terms of sheer numbers, so that women have low statistical visibility, as well as in terms of existing power relations.[14] Prah (2003) discusses how the low statistical visibility of females has implications for the number of women who will occupy policy-making positions in the university, since it is academics of high rank who get to sit on the influential policy-making boards. She cites how in her own institution, the University of Cape Coast (UCC), between 1995 and 2000 no more than three women sat on the Academic Board at any given time. At the University of Ghana, the picture has been friendlier: between 1995 and 2007 the proportion of women on the Academic Board ranged between 10 and 16 per cent.[15] Prah (2003) argues that groups with high statistical visibility may perceive those with low statistical visibility as weak, unimportant and lacking in status. This affects the balance of power, because those considered to be insignificant are not likely to be considered for influential and high-ranking positions, neither are they likely to be consulted on matters viewed as important unless it is absolutely necessary, as for instance in situations where there is a need to woo all groups in order to build a strong consensus. She contends that a group's low statistical visibility may also affect the self-esteem and confidence levels of its members. For instance, members of such a group might not be motivated to become high achievers because there are very few of them. I have felt this invisibility most sharply when it has come to the use of language. In so many contexts – official meetings, open fora, pubic lectures and on one occasion even in an advert for a deanship – the language refers to a 'he', as if women could not possibly be available or contribute in the capacity under discussion. The language thus excluded me.

Second, within the university system little or no thought is given to

---

14. The average percentage of female academic staff in the three oldest Ghanaian universities in the 1960s, 1970s, 1980s, 1990s was 11 per cent, 9 per cent, 9 per cent and 13 per cent respectively (Brown, Anokye and Britwum 1996).

15. The Academic Board is an important and influential forum chaired by the vice chancellor and currently comprises all professors and associate professors of the university, deans, vice deans, directors of institutes, heads of department and centres and representatives of various units. It is here that major university policies are formulated and discussed. At the University of Ghana, where I teach, 42 of the Board's 285 members were female as at October 2007.

providing support structures that will enable females to perform their work efficiently – support such as the provision of childcare facilities, the organisation of meeting times such that women can still take care of domestic responsibilities, access to accommodation which allows women to perform their multiple roles, and so forth. What all of this means is that before women even begin to think of the time constraints imposed by these multiple roles, they have to deal with the structural barriers that make teaching and research a challenge. Women who choose a way around this by prioritising their careers are perceived as abnormal and frequently made to feel guilty.[16]

Thirdly, female academics would appear to have access to fewer resources either as a result of ignorance about what is available, in itself a built-in structural constraint, and also as a result of more direct discrimination. Female academics themselves certainly perceive that they are discriminated against when it comes to the distribution of resources.[17] Certainly it was my own experience when I was a young researcher that male colleagues knew about opportunities for travel or funding long before the official memorandum reached my institute (and hence me). By this time, the application deadlines were too close, if they had not already passed, to write a decent proposal. These domains remain areas of continual struggle for many women.[18] I have survived within the academy, as well as in my efforts to be an activist and a consultant, for several reasons. First, I have been blessed with an extremely supportive family. Over the years, particularly when my daughters were young, my mother-in-law and her household provided childcare and other forms of domestic support whenever my husband and I have needed these. So, like my male colleagues, I have had access to a wide range of (female) domestic and reproductive services. This support has been provided without any questioning of my maternal competence from those closest to me. Quite the contrary, I have received encouragement and my perceived achievements have been celebrated. I fully recognise that this is a

---

16. Following the work of a visitation panel between 2007-08, the University of Ghana is undergoing major structural reforms, including the implementation of gender-specific actions to support female faculty and students. The Centre for Gender Studies and Advocacy is leading the development of a gender policy, which it initiated in 2006.

17. Respondents in Prah's study (2003) argued, for example, that access to resources has less to do with scarcity than with how these resources are distributed by those in power, that is male academics and administrators.

18. The arrival of the internet in the late 1980s and the recent adoption of intranet for university communications have significantly reduced some of these disparities in access to information.

privilege that is not shared by many of my female colleagues and is one that I should not take for granted. Second, I have been blessed to have had as mentors women and men who guided and nurtured me intellectually, who helped shape my work, many of them having been my friends as well. This shaping and support has come from academic colleagues both in Ghana and abroad. My collaborations with women and men in activist/civil society organisations have also provided insights 'from the field', and new and exciting opportunities to share my research.

Some of the Politics of Gender Research

It is important to recognise the dominance of particular approaches to doing work on gender, ranging from the purely technocratic work conducted in much of the development industry, to work that services hegemonic development discourses. Thus there often exists a tension between researchers who identify as feminists, whose scholarship is rooted in a feminist consciousness and who foreground gender and issues of inequality in their work, and those who adopt a more 'pragmatic' approach, who generally focus on one or more topical issues such as female genital mutilation (FGM), violence and so forth and who may not necessarily identify as feminists (Adomako Ampofo, Beoku-Betts, Njambi and Osirim 2004). Many of those who fall in the latter category point out that the experience of gender is not shared by all women (or men) and that there are many particularities, such as political crises or poverty, that better explain the relative conditions of women and men. In between these two poles, of course, are the many scholars who work in particular areas such as HIV/AIDS or domestic violence, and who, within these, draw on feminist theorising to link women's conditions to female oppression.

Here I will return to the issue of role-juggling between being an academic, a consultant and an activist. Because of the inevitable drains on one's time, energy and emotions, an intellectual distancing by social science researchers from society often occurs so that we go through the motions of doing research, teaching and even so-called activist work. Often we churn out 'policy-oriented' research for state or international agencies. The power relations that structure knowledge production both locally and internationally stymie our efforts even further. It is so important for us to question who produces 'knowledge' and how and where it is disseminated, whose voices are privileged and which forms of scholarship are legitimated (Mkandawire 1997; Tetteh and Pupulampu 2000). Partly because 'Western' epistemologies and the cultural worldviews of 'traditional' disciplines have largely failed to take into account local explanations for phenomena which affect local peoples, 'Culture' has (re)emerged as the place where gender is most passionately contested and (re)invented in oppressive forms. In the name of 'Culture', then, women continue to be oppressed, and 'Culture' becomes the scapegoat, whose fault it is that Africa fails to 'develop'. Yet almost by definition, contract work for a donor agency, or an academic publication for a 'peer-reviewed' international journal, must craft gender issues in Africa from a perspective which denies people their agency and allows the prescription of pre-formulated models.

In the academy, we far too often find students writing a graduate thesis, and even some faculty writing for publication, feeling compelled to include a 'policy recommendations' section. I agree with Tetteh and Pupulampu (2000) that if we are to focus primarily on 'policy-oriented' research (read: practical/useful), we may risk weakening our theoretical enquiries. Perhaps the issue is not whether we should do policy-oriented work or not, but what kind of 'policy' work we do, and on whose terms. As I see it, it is crucial that as researchers we should consciously seek to meet the needs, either directly or indirectly, of the communities that have privileged us, and in which we live.[19] I think that this is even more critical for feminist researchers, because most of us believe that our teaching and research must ultimately contribute to improving the lives of African women and gender relations.

Early in my career at the University of Ghana, in true social-demography mode, I wanted to carry out a study of attitudes to (pre-marital) sex among adolescents in Ghana. I put together what in later years I realised was a rather passionate and journalistic proposal and begun walking from institution to institution in Accra to see if some organisation might be interested in what I was interested in. One afternoon I walked into the offices of the then director of Maternal and Child Health (MCH) at the Ministry of Health (MOH). I told her what I wanted to do and asked if the Ministry might be interested in funding my research. It so happened that the MCH division of MOH was interested in looking at the 'reproductive health' of adolescents, and the Director was working with a UN Population Fund

---

19. An example of how a small contribution can be made may suffice. During my PhD research on reproductive decision-making among couples, I discovered that many couples wanted to understand more about contraceptive options as well as infertility. I decided, after asking respondents if they thought it might be useful, to conduct a seminar on these issues. My husband, an MD, was the resource person, so I had to pay for only the venue and refreshments.

(UNFPA) representative to design a framework for a situation analysis. They 'hired' me and also gave me a free hand to design the study. In return for their supporting my budget, I had to provide them with a report and participate in some dissemination workshops. As part of my research design, in secondary schools students viewed a highly acclaimed Zimbabwean feature film and held discussions about the plot, the protagonists and sex in general.[20] The MOH had the information to guide policy design and the setting up of an Adolescent Reproductive Health Steering Committee that it wanted (and which I joined), and I was able to carry out a critical enquiry and collect masses of data from across the country from which to theorise about adolescent behaviours and attitudes. I was also able to inject my report with nuanced analyses of young people's notions of sexuality and morality. I also learned a great deal about young people's agency, and the fact that many of them were, contrary to prevailing popular thought, not interested in engaging in sex. And I had a great deal of fun. The dynamics of this inter-generational mutual learning process is something that I have since become very interested in theoretically.

Collaborative encounters have been where much of my learning has occurred – through dialogue, hearing different perspectives, being exposed to new scholarship and even disagreements. Not only can collaborative encounters be intellectually stimulating and enhance our learning, they also often make it easier and cheaper to do research. It is true, collaboration and sharing make one vulnerable. Some people will use your ideas or work without acknowledging your input, not even in a cursory footnote; others may patronise you; and yet others not take on their share of the workload either technically and intellectually. However, collaborations enhance our personhood and strategically they tell people that we are team players. At the University of Ghana, where I work, I have since 2005, in addition to being a professor at the Institute of African Studies, headed a new Centre for Gender Studies and Advocacy. This has truly been a collaborative endeavour with my Deputy Head, Dzodzi Tsikata, as well as colleagues from around the university, women and men, from the Humanities as well as the Physical and Applied Sciences, who work on one or more of our sub-committees.

---

20. The film tells the story about two bright and attractive teenagers who fall in love and eventually have sex. The girl falls pregnant and, even though they try to work things out, the relationship falls apart because the boy wants to take up a prestigious university scholarship. School is a struggle for the girl but eventually she is able to make something of her life, while the boy does not seem to do too well.

It has been this collaboration that has helped us navigate the university bureaucracy and build this young centre with the help of colleagues who come with diverse skills and who are represented on different boards and committees in the university.

One of the major challenges for intellectual work is the recognition that we need dialogue and collaboration with our colleagues in the North, despite all that has been said about the myths of global sisterhood, and despite any pressure we might experience towards relying on Western methodologies, ways of conceptualising and theorising that we may sometimes resent as attempts at subverting our personal, professional and intellectual autonomy. Nnaemeka (2005) notes that after years of struggle and stock-taking, she came to the conclusion that the theorising of feminism created structures of power in the feminist movement analogous to those for which patriarchy is attacked. As positions of margin and centre became delineated, the resistance of the marginalised to the imperious hegemony at the centre became more apparent. Many of us have bitter stories of such colonial encounters that started out promising to be exciting but soon turned out not to be partnerships of equals: decisions are questioned and over-turned without consultation let alone discussion, the budget is not transparent, co-researchers are played off against each other in a soap-opera like game of power, work we produce is not acknowledged because we have been paid (as consultants) for our knowledge and we are not seen as knowledge-producing collaborators. Yet those of us in the Global South and those in the Global North need each other: because context matters in defining perspective; because feminist theorising benefits from these diverse perspectives; because feminists in the Global North rarely speak our local languages and need us to help them enter our space; because northern-based researchers have access to more and better resources to carry out research and to publish (they hold gate-keeping positions in journals and funding agencies); and because space-sharing is a feminist thing to do. However, the issue of gate-keeping requires some discussion, because these gates are often kept tightly shut, or are only opened a crack periodically, thus serving as a disincentive for African researchers to publish in 'international' journals or to seek to write books with 'international' presses. It is far easier to focus on preparing research reports for funding agencies anyway. As African feminists, we need to be able to represent our continent in the works that get published and cited, for we are often as authoritative, if not more so, when it comes to the lives of women on the continent – after all, too often this is our lived experience, or that of our mothers, sisters and aunts. We might also provide a more sensitive perspective.[21] This kind of gate-keeping ultimately has implications for the production of knowledge, the development of concepts and theories and for policy. We need to be critical, and loud, about this kind of hegemony that essentially subordinates our own knowledge and experiences.[22] We want our sisters (and brothers) in the North to accord our work the same legitimacy they accord their own. They can do this, for example, by using our works in their courses, as some are already doing, and by seeking to include us in positions of influence. We expect that our African sisters, who are now located in the North, whether by design or accident of history,[23] will show us special support. One of my own most fruitful long term transnational collaborations has been with two colleagues in North America, Beoku-Betts and Osirim, both Africanists and both sociologists. I cite this example because the mere fact that we have worked together for several years across two continents is testimony to the possible. I met one of these women, Josephine Beoku-Betts, at a conference while I was a PhD student in the US in the early 1990s. She made useful comments on my presentation, and, thereafter she sent me several references and a collegial relationship was built. Over the years, she drew me into a circle of sister colleagues in the Diaspora and together we have forged some exciting collaborations. Through Josephine, I met Mary Osirim, and together we have collaborated on women's caucuses, publications, seminars in each other's countries and international conferences. Both women are slightly senior to me in age as well as status, and yet they have never pulled rank on me or expected me, as the younger partner, to do most of the work in our engagements. Our commitment to an African feminist agenda and each other's professional

---

21. I was initially interested in, and then appalled by a publication I received in the mail. It was a coffee-table type book with an attractive cover showing a group of smiling African children against the backdrop of peaceful-looking mountains. The title of the volume is *African Poverty* (White and Killick 2001). While the book's cover is not a statement about its contents, and whether the authors were collaborators in the selection of the cover design I cannot say, but the fact that African poverty had now moved from merely being the flavour of the moment to being romanticised at the expense of African children I found deeply disturbing.

22. I recognise that issues of commodification (Tetteh and Pupulampu 2000) are an important part of the practice of gate keeping; however, it is beyond the scope of this paper to enter that discussion. In any case, Tetteh and Pupulampu (2000), as well as Yankah (1995) and Mkandawire (1993, 1997) provide adequate analyses elsewhere.

23. We certainly do not expect to hear any of the arrogance displayed by a "well-known French Africanist [who] concluded only recently that there was only 'one intellectual in the whole of Black Africa'" (see Mkandawire 1997:15).

development is reflected in the sharing of information, materials and the conscious support for each other's work.

I Work Hard for My Money: Consultancy Work

The chronic shortage of funds to do research in our universities has been exacerbated by the implementation of neoliberal economic perspectives which, in the 1990s, called for cuts in government subsidies to tertiary institutions (Adomako Ampofo 2002). The new millennium saw the World Bank and International Monetary Fund revise their position and tertiary institutions are back on the agenda. However, a deep harm has already been done, for where funds were unavailable for research or other forms of professional enhancement, consulting or NGO-ing enterprises became the way to survive (Diouf and Mamdani 1994) and the practice can become quite addictive.[24] The development industry in particular is now having unforeseen effects on scholarship. The emergence of women in development as a field of policy and project activities has impacted women's studies and gender research (Mama 1999) by problematising women's lives along particular basic needs lines such as reproductive health, education, access to credit and so forth, frequently leaving more fundamental issues of equal citizenship untouched.

While scholars outside the continent also undertake consultancies, they may need them more for professional advancement and status and less for their daily bread than we do in Africa, hence they are less frequently found to be in conflict with research and teaching responsibilities. Yet even for us in Africa, contract work does not have to be in conflict with academic research and the two can, in fact, be mutually supportive. For example, the data from a consultancy report can sometimes be translated into an academic article, and students can participate in data collection so that they gain 'field experience'. By these means, the space can become an activist space where we teach about relations between theory and praxis and draw on students' suggestions on how transformations might occur.

The typical scenario for a consultancy is that we are hired by an organisation to carry out an empirical study, an evaluation or a training programme. We are presented with specific Terms of Reference (TOR), a timeframe

---

24. In this paper, I do not examine the trend for many academics to be involved in NGOs, nor their membership of external 'Centres' and 'Think tanks'. Suffice it to note, however, that NGO work is not necessarily a political, altruistic, voluntary practice devoid of the economic benefits normally associated with undertaking consultancy work.

within which to complete the assignment and are offered a fixed, or sometimes negotiated payment for our services. Sometimes we apply for these consultancies on a competitive basis in response to an advert, or because we have been recommended by a friend or colleague. Other times, someone in the organisation that needs the job done approaches us directly and asks us if we can carry out the particular assignment. Because of the TOR and the often-rigid timeframe that the contracting agency imposes on consultants, we come under a lot of pressure to produce an output (usually a report) by a fixed date. Further, because some of us juggle a number of consultancies simultaneously, we are not able to give of our best. This is unfortunate. None of us wants to be accused of being part of the phenomenon of "new patterns of data gathering and consumption that lead to highly selective collection of data, fudging of data to meet deadlines and to fit the predisposition of clients" (Mkandawire 1993,135). When we produce shoddy work, this closes the doors to other researchers and reinforces the role of expatriates in research and consulting. Mkandawire (1997) estimates that by 1997 Africa was paying foreign experts an estimated total of $ 10 billion per annum. Shoddy work on gender issues is also a huge disservice to the cause of gender transformation, often leading people to discard the entire enterprise of engendering research.

Our consultancy work can be helpful beyond providing an income and occasional hotel stays away from home. It can also be relevant to our teaching. In 1990, soon after I joined the University of Ghana, I was roped into a study a senior colleague, Takyiwaa Manuh, was undertaking for the (Ghana) Statistical Services. The work required us to carry out analyses of data on women from the three national censuses undertaken up until that time. As an introduction to the analyses, we decided to provide a discussion of some of the conceptual and methodological limitations built into the censuses. For example, in our report we critiqued the conceptualisation of the 'household' and 'economically active' persons, and the effects these have on women's positions, such as making women's work invisible because it is not defined, much less counted. This may be common fare today, but 19 years ago these efforts provided new impetus for our teaching of Gender and Development in African Societies.

To cite another example, from 2000-04 a male colleague, Kweku Yeboah, and I carried out three National Reproductive Health Baseline Surveys for Save the Children Fund (SCF), Ghana. While we defined the research issues together with SCF and recommended how the data be collected, the ultimate focus was SCF's prerogative. However, we got paid a decent amount of money and were armed with a wealth of data. The data we gathered included a rich collection on health issues for which little data were available, such as on breast-feeding, 'female genital mutilation' and the use of herbs to dry the vagina for sex. These data have been most useful in providing very recent empirical findings on many issues for which I previously relied on anecdotal evidence or small-scale qualitative studies in my teaching. The data, experiences and insights that have been gained from consulting work have also helped me frame or refine research questions, interrogate concepts and methods and reconstruct my own research philosophies.

For me as an academic, the challenge lies in being able to earn an income from a consultancy while still carrying out critical analyses of the data and publishing from it, being true to one's ideological positions, and not being torn apart as a person because of the sheer workload. The privilege of being an elite woman brings responsibility – the responsibility to draw from my multiple contexts and experiences. The resources that consultancy provides are extremely useful for activist work – the money, connections to powerful and influential organisations and people, the networks with individuals and groups and the technical information. Personally, I do not see how we can afford not to be activists – the immediacy of the issues that face us, the position of women and the terrain we fight for compels us. Can our consulting for various organisations also bring about change in the lives of African women? It can if we take the lessons learned into new places – the written page, the classroom, as well as engagements with civil society and state. Osirim (forthcoming) notes how African and African American women scholars are strongly committed to both research and activism in their professional lives, and that for them a division between scholarship and activism would seem artificial. Drawing on work by Patricia Hill Collins, Osirim emphasises that theory-building for these feminist scholars is related to their experiences in the world – their engagement with the real world problems of development, state-formation and gender relations that they see themselves, their communities and their nations facing. The same is true for all feminist scholars in the Global South.

I am Woman, Watch me Roar: Advocacy[25]

In December 2000, the people of Ghana voted a new government into office. This government was re-elected in 2004. Whatever our political per-

---

25. Borrowed from the 1972 hit song "I am woman" by Helen Reddy.

suasion, most well-intentioned Ghanaians, I believe, were interested in a 'positive change'.[26] The New Patriotic Party (NPP) government established a new ministry, initially the Ministry for Women's' Affairs, MOWA, later revised to include children, hence MOWAC. While many women activists were, at best, apprehensive about the ability of this ministry to bring about change for women,[27] the collective of women activists recognised the creation of the ministry as an opportunity for verbalising our own political agenda and vision for women of Ghana.[28] A variety of civil society organisations, under the rubric of the Domestic Violence (DV) Coalition, have worked with MOWAC and other state agencies to address issues of violence, citizenship and rights. I have been part of this process as a member of the coalition and also as a scholar interested in the subject of gender-based violence. I have joined the DV coalition on marches, press and other public events. However, I feel that my major contribution to the efforts to get the legislation passed came from my role as a scholar. I contributed to drafting press releases and other statements, and served as a resource person at dissemination or advocacy events on gender-based violence, such as a session with members of parliament.

I am certainly not unique in living with a sense of mission – there are hundreds, nay, millions of African women like me feeling that we must participate in some way in acting out our concerns over the economic crisis facing our country and continent, while at the same time working to change gender inequalities and perceptions of gender and gender relations. We are challenging the silences around gender relations and what those silences mean for women – the inequities, but also specifically violence, the state's relations with us and its policies (or lack thereof). We engage in public discourse whether at public forums or in the media. We are willing to be controversial and to be attacked. We are strategising for political and economic ends. For me, perhaps, two of the most rewarding areas of activism have been in the church and in the classroom. The church is a traditionally patriarchal institution where men have been in the forefront of leadership, if not necessarily always in decision-making, and it has been very rewarding, educative and humbling for me to be accorded space by both men and

---

26. This was the slogan of the NPP government during its election campaign.
27. See Tsikata (2000a, b) for a discussion of the history of women's bureaux in Africa and their general failure to deliver.
28. Elsewhere, I discuss in greater detail the rocky nature of MOWAC's relationship with civil society, especially over the passage of domestic violence legislation (Adomako Ampofo 2008).

women to transform gender relations and our thinking around theology. While perhaps I have often been non-confrontational in my 'style', the issues have not necessarily been without contestation.

African feminist scholars see the classroom as an activist space. Osirim (forthcoming) notes, "In our teaching we strive to remove/reduce hierarchies in the classroom ... [W]e often strive to unite theory with praxis and choose to teach and engage students in service-learning courses ... [We] engage in scholar-activism in the classroom". Beoku-Betts and Njambi (2005,126) assert that they "attempt ... to disrupt the normalised images of African women ... including those of victimhood". Since the early 1990s, I have taught or co-taught two graduate courses in Gender, always from a transformative perspective with the goal of getting students to critically question what is seen as 'normal' or 'natural'. Of course, even if our reputations have not preceded us, students soon recognise our own values. Nonetheless, apart from some heated debates, I have never experienced any resentment from students. Most gratifying have been the testimonies, even if embellished to make the student look good, about male students' wives who have praised them for becoming more sensitive, or female students who provide anecdotes of negotiating change in the relationships or spaces they find themselves in. Since then, the setting up of the Centre for Gender Studies and Advocacy, CEGENSA, at the University of Ghana, which has grown out of the small Development and Women's Studies programme at the Institute of African Studies, has provided a formal space in which to make gender a legitimate part of university business through curriculum development, policy design, research, mentoring, extension and advocacy, provision of resources and the creation of a sexual assault crisis unit. Although ostensibly set up by the University Council in 2004, CEGENSA's existence as an academic and service centre is the result of efforts by the local women's movement, international collaborations and the individual and collective efforts of feminist scholars. It started as a programme to link the academy to policy, then we designed courses to be co-taught by faculty around the university, and later the programme benefited from collaborations with colleagues in UK institutions through formal Ghana-UK links. In 2000, several members joined the Gender and Women's Studies for Africa's Transformation project coordinated by the African Gender Institute at the University of Cape Town. That project provided an opportunity to be part of curriculum development workshops. CEGENSA has since held two curriculum workshops that brought together teachers of gender from tertiary institutions in Ghana.

In Conclusion: "One Who has Strength – She has the Truth"

The point of the proverb that begins this paper is not to suggest that truth is relative, but to indicate that in this world we live in, 'the truth' survives if those of us who have it and care to share it survive ourselves. We need to be resilient, but we also need to be wise. Sometimes I have been stretched to the limit as I have tried to write and rewrite articles whose submission dates were yesterday, mark student papers, prepare reading material for my classes, write research proposals so that I can have money to do some of the work I am interested in, carry out administrative and other university responsibilities, and meet the deadlines of the agencies for whom I occasionally do consulting work.[29]

The three roles of researcher, consultant and advocate, as I have argued, are not mutually exclusive, nor, in spite of the time demands, mutually upsetting. On the contrary, they can be mutually supportive. Research provides intellectual meaning and a sense of identity, legitimacy and status within the academic community. Consulting offers a livelihood and can provide avenues for publishing and teaching while building a professional reputation. Consulting also provides empirical data that can be used towards the production of an (academic) publication. It provides opportunities for students to gain experience and earn some money as assistants. It allows entry into places with influential persons and can enhance our CVs, thereby increasing the chances of success in seeking funds for research work. Advocacy and activism provide a sense of purpose and satisfaction as we witness change.

Consultancy work and the reports emanating from it can also be used to leverage funding for activist research projects and vice-versa. Late in 2007, CEGENSA, together with two activist organisations, put in a research grant application for a multi-layered study on gender violence and HIV. Our research focuses on young people in three tertiary institutions, as well as on HIV-positive women in selected communities. The study, in turn, will: feed into the services each of our organisations offers our constituents; enhance women's opportunities to participate in familial, local and national discourse and decision making; strengthen women's abilities to resist and respond to violence; and strengthen legal and psychological support to survivors of vio-

---

29. As a rule, I never undertake a consultancy for which I have to carry out a major revisiting of the literature. Unless I can find a collaborator, I also never take on assignments for which I have insufficient technical expertise. I rarely take on more than one consultancy a year as, with increasing responsibilities at the university, I have found that this is as much as I can reasonably manage and still remain sane and true to the agencies.

lence and HIV+ women through working with civil society organisations as well as duty bearers. Not long after our proposal was approved for funding, I was offered a contract assignment to evaluate the work of an activist organisation that has had many years of experience in the area of gender-based violence. The preliminary research for the proposal strengthened my understanding of the work required for this consultancy, while the consultancy work has provided deep insights into the possibilities for community work by activists and duty bearers in the area of gender-based violence. At the same time, the insights from both the consultancy and the research work, and CEGENSA's collaborations with the two activist organisations, significantly strengthened a recent article of mine on the women's movement and the passage of domestic violence legislation in Ghana (Adomako Ampofo 2008). The lessons and experiences also find their way into the classroom when my students and I discuss the politics of social movements.

Ultimately, however, whether we are in the field collecting data for our pet research or a consultancy assignment, in the classroom, at our computers typing away at an article, we are engaged in activism. While economic issues may determine some of the consultancies we take on, a feeling that we owe our continent something determines the kinds of consultancies we accept, the subjects of the research we pursue and the courses we teach.

References

Adomako Ampofo, Akosua, 2002, "Introduction: Teaching and Learning in Ghana; Historical and Contemporary Issues", *Ghana Studies* Vol. 5:1–20.

—, 2008, "Collective Activism: The Domestic Violence Bill becoming Law in Ghana", *African and Asian Studies* (7):395–421.

Adomako Ampofo, Akosua and Josephine Beoku-Betts, Mary Osirim, and Wairimū Njambi, 2004, "Women's and Gender Studies in English Speaking Sub-Saharan Africa: A Review of Research in the Social Sciences", *Gender and Society* Vol. 18(6):685–714

Achebe, Nwando and Brigid Teboh, 2007, "Dialoguing Women", in Catherine M. Cole, Takyiwaa Manuh and Stephan Miescher (eds), *Africa after Gender*. Bloomington: Indiana University Press: 63-84.

Atteh, S.O., 1996, "The Crisis in Higher Education in Africa", *Issue* 24(1):36-42.

Beoku-Betts, Josephine and Wairimū Njambi, 2005, "African Feminist Scholars in Women's Studies; Negotiating Spaces of Dislocation and Transformation in the Study of Women", *Meridians: feminism, race, transnationalism* Vol. 6(1):113–132.

Brown, C.K., Anokye, Nana Amma, and Britwum, Akua O., 1996, *Women in Public Life*. Accra: Friedrich Ebert Foundation.
Court, D., 1982, "Scholarship and Contract Research: The Ecology of Social Science in Kenya and Tanzania", in L.D. Stifel, R.K. Davidson, and J.S. Oleman (eds), *Social Science and Public Policy in the Developing World*. Toronto: Lexington Books: 321–346.
Diouf, Mamadou and Mamdani Mahmood, 1994, *Academic Freedom in Africa*. Dakar: CODESRIA.
Manuh, Takyiwaa, Sulley Gariba and Joseph Budu, 2007, Changes and Transformations in Ghana's Publicly Funded Universities: A Study of experiences and Opportunities. Oxford: James Currey.
Mkandawire, Thandika, 1993, "Problems and Prospects of Social Sciences in Africa", *International Social Sciences Journal* 45:129–140.
—, 1997, "The Social Sciences in Africa", *African Studies Review* 39(2):15–37.
Mikell, Gwendolyn (ed.), 1997, *African Feminism. The Politics of Survival in Sub-Saharan Africa*. Philadelphia: University of Pennsylvania Press: 232–256.
Mohanty, Chandra T., Ann Russo and Lourdes Torres (eds), 1991, *Third World Women and the Politics of Feminism*. Indiana: Indiana University Press.
Momsen, Janet H. and Jane G. Townsend, 1987, *Geography of Gender in the Third World*. New York: State University of New York Press.
Nnaemeka, Obioma, 2005, "Bringing African Women into the Classroom: Rethinking Pedagogy and Epistemology", in Oyeronke Oyewumi (ed.), *Afrcian Gender Studies, A Reader*. New York: Palgrave Macmillian.
Osirim, Mary, 2005, "Contested Terrain: Transnational Attempts at Theorizing about Feminism and African Women's Lives". Paper presented at Women's Worlds 2005 – the Ninth International Interdisciplinary Congress on Women, Seoul, Korea, June 2005.
—, 2009, "Mobilizing for Change Locally and Globally: African Women as Scholar-Activists in Feminist and Gender Studies," in Muna Ndulo (ed.), *Power, Gender and Social Change in Africa and the African Diaspora*. Oxford: James Currey Press.
Peirera, Charmaine, 2007, *Gender in the Making of the Nigerian University System*. Oxford: James Currey.
Prah, Mansah, 2003, "Gender Issues in Ghanaian Tertiary Institutions: Women Academics and Administrators at Cape Coast University", *Ghana Studies* Vol. 5:83–122.
Sawyerr, Akilagpa, 1994, "Ghana: Relations Between Government and Universities", in G. Neave and F.A. van Vught (eds), *Government and Higher Education Relationships across Three Continents: The Winds of Change*. Paris: IAU Press and Pergamon, 22–53.
Tsikata, Dzodzi, 2001a, "Introduction", in Dzodzi Tsikata (ed.), *Gender Training in Ghana. Politics, Issues and Tools*. Accra: Woeli Publishing Services: 3–32.

—, 2001b, "Gender Equality and Development in Ghana", in Dzodzi Tsikata (ed.), *Gender Training in Ghana. Politics, Issues and Tools.* Accra: Woeli Publishing Services: 259–272.

Yankah, Kwesi, 1995, "Displaced Academics and the Quest for a New World Academic Order", *Africa Today* 42(3):7–25.

CHAPTER TWO

Connections to Research
The Southern African Network of Higher Education Institutions Challenging Sexual Harassment / Sexual Violence, 1996–2001

Jane Bennett

Introduction

Battling with neither grace nor panache against the institutional culture of an American graduate programme, I wrote a doctoral dissertation on the politics of representing rape in the same years in which I worked as a hotline counsellor at the Rape Crisis Centre of the city. As the need to keep a roof over my head meant full-time work during the day, my nights were divided between the small, brightly lit cubicle housing the hotline phone and the cocoon of my own apartment, where the computer hummed and the 'secondary literature' lay in disorganised, pliant heaps on the floor.

The difference between the two zones was dramatic: with all the training in the world, there was no way of being completely prepared for the moment the hotline phone rang. The calling voice could be coming from any street or crevice in the city, driven by shards of loneliness and pain (who calls a hotline? and when?), telling stories in no predictable words or pattern. The 'control' I had as the woman answering the phone was limited to my convictions about the importance of doing that answering and the recognition that my access to 'control' – in that cubicle – was beside the point. On the nights on which I worked at my own desk, however, control was everything: designing command over others' (written) words, revealing my manipulation of theory and paradigm, organising data (an interesting term), arranging myself – for the panoptic omniscience of examiners – as knowledgeable.

If one difference between the zone of the hotline and the zone of the computer lay in issues of control, another – not unrelated – lay in the significance of the experience of rape and the politics of that significance. The epistemological principles guiding the process of listening to an unseen stranger's autobiographical narrative of rape prioritised her (usually, not always, *her*) right to construct that narrative as a critically political right. Reconstructive moves from the listener ("are you sure it happened like that?", "that doesn't make sense", "what about putting it another way?") would have been unthinkable, the behaviour of someone invested in the cannibalisation of the autobiographer's body (systemically akin, in fact, to the raping assailant in her story). While all counsellors worked within a framework well versed in the connection between one rape and another, and used insights drawn from these connections to attune themselves to the nuances of each new autobiography, it was never assumed that one story could be replaced by another or that a counsellor's previous listening experience could predict the shape, complexity, silences or depth of the next narrative she would encounter. From the perspective of the hotline counsellor – in the moment when she picked up the ringing phone – one experience of rape bore whole, unique and sufficient witness to the nature of late 20th century urban American patriarchy, but did so from the irreplaceable authority of the woman or man speaking about what had happened to/in them.

The work of the dissertation author, however, involved the integration of representations of rape into scaffolds of theory on discourse and required that I myself become the architect of those representations' salience: a deferential architect, one whose skill would be appraised by sociolinguistic experts (not one of them self-identified as either rapist or raped) – an architect whose connection with those telling autobiographical rape narratives was more a focus of scientific scrutiny concerning verifiability than a zone raising ethical or political questions. The epistemological paradigms through which I acquired status as an educated woman demanded that I own my 'data', and that I take full intellectual responsibility for that colonisation.

I recognise, as I write, the anger still alive within my blood as I recall the deictic imperatives of doctoral performance. It may be an illegitimate anger, rooted in the infantilisation inherent in postgraduate research, an anger projected on to questions of epistemology, evading deeper anxieties about my scholarship or credibility. It is certainly true that the process of engaging with language through diverse theorisations of discourse, offered me extraordinary intellectual adventure. It is also true that my particular experience of graduate school supervision was not markedly brutal. In an article on the politics of writing, I once introduced myself through a debate with a feminist colleague:

> A feminist friend and I have an ongoing debate about the meaning ... of reading (and writing) as a sphere of primary experience. Her position is that despite the value of the written word to her life, the most important things she knows come from direct experience of the body, unmediated by any text. My position is that reading has been so critical to what (I feel) I know about being that I am willing to prioritise textual voices as essential sources of my experience.[1]

It is irrefutable that my sanity, and whatever capacity I have to move beyond the sepulchre of my ancestry, is indebted to literacy, and although the readings which have most deeply resoldered my neural highways have not – on the whole – been those recommended by course readers or research supervisors, they have nonetheless often been discovered in university libraries, discussed as touchstones with peers and shared (over, now, 20 years) with those I've had the privilege of teaching. This is especially true of feminist writing, a vast and complex field whose contestations and vitality continue to exasperate, goad and energise me. As a thinker and researcher, I am shaped by academic conceptions of rigour, value, purpose and integrity in more ways than I can enumerate: I am capable of *speech on behalf of*.

And yet.

And yet, the epistemological clash between the world of the hotline counsellor (for whom the voice at the other end of the phone holds powerful authority over her/his own experience) and the world of the academic writer (who must forge links between one voice and another, metalinguistically commanding the terms of this negotiation) is visceral. It is felt at the level of the body, articulated in bitter arguments between NGO workers and academics about the direction or ownership of knowledge and soaked in the bloody legacies of colonialism, racism and classism. No discussion of research ethics quite captures the material palpability of the tension of this chasm.

Hippocratic Oaths: Feminist Research Ethics

One of the most persistent anxieties in writing on feminist research involves the possibility of violation through the process of the research, the likelihood of 'doing harm'. There is, in fact, an inevitable logic to this anxiety: in many contexts, public theorisation on 'doing women's studies' was rooted in sharply focused analyses of the androcentric epistemologies which underlie

---

1. Bennett, 2000, pp. 3-12.

discipline-based canons of knowledge, and discussed the incontrovertible evidence of these canons' capacity to cause damage to women and to gender relations. The connection between epistemological frame and ontological injury is fundamental to feminist theory.

In 1970, in New York, Kate Millett's *Sexual Politics*[2] – reading literary texts as unmediated illustrations of male psyches – made contemporary Northern feminist history as a model of epistemological analysis;[3] Adrienne Rich's collection of essays, *Lies, Secrets and Silences*[4] is a more complex example of classic 'Second Wave' theory in the Northern late 1970s and 1980s, in which every discipline was subjected to the epistemological scrutiny of feminist analysis.[5] Despite the disciplinary differences among these theorists (and as the 1980s wore on, the increasingly nuanced debates emerging between feminists working within particular fields), their epistemological unity is (especially in retrospect) dramatic: academic knowledge was conceptualised as the encyclopaedic alphabet of patriarchal class interests, designed as a code for the exclusion of women and deeply implicated in the material effects of sexism. The recognition that the construction of hegemonic knowledge caused lasting, vicious and deliberate wounds was articulated as *personal*[6] and as deeply, politically, inhumane – 'unethical'.

The ignorance of race (and of its implication in class interests) in much mid-1970s/early 1980s Northern feminist theory on epistemology is staggering, revealing (among other things) its conscious grasp of 'epistemological injury' as thin. Two decades of debate have elaborated the significance of locating racism within the construction of canonical knowledge in the North,[7] but it is only within the writings of critical race theorists such as

---

2. Millett, 1970.
3. Kate Millett's was not the first text to do this by a long shot: see Virginia Woolf, Simone de Beauvoir.
4. Rich, 1979.
5. Anthropology: Karen Sacks, Rayna Rapp; History: Joan Kelly, Nancy Stepan; Psychology: Jean Baker Miller, Nancy Chodorow, Juliet Mitchell; Sociology: Zillah Eistenstein; Biology: Evelyn Fox Keller; Religious Studies: Mary Daly.
6. This idea was hardly new – the interaction of 'knowledge-production' with class interests is one of the founding principles of Marxist-based epistemological theory. Nevertheless, besides feminist writings, there is no other example of so large an 'indigenous literature' written within the institutions of the 'coloniser' against the organising epistemologies of the institution.
7. See the work, for example, of Paul Gilroy, Henry Louis Gates, Patricia Hill-Collins, Trinh Minh-ha.

Kimberle Crenshaw[8] that multiple deixis animates analysis of justice, of policy on redressing the injuries caused through epistemological exclusion.

Researchers' self-reflexivity is demanded as a key skill in much feminist writing, and classifications of racial, class, gender and sexual identity are often integrated into authorial signature as shortcuts into positionality. Difficult to interpret beyond the essentialisations enforced through hegemonic oppressions, researchers' self-descriptions as 'white', 'born in Northern Tanzania' and/or 'Catholic' sometimes bring little illumination to the deeper task of epistemological self-reflexivity. Such a task requires not simply that a writer self-categorise, but that he/she explore the consequences of mobile subjectivity and efficacy for the political direction of her/his own work.

While most African feminist writers are likely to be embedded in middle class conditions of labour – given the current conditions of access to higher education and the resources required by researchers – my own experience leads me to think that it is fairly unusual for African-based researchers and writers to be confined within the universe of professional publication. Questions of epistemological ethics travel beyond the 'researcher-subject' interaction into zones of advocacy, service provision and policy consultancy. Such journeys may offer insight into the texture of African feminist *living*, in contexts where location as an 'intellectual' complements, complicates, facilitates and endangers work in NGOs, religious and artistic communities, parliamentary fora or training rooms.

While I have found theorisation of feminist research ethics around 'positionality', 'self-location' and 'self-reflexivity' provocative in its insistence on the centrality of the (privileged) representing voice to the significance of the text, I remain interested in exploring research as a process encompassing the possibility of *multiple* deictic positions for those involved. It is not that I imagine such exploration will obviate or simplify questions of epistemological injury or allow for cleaner explication of the 'principles' of ethical, feminist writing and research. It is, rather, that I believe an approach to research which acknowledges the mobility of participants may reflect more accurately the reality of the conditions under which feminist research is negotiated. Such an approach may also transform the definition of *research*, moving the term from primary reference to a dynamic between researcher and subject participants towards a mesh of interaction (textual, communicative, organisational and individual), which gradually uncovers 'new' information and facilitates fresh and unexpected inquiry.

---

8. Chrenshaw et al., 2001.

NETSH: The Growth of a Network

It is in the context of this claim that this chapter explores an initiative undertaken by individuals working in diverse Southern African institutions of higher education to establish a network capable of challenging sexual harassment and sexual violence on campuses. The work of this initiative addresses the seeming impossibility of creating conversation between the need to hear survivors' authority and the task of discursively astute and directed negotiation with institutional conventions about power, discipline and culture. The term 'address' I use advisedly: the tension between the authority of those who experience systemic, albeit personalised violation and conceptions of authority based on the thinking of researchers (and managers) consciously trained against subjectively derived deduction is not one that can be 'bridged' or 'resolved'.[9] What the example of NETSH (Network of Southern African Higher Education Institutions Challenging Sexual Harassment/Sexual Violence) suggests is that interesting political questions, difficult realities and compelling epistemological debates can become illuminated through deliberate engagement with the lack of connection between survivor and institution: *research* itself is released from acid debates over loci of authority into a process more concerned with flow than statement, more invested in long-term vision than in the short-term stakes of status and boundary.

In order to explore my claim for NETSH's capacity to contribute to definitions of *research*, the following section describes something of the initiative's discursive and organisational history between 1994 and 2000. Although proceedings from several of the conferences which took place in this period through NETSH are available as 'grey' literature, there is no current writing that attempts to synthesise or comment upon the overall direction of the discussions raised: given their importance, they are summarised in some depth here. The implications of these discussions, and – centrally – of the attempt to continue organising individuals in diverse Southern African institutions, are analysed through this overview of NETSH-based contexts for institutional activism.

NETSH is, of course, far from the only African feminist network designed to effect political change through integrating the experience of women and men into grounded institutional advocacy. The final section of the

---

9. The tension does not occur between poles of equal strength: the dominance of the latter depends, in sophisticated algorithm, on the erasure, cannibalisation and distortion of the former.

chapter looks at NETSH as one example of African feminist networking, not because it is an example of particularly powerful solidarity or especially effective institutional change, but because the process of *understanding sexual violence* is radically reshaped through concrete interaction with those working in higher education institutions at the frontlines of violation: survivors, residence administrators, friends, deans, counsellors, priests and imams, secretaries or disciplinary officers. As will be explored, the difficulties of sustaining networks – through donor funding, local institutional hospitability and individuals' workloads – are formidable. While my interests here certainly involve some documentation and exploration of a particular effort to confront gender-based violence, they also centrally concern an argument defining theoretically-oriented feminist research as quintessentially uninterested in the polarisation of 'author' and 'subject', 'theory' and 'experience', 'intellectual' and 'activist'.[10]

Over the past five years, Southern African institutions of higher education have moved, through a combination of restructuring initiatives and projects explicitly dedicated to the improvement of the quality of life on campus for educators and learners, into increasing acceptance of their seminal role in the leadership of democratic strategy and practice in the region.

Since its inception in 1996, the African Gender Institute (AGI) at the University of Cape Town has been committed to working within higher education as an appropriate zone in which to initiate and drive diverse programmes of capacity-building. These programmes have included funded projects which support African women researchers' development; the design and delivery of workshops in organisational transformation and in gender analysis for research purposes; the delivery of on-campus teaching programmes within the University of Cape Town's undergraduate and graduate faculties; the initiation of projects which – through several routes – will strengthen gender/women's studies on the continent; and, together with key individuals from many other universities and technikons, the co-development of a Network of Southern African Higher Education Institutions Challenging Sexual Harassment/Sexual Violence. A focus on sexual harassment and sexual violence on campuses allowed for the recognition of the multiple routes through which individuals may become vulnerable to violence and fear: a 'case' of sexual harassment or sexual violence is always

---

10. This does not entail the collapsing of the terms. As will be argued in the third section of the chapter, such terms are used to defend particular epistemological claims and demand political deconstruction as they are encountered and deployed.

embedded in institutionally specific dynamics of 'race', sexuality, nationality, gender and culture.

From my location within the African Gender Institute, the logic of beginning the story of NETSH's design in the mid-1990s within the sphere of my own environment is seductive. It is also deeply flawed. While there is a version of the story connected to the African Gender Institute, and in which I am an active character, the sheer fact of a network's initiation entails the presence of multiple 'beginnings', tales of diverse individuals within different locales, thinking about the sexual attacks encountered on their campuses and taking on the responsibility for understanding the nature of those attacks and stopping them. I proceed, therefore, in describing the evolution of NETSH's conceptual and practical strengths in the years 1996-2001, in full acknowledgement not only of the partiality of my view but also in recognition that all these voices together, from other universities and countries, would present a much *richer* perspective on the network's potential.

Early Reports on Sexual Harassment

By the late 1980s/early 1990s, university and technikon students on different campuses in the SADC region were identifying sexual harassment and sexual violence on their campuses as sources of outrage. In the following, three different reports will be brought forward. First in 1987, from the University of the Western Cape, Collette Solomon reports[11] on women students' activism on campus when the reported rapes of peers attracted no serious administrative attention from university management. The student activists protested in several ways and encountered intense hostility – both from most university officers and from other students on campus. Solomon writes:

> We were told that we had sidestepped certain structures on campus. Structures which I hasten to add had knowledge of the incidents, but had done nothing constructive. We were told that we were behaving like feminists (as if that is a negative label) because we had organised a women's only meeting, for obvious reasons, where the victims were present and related their expe-

---

11. Collette Solomon, journalist for article for Campus Newspaper entitled "International Women's Day celebrations focus on rape!", given as addendum to paper by Bernadette Johnson, UWC Student Representative Council Gender Officer, on "Student Organising and Sexual Harassment" at Southern African Conference on Challenging Sexual Harassment within Tertiary Education, 29-30 October 1994, held at University of Cape Town, hosted by the Equal Opportunity Research Project.

riences. Because we had organised in this fashion we were also labelled as being divisive. We were told we were being emotional about this issue ...We were actually even asked why we were so angry about the issue when the victims had probably not even been virgins at the time of the rape.[12]

Solomon's article hints at an institutional climate in which, while the concept of protest against structural injustice was well embedded in campus culture,[13] the demand for women's safety led very quickly to reactive discourse saturated with hostility to feminist principles about gender equality.

A similar discourse erupted over the second report, describing an intervention initiated by the University of Botswana in 1992. In March 1992, the Student Representative Council received complaints from women students that certain faculty were guilty of sexually harassing them: intimidating them when they refused sexual overtures, marking students on the basis of their perceived sexual attractiveness and inviting them to visit their offices for sex.[14] Unlike the situation described at UWC, report authors Sheila Tlou and Lebohang Letsie describe the university administration's response to the SRC's complaints as proactive: the University's Gender Policy and Programme Committee was commissioned to initiate immediate research into the issue and the Vice Chancellor made it clear that one complaint of sexual harassment would justify the development of formal policies. Such executive support did not, however, protect the researchers from the hostility of the institutional culture to the work. Not only did the researchers struggle to collect information from students, but also academic and non-academic staff were very reluctant, overall, to fill out questionnaires or participate in any form of live interview. In addition, the researchers were vilified:

The researchers conducting the study were brought under scrutiny – they were labelled as freaks, as uninformed, as culturally alienated and as victims of feminist propaganda from the West. Their credentials as 'good' women were questioned. The male researchers were branded as having been pressured into accepting culturally unacceptable notions of manhood and womanhood.[15]

Lastly, the University of Cape Town's 1991 Report on Sexual Harassment at the University introduces the issue by quoting from an anonymous

---

12. See footnote 11.
13. The University of the Western Cape was one of the most active anti-apartheid South African campuses.
14. Tlou and Letsie, 1997.
15. Tlou and Letsie, op.cit., pp. 18-19.

pamphlet circulated on the campus in September 1989: "Some men on this campus have declared war against women. They have claimed the right to decide where women should be and when. They are dictating to women what they should wear and how they should live their lives".[16]

What is also included in the pamphlet is an invocation of one of the most powerful moments of anti-apartheid struggle organised by women:

> you've struck the women, you've struck a rock
> women on this campus shall not be intimidated
> women reserve the right to walk around as they please
> women shall organise and mobilise

This invocation places the pamphlet in performative synchrony with a very particular history, that of black South African women's rejection of institutional coercion and harassment under apartheid. The focus of the pamphlet's outrage is on the *climate* of misogyny facing women students, a climate explicitly named as military oppression, including a range of assaults (from 'dictation' about dress and behaviour to physical and sexual attack).

The UCT Report tries to unpack the social and academic culture of students by analysing questionnaires distributed in men's and women's residences (n =200) and by careful and detailed interviews with students, residence wardens, university management and others. Despite the complexity revealed in the report,[17] it concludes that sexual harassment and sexism are widely accepted within the residence systems and that complaints about sexual harassment – formal or informal – were met with political scepticism, hostility or derision.

---

16. Simons et al., 1991, p. 8.
17. By the late 1980s, the University of Cape Town had taken critical steps to begin intervention in the apartheid-based elitism of the university's student population. Whereas in 1985, white students made up 91 per cent of students in residence, by 1990 the profile had shifted so that black students ('African', 'coloured' and 'Indian') comprised 50 per cent of the residence population. The meaning of 'race' dominated struggles over identity, authority and issues of cultural control over university membership, and the UCT Report traces debates on sexual harassment, which are embedded in struggles against racism. The theoretical point is clear: for the UCT students surveyed, issues of discrimination could not readily be flattened into single-axis analysis. Black women students' experience (despite their diversity) differed markedly from that of white women: black men did not share social, linguistic or political relationships to masculinity with white men.

There are substantial differences between the studies from the University of the Western Cape, the University of Botswana and the University of Cape Town. Each campus is enmeshed in historically specific conditions concerning resources, access and national policies on higher education and development. In addition, the abovementioned reports demonstrate – dramatically – the meaning of 'partiality' in the analysis of sexual harassment and sexual violence. Bernadette Johnson's paper, on which Collette Solomon's UWC report is based, speaks with the voice of a student activist to the growth of a vigorous feminist movement on campus, encompassing the development of women's studies, the provision of training in residence and political protest against rape – the focus is on institutional combat. Sheila Tlou and Lebohang Letsie, as senior researchers, are empowered to explore particular complaints by students, complaints which target male lecturers[18] and demand interrogation of academic culture. The UCT Report, commissioned through a Deputy Vice Chancellor and written as the work of a Committee, focuses on residence students' experience (mostly) of other students and of their residence environments.

At the same time, all three reports bear witness to the hostility of the environments in which the authors are working. Not only was sexual harassment and sexual violence prevalent, but the articulation of protest, analysis and demand for change encountered an arsenal of 'erasers': the facts of sexual harassment and sexual violence were threatened by political arguments on appropriate struggles, socio-anthropological claims about gender-identity, academic trivialisation, physical and verbal bullying, economic predictions about the value of those who insisted on taking gender discrimination seriously and personalised vitriol.

Bodies of Voice: Conferences in Cape Town, Gaborone, Harare

Cape Town Conference 1994

Such negation was expressed differently within each institution. It was collective recognition of the *impact* of sexual harassment, an impact which reverberated through survivors' bodies and minds into the lives of anyone who reacted with concrete action against the abuse, which forged an extraordinarily consensual space for the initiation of regional solidarity among

---

18. In later research by Lebohang Letsie, she turns her analysis to administrative staff issues, and uncovers a broad band of sexually harassing behaviours experienced by secretarial staff.

individuals working in higher education. At a 1994 conference held at the University of Cape Town, over 100 women and men based at higher education institutions participated. The level of regional interest in the issue, for which the conference organisers had been unprepared, energised a programme of discussion which positioned higher education campuses as zones in which substantial – and holistic – political work on gender needed to be undertaken. The opening address at the University of Cape Town by Mamphela Ramphele set the tone:

> At a recent Conference in Kenya on the connection between economic policy and human rights violations, John Njenga (the Catholic Archbishop of Mombasa) pointed out that: "Education as a human right is increasingly becoming an impossible ideal for many who have suffered the consequences of unfair 'economic policies'"...

In many discussions about the need for connections between the legacy of colonialism and the need for economic and social change, education is invoked as one of the most important areas in which policy-makers' intervention can make a difference to the future ...What does not get discussed is the fact that gender alters the meaning of 'educational opportunity' and that this is particularly important for tertiary education.[19]

I was present at the Conference as a part-time contract researcher in the Equal Opportunity Research Project directed by Ramphele, charged with the task of initiating research into the implementation of the university's sexual harassment policy. What was momentous for me within that conference room was the solidarity of the participants.

Rather than summarise the individuals' input, the Conference Report collated collective perspectives on different zones of activity through which sexual violence and sexual harassment could be tackled: policy formation, research, training, public protest, advocacy around new – or better – service provision. The collation of the Conference voices as a whole strategy, despite the vast differences among Southern African campuses, may strike one at first reading as slightly simplistic. In retrospect, however, the Report strikes me as the reflection of a – yes, simple – solidarity, in the face of survivors' pain.

Although the Report assumes survivors, and includes quite intensive discussion on definitions of sexual harassment which would explain its

---

19. M.A. Ramphele, "Challenging Sexual Harassment: Strategies Within Tertiary Education", Conference at University of Cape Town, 29-30 October 1994. Unpublished paper, available from the African Gender Institute, contact jane.bennett@uct.ac.za

psychological, physical, spiritual and/or economic impact, there is no first person witness in the report's pages. Although many presentations included side-references to 'personal' experience of (for example) being harassed by particular words, no presentation concentrated on an autobiographical experience of rape or sexual harassment. Nevertheless, conference spaces unfilled by papers and panels – teatimes, evenings, lunches, conversations in the bathrooms – were packed with exchanges about personal experiences. Such experiences included narratives of others (staff, students, friends) who had been attacked and direct discussion of storytellers' own encounters with assailants and bullies. In a room full of confident, vocally skilful and interesting men and women a current of respect for mutual knowledge of a very particular evil gave *body* to the talk of presentations, a body which demanded attention.

The year following the 1994 conference gave shape to participants' explicit interest in moving beyond individual contexts and perspectives through the formation of a Coordinating Committee of people charged with finding an appropriate activist forum, to a shared regional conviction that campus-based sexual violence and sexual harassment were intolerable. The Committee's composition attempted both representativity and realism: membership needed to bring geographical and contextual differences to the table and, simultaneously, to recognise that none of us had job responsibilities in which challenging sexual harassment and sexual violence constituted a primary (or, in some cases, even 'valid') focus for daily work.

Over the next five years, NETSH developed as a collective of diversely placed people working on SADC campuses. This development took place through moments of concerted, intensive interaction during Coordinating Committee planning meetings, workshops and conferences, as well as during long periods when the only possible collective activities involved database work, resource dissemination, e-mail communication and fundraising. From the perspective of any one institution, since NETSH was based on individual affiliations, the network's impact would be very uneven, perhaps in some cases barely discernible.

The choice to develop NETSH through individuals' commitment was a political one: in the face of institutional hostility to any form of feminist activism, it would have been naïve to canvass for participation based on institutional 'membership' signed on at executive levels of management. More importantly, it was recognised that the coal-face work being done to shift dangerous and sexist campus cultures was initiated and implemented by individuals, often working beyond the borders of their professional responsibilities, inspiring others through creativity, dedication and a savvy strategic consciousness about the need for long-term vision. Rooting the body of the network in individual volunteerism was politically appropriate, but it meant placing huge responsibilities on the shoulders of already burdened staff and student leaders. The narrative of ongoing work on challenging sexual harassment and sexual violence across dozens of campuses was intimately embedded in local institutional contexts, and the decision to create a linking network risked tough questions about the possibility of visible impact on a day-to-day level.

An overview of the five years' work of NETSH, however, illuminates an astonishing trajectory of discursive and practical development in coming to terms with the prevalence of sexually harassing and abusive behaviour on SADC campuses. A synopsis of 'events' coordinated shows two regional conferences, one held in Gaborone (1997) and the other in Harare (2000), and at least six substantial workshops and regular meetings of Coordinating Committee members. While I suspect that this trajectory merely hints at the locally rich battles over sexism, democracy, resources and authority waged on different SADC campuses during these years, the opportunities built through NETSH for cross-institutional discussion did facilitate deepening comprehension both of 'sexual harassment' and, as crucially, of the size of the transformational tasks ahead.

Gaborone Conference 1997

The National Institute of Development Research and Documentation at the University of Botswana was responsible, through the leadership of Lebohang Letsie with other Coordinating Committee members, for organising a Conference in Gaborone in 1997. One goal of the Conference was to bring back together as many as possible of the 1994 participants, expand the participation of Botswanan allies and formalise the structure and organising principles of NETSH.

The concluding remarks of Ansu Datta, then the Director of National Institute of Development Research and Documentation at the University of Botswana, capture something of the direction in which regional theorisation on sexual harassment and sexual violence was moving. In 1994, although of course individual participants brought particular perspectives with them, the overarching discourse was thematised, through shock and outrage, around the need to tackle institutional culture holistically. By 1997, however, Datta concluded:

> From the deliberations it has become clear that sexual harassment on university campus is only the tip of a proverbial iceberg ... yet, the battle on campus is notable for several reasons. Sexism here can be a most subtle kind of hidden agenda; the ideology sustained sexism is likely to be garbed in its most sophisticated form; and perhaps it is at this level that we may find the most blatant hypocrisy regarding the gender issue – the yawning gap between what is avowed and what is met in practice .. [I]t came out quite clearly from the Conference that sexism, the bedrock of sexual harassment, is a complex phenomenon and that unless we are careful we stand the risk of indulging in what may be called quick-fix remedies, simplistic solutions to involved syndromes.[20]

Datta's suggestions capture the shape of a very particular difficulty facing conference activists: where behaviour experienced as impossibly destructive by survivors is discursively protected (such behaviour is 'natural', 'normal', 'culturally prescribed', 'innocent'), the work of voicing resistance needs long-term, intricately strategised theorisation. There is a terrible tension between the immediacy of an outraged response to a specific sexual attack and the insight Datta explicates – institutionally, there is no option of 'fighting back' through the deployment of clear force or clean retribution. Feminist epistemologies, revolutionary in their logic concerning what McFadden names as "bodily integrity",[21] are met institutionally by a traditionally powerful split. Aspects of feminist theory and its implications for practice can be assimilated via the prism of the 'public', while the 'private' – the bordered zones of bodily interaction most intimately, nakedly, involved with reproduction and sexuality – must remain 'untouched', private. Thus feminist invitations to examine the meaning of community under gendered laws of access to humanity, find themselves acceptable to language concerning the right to (say) education but offensive to scripts of the body, to discussions on bodily significance.

Datta's remarks on hypocrisy and gaps are in conversation with those of Patricia McFadden, then the Director of the Feminist Studies Centre in Harare. McFadden opened the conference with a passionate attempt to lay bare some of patriarchy's discursive tools against the recognition of women's bodies as 'unownable' (a recognition reasonable enough in postcolonial environments fully apprised of what it has meant, historically, to trade in the ownership of African bodies). Her presentation surveys the contempo-

---

20. Datta, 1997 , p. 61.
21. McFadden, 1997.

rary constructions of African women's sexuality, polarising 'femininisation' against 'othering'. While the former, she argues, accounts for cultural permission to 'parade' young naked women before SADC heads of states in nationalist ceremonies, the latter positions resistance to violations of women's bodily integrity as (literally) 'other': Western, foreign, overeducated, unpalatable, unAfrican, beyond culture, inhuman – 'unfeminine'.[22]

McFadden and Datta both move the description of sexual harassment from a conversation stretching for connection between diverse experiences, in blind faith that such connection could clothe over the exposures and humiliations of sexualised assault, into forensic analysis of the *interests* galvanising such assaults. Although it is certain that several participants at the 1994 conference were deeply conscious of the complexities at the heart of sexual harassment, the surface discourse concentrated on the straightforward injustice of sexual attacks and the conviction that institutions, like universities and technikons, could 'eradicate' them through a web of planned policy-focused processes. In 1997, contained between Datta and McFadden, presentations did not abandon the work of designing activist interventions, but the political depth of the epistemological, discursive, contextual and physical battles participants were undertaking was visible. Daily 'energisers' reflected this: Nozipho Kwenaite, Dean of Students from the University of North, led participants in the lighthearted but/and military chorus – "*amajoni, amajoni wesexual harassment*".[23]

The theorisation of gender, culture, sexuality and violence crafted through the two conferences is the result of a research process realised through discussion and unmarked *as* research. There were (as already described) several pieces of work formally identified as 'research', such as that brought to the Conferences by Lebohang Letsie, [24] one of a number of sociological surveys looking at attitudes, experiences and policy environments. These formal studies played a critical role, first in creating – through the printed word – a collective of intra-institutional voices with information about sexual harassment and sexual violence and then, within the conference sites, as touchstones through which to offer traditionally 'academic' validity to problems denigrated as trivial or irrelevant.

---

22. McFadden, op.cit, p. 12.
23. A translation of this line: the soldiers, the soldiers of sexual harassment!
24. The first research done in South African universities was done at the University of Natal, followed closely by the research at UCT and research undertaken by Amanda Gouws and Andrienetta Kritzinger at the University of Stellenbosch, see Gouws and Kritzinger, 1995.

Reading the Conferences themselves, however, as points within a research process whose perimeters went beyond individual institutions reveals an ever-deepening conceptual complexity achieved as much through attention to particular position papers as through the organisational work required to bring dozens of people together. Who wanted to come, which professional portfolios claimed authority, which institutions made it possible for ten (rather than one) of their members to participate, how discussions negotiated regional, linguistic, racial and gender differences – all these questions came to inform questions about the place of political activism on sexual violence in higher education. There were increasingly complex discussions about whether activism against sexual harassment and sexual violence should be driven by management structures and focused primarily on policy development, or whether the voices of much less powerful sectors of the campus (residence wardens, counsellors, junior lecturers, administrative staff, students themselves) constituted the primary base of solidarity (and strategic decision-making) for the campus. There were also debates about epistemology. Some voices were deeply embedded in radical African feminist politics (such as Pat McFadden's, arguing passionately for the *bodily integrity* of African women, during the opening of the Gaborone Conference). Others, rooted in religious constituencies and faith-based philosophies, approached the issue of gender-based violence more from the perspective of 'good' Christian or Islamic practice than from the notion of transgressive gender-advocacy. There were strengths to both approaches – what was interesting to the researcher in me was the organic emergence of critical theoretical debates on gender and sexuality, and the possibility of containing actually quite distinct perspectives within one auditorium.

Harare Conference 2000

The emerging theoretical complexity of NETSH's work became particularly clear as the new Coordinating Committee began work in the years following the 1997 Conference. New fundraising work needed doing, a network membership needed development, local workshops needed design and delivery and the University of Zimbabwe had been nominated to host the next regional conference. The work of creating an environment hospitable to hosting this conference took ingenuity and political savvy among those within the Gender Studies Association/Affirmative Action Project at the University of Zimbabwe, and the work of NETSH was skilfully 'absorbed' into plans to hold a regional conference on Gender Equity, Democracy and

Human Rights in Institutions of Higher Education in Southern Africa.

This Conference, held in July 2000, occurred a month after the Zimbabwean parliamentary elections that returned ZANU-PF under Robert Mugabe to power, amid deep anxiety over government economic policies and a sense that Zimbabwean activism was facing enormous challenges of direction. Dr. Hope Sadza, then a University of Zimbabwe Council member, opened the Conference with direct appeals to participants to consider the full meaning of democracy in the post-election climate and yoked the question of gender discrimination to national policies on human rights. The Conference programme was complex: NETSH membership lists had been the basis for invitations and through well-placed presentations on sexual harassment and sexual violence, the NETSH agenda was subtly woven into 'broader' analyses of curricula, institutional cultures and – critically – the construction of masculinities.

At one level, the discussion of sexual harassment and sexual violence on campuses found itself submerged in a kaleidoscopic approach to 'gender', 'democracy' and 'equity'. At another – much more powerful I would argue – the theoretical language of sexual assault, developed through the Gaborone encounters, had found appropriate location within debates on gender identity, definitions of human rights and painfully complex avowals about democracy (in the presence of national definitions concerning democracy not palatable to all in the room). While new connections (between those initiating gender studies programmes and those battling sexist cultures in residences, for example) were forged, older links between those who had worked within NETSH purely through the focus on sexual harassment and sexual violence were challenged, especially through the conference's exploration of masculinities.

NETSH arranged for Tony Sardien, then a trainer with the Gender Education and Training Project (GETNET) in Cape Town, to bring a workshop on masculinities to the Harare Conference. In addition to this, a powerful student-focused research project run by the Department of Sociology at the University of Zimbabwe led to the presentation of a number of papers on gender identities on the campus, several of them authored by students, male and female. Many of these papers have since been collected into a book[25] and although academically uneven, they are extraordinary examples of analytical engagement with the links between class, ethnicity and gendered identities on a campus, identities through which students either survive their aca-

---

25. Gaidzanwa, 2001.

demic lives or – through deprivation, isolation or duty – fail. The Conference audience included nearly equal numbers of men and women: however, for some NETSH members permission for an overt focus on masculinity destabilised something of the earlier Conferences' political solidarity.

Within the public Conference discourse, performances of masculinity ranged from verbal sexual harassment in response to a keynote address by Amina Mama (she was asked whether she wouldn't prefer being the questioner's wife to giving public addresses on equity), through complaints about male peers' intolerance of those men interested in gender studies, to heartfelt male requests in Tony Sardien's workshop to have traditional 'masculine roles' (such as paying lobola, or being expected to tolerate aggression from other men) re-examined.[26] At the end of the Conference, participants were asked to stand up and collectively recite a poem:

> For every woman tired of acting weak when
> She knows she is strong, there is a man weary of appearing
> Strong when he feels vulnerable
> For every woman sick of acting dumb, there is a man burdened
> With the constant expectation of 'knowing everything'…
> For every woman feeling tied down by having children, there is a man denied
> The full joy of sharing parenthood.
> For every woman denied meaningful employment or equal pay
> There is a man bearing full financial responsibility for another human being
> …

For many participants, this poem was entirely congruent with the sense of new gender paradigms suggested by Conference discussions, and hinted at gendered warmth and reciprocity. Some others were appalled by the seeming loss of analysis of patriarchy:

"What utter rubbish – what are we going to be saying next: for every woman raped until she can't move, there's a man wanting to have his life destroyed?? What about the truth: for every woman deprived of a job, there's a man who is happy to control her – why does equality have to be so blind?"[27]

---

26. Not all men in this workshop were interested in such re-examination. In response to the question, "what is hard about being a man?", several answers suggest deep conservatism about gender identity: "feeling bad when provided for by a woman", "losing job to a woman", "seeing your daughter go out with another man".

27. From e-mail correspondence to author post-conference. The sender prefers anonymity, but has agreed to use of quotation here.

While six years earlier, in the 1994 Conference, Ramphele had argued for the transgressive construction of 'new' genders, among participants, many of whom were already sophisticated gender analysts, it took until 2000 for the implications of commitments to different incarnations of gendered identity to become fully embedded in public theoretical debate. Explorations of sexual harassment had shifted from appalled recognition of women's vulnerability to engagement with the masculinities responsible for male perpetration. This was a move painful in its illumination of conflict and confusion about whether masculinities could be reconstituted in ways that didn't fundamentally alienate them from 'womanhood', but a move essential to realism about the shape of the institutional battle against sexual harassment and sexual violence. International literature and regional research and publishing on masculinities certainly influenced the move, as did increasing donor interest in projects that tackled men's relationships to gender equality. Within the network of those whose focus was on sexual harassment and sexual violence in SADC higher education, however, the NETSH-co-organised conferences offered opportunities to research understanding of gendered violence in incrementally deepening ways.

The survey of Conference-based discussions suggests the development of indigenously-rooted theories of gender, sexuality and violence, spearheaded through collective exposure to the narrative of sexual assault on different campuses. There is no doubt in my mind that my thinking about such assaults has been strengthened by immersion in the organisation (through several different roles over the years) of occasions designed to effect – primarily – political activism in a specific area. That strength is not merely the obvious side-effect of taking other people's opinions and experiences seriously. It is more the result of negotiations of agency, mobility, identity and voice that occur in the process of transforming oneself from the 'author' of theorised experience into a member of a complex collective, visible at certain points, irrelevant at others, influential in some zones, naïvely powerless in others, successfully cooperative in places, radically isolated and maverick elsewhere. Such fluidity and its lessons were critical to the work of co-organising NETSH events.

Bodies in Action: Organising NETSH Activities – Tensions and Challenges

In 1997, at the Gaborone conference, participants spent a good half of the programme time in the systematic coordination of principles though which a network could become formalised as a body, empowered through constituency mandate to initiate and support local projects, to receive resources where possible and to demand inclusion in institutional policy discussions. Through intensive group-based debate, language was formulated to encompass statements of vision, mission and strategic aim and the structure of the proposed network was agreed upon.[28] NETSH was to be organised at three levels: a membership of 'signed up' individuals working in different ways on their campuses to challenge sexual harassment/sexual violence; a Coordinating Committee on which at least one person from every country represented within the membership sits; and a secretariat located at the African Gender Institute. Of these levels, the Coordinating Committee was to be the most powerful, directing and planning workshops, resource initiatives and local public advocacy work. By 1997, five countries were represented on the committee (Botswana, Lesotho, South Africa, Swaziland, Zimbabwe) and explicit commitments were made to develop membership and Coordinating Committee participation from other SADC countries: Zambia, Malawi, Namibia, Mozambique and Angola.

The process of designing a network structure raised questions which illuminated the politics of advocacy against sexual harassment at two levels. *Firstly*, tensions about representativity arose: were prospective NETSH members to 'represent' the institutions in which they were based as workers or students? Were Coordinating Committee members to 'represent' the interests of all institutions in the countries from which they came? All democratically-built organisations face debates about representation. What was peculiar to the NETSH tensions was the knowledge that no individual interested in NETSH's mission or aims carried the full support of her/his institution: while a vice rector here, or a committee there, had shown support for challenges to sexual harassment and sexual violence, as institutions each university was economically, culturally and intellectually largely hostile to the kinds of changes envisaged. Individuals could *not*, with integrity,

---

28. In 1997, these were articulated as follows: "Statement of Vision – Sexual harassment and sexual violence damage and distort the opportunity to work and to learn within Southern African institutions of education. The Network is committed to eliminating sexual harassment and sexual violence within education, and thereby, to contribute to the creation of Southern African societies where all sectors of life are free from sexual harassment and sexual violence. Statement of Mission – The Network's mission is to contribute to the elimination of sexual harassment and sexual violence in all Southern African institutions of education. The Network's initial focus will be on the elimination of sexual harassment and sexual violence in tertiary education".

'represent' their institutions – to do so would have meant constant rehearsal of covert misogyny, overt scepticism about the value of concentrating on sexual harassment, contradicted by flashes of feminist brilliance and energy. In addition, to work towards a structure comprised of 'institutions' would most likely exclude the participation of exactly the individuals most interested in challenging sexual harassment and sexual violence: people, for the most part, without much professional authority.

Coordinating Committee members faced slightly different dilemmas of representativity. They were more familiar with traditional political dilemmas of accountability, and the questions for them involved the diversity and numbers of institutions within the countries they came from. South African members could not be expected to fairly represent the interests of the (at least) 30 institutions of higher education in the country,[29] while members from Swaziland could find themselves accused of having access only to the viewpoint of a very small (relatively) single institution. As critically, given the inevitable difficulties of galvanising work in one institution, how were Coordinating Committee members to access the authority to inspire connections and new projects in institutions at which they were not workers or students without risking the 'denigration' of their own campuses?[30]

Wrestling with these issues continued over three years' worth of Coordinating Committees and in training workshops organised by NETSH in different countries. Immediate solutions took the shape of naming Coordinating Committee members based on the individual's access to resources, energy, political grasp of the problems and ability to gain respect within their local context. Such solutions risked compromising deep democracy and simultaneously increased the likelihood that those already with strong (even contentious) local profiles and individual resilience would be asked to take on the leadership of NETSH activism. The job responsibilities of these individuals were likely to be intense: in the years in which I worked among Coordinating members, several suffered severe bouts of ill-health as a result of institutionally based overwork and environmental hostility to their feminism.

---

29. The number of the institutions would have been the least of the difficulties here: apartheid education policies radically segregated South African education systems, leaving huge disparities in resources between them and deep ideological divisions.
30. In order to create joint institutional projects on challenging sexual harassment, it has to be acknowledged that sexual harassment does in fact take place. Where there is no permission for this, an individual who discusses cases of sexual harassment. occurring on her/his own campus with people from other campuses can be accused of 'disloyalty' or 'troublemaking'.

Questions of representativity, therefore, became shaped as much by the terrain in which the network wanted to work as by predictable organisational negotiations about power and accountability. The process of building a network found itself embedded in the dynamics of sexual harassment: successful and communicative activism had to find ways of combating institutionally effective ways of silencing feminist voices and marginalising feminised (women's, usually) bodies. While it would be stretching a metaphor to identify the NETSH process as a 'survivor', to recognise that organisation against sexual violence engages the complex aggression of 'normal' institutional authorities would not entail exaggeration. One of the earliest observations of sexual harassment researchers was that the performance of institutional hostility to their public exploration of abusive gender dynamics mirrored the interests of perpetrators. It is not surprising, therefore, that engagement with building a whole network of inter-institutionally-based individuals meant that we struggled to find straightforward ways of bringing directed energy to the task of challenging sexual harassment regionally.

Secondly, the organisation of NETSH raised dilemmas over resources. While at a constitutional level, the Coordinating Committee held leadership in the direction and flow of NETSH projects, the secretariat (at the African Gender Institute) was accountable for the management of funds raised to support NETSH work.[31] Coordinating Committee members thus had no independent access to NETSH funding and were dependent on administrative procedures far beyond their institutional control for integration into Committee meetings and into local negotiations over prospective new projects. Members based at the African Gender Institute, on the other hand, needed regular information and communication with Committee members in order to implement plans: this was rarely effected without delays, the need for clarification or problems of connectivity.

Well aware of the political difficulties at the African Gender Institute, Coordinating Committee members and others spoke of the hope that the secretariat could rotate, a hope supported by everyone at the African Gender Institute. The reality was, however, that African Gender Institute participants came to be seen as key to NETSH life and where these participants were forced to take on new responsibilities, changed portfolios, or left the Institute, NETSH cohesion suffered. Accusations and self-accusations about commitment, connection and agency occasionally coloured Coordinating

---

31. In the years 1994-2001, nearly all these funds came from the Ford Foundation. NORAD also contributed funding to the Gaborone Conference.

Committee meetings. Despite the positive evaluations made by people in a range of training workshops about the quality of NETSH members' grasp of sexual harassment issues and of the value of creating linkages between individuals to help them develop institutionally-specific strategies, people who had taken on large organisational roles within NETSH experienced fatigue, isolation and the sense of being pushed to the limits of what was possible.[32]

The organisational issues here are, like those of representativity, not uncommon in the work of alliance-creation, advocacy and movement-building. I would argue, however, that organising against sexual harassment and sexual violence creates particular difficulties for those with leadership responsibilities. Public 'expertise' in the area puts one very directly in connection with resource needs: for training, for advocacy work, for meeting survivors' needs (safe housing, academic support, travel to supportive space, healthcare, etc.). It is extremely difficult to sustain effective local challenges to sexual harassment and sexual violence without both high-level political support *and* access to resources. Where the only resources for the work are funnelled through a geographically distant (albeit strongly collegial) connection, one is placed in a position of dependency that compromises autonomous initiative: one is in fact 'feminised'. Coordinating Committee members undertook the organisation of conferences within their 'own' institutional space (Gaborone in 1997 and Harare in 2000) and simultaneously had to negotiate the politics of energising and building local conference committees and work with the NETSH secretariat. Colleagues at the secretariat rarely understood the full complexity of the local dynamics faced in Gaborone and Harare and also needed information acceptable to the University of Cape Town's administrative systems.[33] Both Coordinating Committee members who did this (Lebohang Letsie and Rekopantswe Mate) worked with immense political skill and inspirational dedication across the borders of institutions and countries (negotiating with diverse local inter-

---

32. An evaluation of NETSH was commissioned by the African Gender Institute in July 2001, with Hope Chigudu conducting it. While the evaluation confirmed that NETSH training workshops were valued by participants and that the NETSH vision and goals resonated strongly with members surveyed, it also described the AGI convenor's (then Bernedette Muthien, now Director of the NGO, Engender) levels of pressure and sense of isolation.
33. As the AGI is located within the University of Cape Town, this meant that all financial transactions – such as the transfer of monies from a donor fund for the support of a project – were administered through UCT systems.

ests as well). Positioned from within the African Gender Institute as part of the secretariat, I frequently experienced my work as that of an ignorant bully – asking for budgets and plans, from a position of financial 'authority' and simultaneously cavernous ignorance of the waters being forded by my Committee colleagues.

Regular Coordinating Committee meetings did much to renew and refresh lines of communication fractured by distance, contextual difference and the fact that we collectively shared no 'discipline', 'professional role' or institutional status. The value of face-to-face meetings, discussions and in-depth planning was visible not simply in the organisation of concrete projects (training, conferences, advocacy tools). Questions endemic to organising (representativity, financial power, leadership, communicative integrity) become saturated with the significances of gender, race and class, coagulations into powerlessness. Such powerlessness can be engineered overtly, or may be the result of simply not recognising the inevitable trajectories of 'normal' routes into community. Whatever the case, it is infused with the salience of structural oppressions. Thus, within NETSH organising, positioned accountabilities had the potential of becoming patterned into meanings of gender and class/race dynamics. Along such lines, the African Gender Institute became legible as 'masculine', 'white', 'South African-dominant' , while another Coordinating Committee member resonated as 'feminine', 'black', 'other SADC country'.

The situation described had, at one level, almost nothing to do with the actual people involved, who worked together with respect, affection and a robust intolerance for preciousness or personalised power-mongering. At another level, the possibility that NETSH dynamics would simply mimic conventionally oppressive forces was real – I *was* white and the African Gender Institute *was* located within South Africa and associated with a university whose colonialist legacy is powerful: the 'masculinity' of this position was indisputable. It took the hours of intensive, direct communication between all Coordinating Committee members to ensure that more complicated relations than 'masculine/feminine', 'white/black' and 'over-resourced/under-resourced' animated NETSH planning. A more kaleidoscopic, angled, poetically sharp[34] palette of recognitions concerning identity and power was demanded in the task of theorising the prevalence of sexual harassment and sexual violence and of acting against it. Such recognitions could not, ever,

---

34. 'Poetic' – meaning panoptic capacity to sustain the seemingly disjunct and the wit and intelligence to reveal incongruence.

discount our vulnerability to crude rehearsals of racial, national or gendered language and performance, but neither could they risk confinement to the very terms through which sexual violation is persistently possible.[35]

Theory Informed by Practice

In 1994, the initiation of NETSH was fuelled from numerous sources: national and regional discourses concerning gender, an astonishing year of political realignments within the SADC region and within South Africa itself and the work of fiercely direct – and diverse -- African feminists. As argued above, however, perhaps the most stimulating energies came from the years before 1994, in which struggles about the meaning of bodies' access to citizenship, education and opportunity had been waged on many campuses (and elsewhere). The political difficulty of representing the raped (or sexually harassed) body as a legitimate zone for solidarity within institutional spaces had been encountered as a shock, even to fairly seasoned social analysts:

> To my surprise, while there was certainly a moment at which it was like, "o no, is it true that a first year was raped in that residence?" and a sense that something wrong had happened, it kind of dissolved, just seeped back into the floor, and when I raised the need to do some serious studying of the circumstances of how these things happen, how we can prevent them, I was treated as though I'd made a very inappropriate and emotional suggestion; I was treated as though I was an embarrassment to the department.[36]

The bodies (and voices) of the assaulted created in complex ways the most compelling sources of insistence that higher educational institutions take sexual harassment and sexual violence seriously. NETSH's 'personal' connection with these assaults was, from the outset, multiple: those interested in joining as members included survivors, witnesses, confused friends, outraged would-be guerrilla-protectors, silenced sympathisers, story-tellers, explorers and service-providers. Although established from within the borders of the academy, and despite the influence of some valuable pieces of traditionally crafted research on the issue,[37] NETSH was not imagined as a research network.

---

35. For more analysis of this point, see Rao and Friedman, 1998.
36. B. Mapetla, lecturer in sociology at VISTA, personal communication, Oct. 1995.
37. See the work of Amanda Gouws and Andrienetta Kritzinger, Thandabantu Nhlapo, Fathima Hafferjee, Carla Sutherland and others.

The process of organising fora through which isolated individuals could be supported in the work of building intra-institutional energies through which to design policies, run educational workshops or negotiate for new resources uncovered the nature of sexual harassment and sexual violence on SADC campuses. Unlike other feminist networks in the region, such as Women and Law in Southern Africa (WLSA), NETSH's primary task was not research-focused and yet the complexity of the connections between gender, culture, violence and sexuality became incrementally deepened, explored and debated as discussions looked for ways to, for example, theorise women students' experiences of being sexually targeted by men lecturers 'alongside' analysis of men students' struggles to survive economically within resource-barren campuses.

At one level, therefore, the succession of NESTH-generated opportunities to devote sustained critical attention to the conceptual and practical work of challenging sexual harassment and sexual violence on different campuses escalated the intensity of theoretical debate on gendered dynamics within higher education. The 1994 questions concerning the isolation, gendered hostility and institutionally rooted secondary victimisation faced by those who 'outed' the insidiousness of sexual harassment had developed by 2000 into intensive heuristic engagement with masculinities. At the Harare conference that year, the work being presented by the University of Zimbabwe students and faculty and the interest in the GETNET masculinities workshop was explicitly connected to the demand to explore 'changing' men. While individuals continued to wrestle with intricate local dynamics of instituting new research, policy change or educational programmes on different campuses, the meta-level of the discourse had shifted – through six years of interaction – from appalled political loneliness to complex, practical and undaunted solidarity.

The capacity of conferencing to deepen the kinds of theoretical and practical questions possible within a field of study is, of course, well documented. A deeper level at which NETSH organising influenced the process of conceptualising sexual harassment and sexual violence in SADC higher education came through the politics of designing, building and sustaining a network. Developing the knowledge necessary to create effective communicative linkages, negotiate issues of fund-raising and fund-management and ensure transparency was a long-term process, which demanded balance and careful respect for others' experiences. The skills required speak to the difficulty of all organisation-building, but are particularly crucial to the work of challenging sexual harassment and sexual violence. Issues of silenced voices, traumatised people, defensive institutional structures and resourcelessness pressurise activists (at all institutional levels) in complex ways, rarely grasped in quick discussion across institutions. The negotiation of a collectively-designed NETSH event, such as a conference, taught as much about institutional dynamics as any paper or presentation.

After the July 2000 Conference in Harare, NETSH received funding for another two years' work from the Ford Foundation. The funding was routed through the African Gender Institute and made provision for a full-time position dedicated to the growth of the Network. This post was taken up by Bernedette Muthien, and, together with a new Coordinating Committee, the years 2001-02 saw new workshops, the development of regional audits of available resources and the design and dissemination of a handbook. From July 2000, my own relationship to NETSH shifted from secretariat member to collegial engagement, wherever possible, with Bernedette Muthien inside the African Gender Institute as her work moved NETSH into new waters.

Summing Up

In 1994, when I first came to the African Gender Institute, my relationship to issues of sexual harassment on SADC campuses involved a part-time job at the University of Cape Town as a consultant researcher, commissioned to explore the implementation of the university's policy on sexual harassment. The work placed me in direct engagement with institutional voices, all of which had integrity, but few of which were in synchrony: disciplinary officers spoke of the 'attrition' of complainants; women students voiced fury, insecurity and confusion; some feminist lecturers bore witness to the way the campus had – in fact – changed for the better in the past ten years; counselling staff pointed to the financial and cultural strain many incoming students endured. My own position was marginal, a footnote to a footnote: I was employed by the Equal Opportunity Research Project, a young non-faculty-based research project set up to support the work of a Deputy Vice Chancellor.

After NETSH was initiated following the 1994 conference hosted by the Equal Opportunity Research Project, I was involved more and more in the day-to-day planning for funding and project design. What I came to 'know' as a *researcher* about sexual harassment and sexual violence on SADC campuses accrued over a five-year process of adjustment, evaluation, self-criticism and (literal) mobility across national, institutional and personal borders. The moments of failure (inability to find new funds, postponed events, confusions around agency) and the moments of accomplishment (a well-run workshop, dissemination of a set of resources, the knock at the e-mail door asking for information and support) have become infused with a sense of growing insight concerning the meaning of being gendered and sexual. Apprehension (even horror) at the sight of the gulf between African feminist recognitions of 'bodily integrity' and neo-patriarchal convictions about the epistemological irrelevance of women's embodied experiences has been, at every turn, offset by the palpable reality that we are not destroyed by sexual assault. Outraged, yes; hurt, yes; individually dislocated and silent, yes often; but in any relation to permanent – collective – death, no.

While the statistics on prevalence or perception and qualitative material narrating incident and case depict – as they must – the profile of African (mostly women's) victimisation, what *research* (here, the intricately communicative, directed, exploration of contextualised sexual harassment and sexual violence over five years) suggests is resilient, intelligent, border-crossing strategy towards reimagining the African body as un-invadable.

References

Ahimbisibwe, J. and D.K. Muhwezi, 2002, "The Gains and Challenges of Sponsoring Women's Education in Public Universities in Uganda: A Case Study of Makerere University", paper presented at Women's World Congress, Kampala, 2002

Bennett, J., 2000, "Introduction: The Politics of Writing", *Agenda* 46.

Bunting, I., 1994, *Legacy of Inequality: Higher Education in South Africa.* Cape Town: UCT Press.

Chagonda, T. and A. Gore, 2000, "Issues of masculinity among UZ students" in Report of the Regional Conference on Gender Equity, Democracy and Human Rights in Institutions of Higher Education in Southern Africa, written by K. Kujinga and D. Chingarande, edited by R. Mate, available from Gender Studies Association, University of Zimbabwe.

Crenshaw, Kendall Thomas, Gary Peller, 2001, *Critical Race Theory: The Key Writings that Formed the Movement.* London: Yale University Press.

Chivaura, I., 2000, "Affirmative Action at the University of Zimbabwe", paper presented at Conference on Gender Equity, Democracy, and Human Rights, University of Zimbabwe, 2000.

Datta, Ansu, 1997, "Closing Remarks" in *Report: Southern African Tertiary Education Institutions Challenging Sexual Harassment/Sexual Violence,* African Gender Institute and National Institute of Development Research and Documentation, Gaborone, 1997.

De la Rey, 1997, *Report on gender and higher education in South Africa*. Pretoria: Government Publications.

Fish, J., 1996, *The African student experience at the University of Port Elizabeth, South Africa*. University of Port Elizabeth: Centre for Organizational and Academic Development.

Gaidzanwa, R.B., 1997, *Gender analysis in the Field of Education: A Zimbabwean example*, in Imam, A., A. Mama and F. Sow (eds), *Engendering African Social Sciences*. Dakar: CODESRIA.

—, 2000, "Academic careers and women at the University of Zimbabwe", paper presented at Conference on Gender Equity, Democracy, and Human Rights, University of Zimbabwe, 2000.

—, 2001, *Speaking for Ourselves:Masculinities and Femininities Against Students at the University of Zimbabwe*. University of Zimbabwe Affirmative Action Project.

Gouws, A. and A. Kritzinger, 1995, "Sexual Harassment of Students: A case study of a South African university", *South African Sociological Review* 7, 2, 1995.

Hallam, R., 1994, *Crimes Without Punishment: Sexual Harassment and violence against female students in schools and universities in Africa*. Discussion Paper # 4. London: African Rights.

Kaplan, B., 1995, *Changing by Degrees: Tertiary Education in South Africa*. Cape Town: UCT Press.

Kasente, D., 2001, "Popularizing Gender: A Case Study of Makerere University", paper commissioned for FAWE and presented at 10th General Conference of the Association of African Universities, Nairobi 2001.

Mabokela, R.O. and K.L. King (eds), 2001, *Apartheid No More: case studies of Southern African universities in the process of transformation*. Westport, CT: Bergin and Garvey.

Mbilizi, M., 2001, "Gender Equity in Malawian Higher Education", paper presented at NETSH Workshop on Sexual Harassment, July, 2001, available from www.gwsafrica.org

Mboya, M. 2001, "Gender Sensitive Qualitative Data: Sample Collection Instrument for African Universities", paper presented for FAWE, at 10th General Conference of the Association of African Universities, Nairobi, 2001.

McFadden, Patricia, 1997, "Sexual Harassment: An Opening Challenge" in *Report: Southern African Tertiary Education Institutions Challenging Sexual Harassment/Sexual Violence,* African Gender Institute and National Institute of Development Research and Documentation, Gaborone, 1997.

Millett, K., 1970, *Sexual Politics*. New York: Ballantine Books.

Mookodi, G., 2002, "Constructing Gender in Botswana: Insights into Male and Fenale Identities make a difference", paper presented at the Women's World Congress, Kampala, July, 2002.

Namuddu, K., 1995, "Gender perspectives in the transformation of Africa; challenges to the African university as a model to society", *Women and Higher Education in Africa.* Dakar: UNESCO.

Ndinda, C. and D.N. Charthaigh, 2000, "Perceptions of race, class, and gender among black female students at the University of Natal, Durban", paper presented at Conference on Gender Equity, Democracy, and Human Rights, University of Zimbabwe, 2000.

Nhlapo T., 1992, "Culture and women abuse: some South African starting points", *Agenda,* 13.

Pattman, R., 2002, "'As a Traditional Man, I take the Missionary Position': Forging Gender Identities and Relations at the University of Botswana", paper presented at the Women's World Congress, Kampala, July, 2002.

Ramphele, M., 1995, *A Life.* Cape Town and Johannesburg: David Philip.

Rao, A. and M. Friedman, 1998, "Transforming Institutions: History and Challenges, An International Perspective", paper delivered at AWID-AGI seminar on Transformation for Gender Justice and Organisational Change, Cape Town, 31 May-4 June 1998.

Rathgeber. E.M., 1991, "Women in Higher Education in Africa: Access and Choices" in Kelly, G. and S. Slaughter (eds), *Women's Higher Education in Comparative Perspective.* Dordrecht: Kluwer Academic Publishers.

Rich, A., 1979, *Lies, Secrets and Silences: Selected Prose 1966-1978.* New York: WW Norton.

Sall, E., 2000, *Women in Academia: Gender and Academic Freedom in Africa.* Dakar: CODESRIA.

Simons, M., F. Molteno and C. Sutherland, 1991, *Final Report of the Committee of Enquiry into Sexual Harassment,* University of Cape Town, Equal Opportunity Research Project.

Stambach, A., 1998, "'Education is My Husband': Marriage, Gender and Reproduction in Northern Tanzania", in Bloch, M., J. Beoku-Betts and R. Tabachnick, *Women and Education in Sub-Saharan Africa: Power, Opportunities, and Constraints.* Boulder and London: Lynne Rienner Publishers.

Sutherland C 1991 "Sexual harassment: a darker side to campus life" in *Agenda* 11, 1991

Tamale, S. and J. Oloka-Onyango, 2000, "'Bitches' at the Academy: Gender and Academic Freedom in Africa," in Sall, E., *Women in Academia: Gender and Academic Freedom in Africa.* Dakar: CODESRIA.

Tlou, S. and L. Letsie, 1997, "Sexual Harassment in Tertiary Education: the case of the University of Botswana", in *Report: Southern African Tertiary Education Institutions Challenging Sexual Harassment/Sexual Violence,* African Gender Institute and National Institute of Development Research and Documentation, Gaborone, 1997.

CHAPTER THREE

Reflections of a Feminist Scholar-Activist in Nigeria

Charmaine Pereira

Introduction

This chapter explores my experiences of trying to carve a space for women's studies within the Nigerian academy, and of linking activism in this sphere with activism on gender justice outside the academy. I reflect on the difficulties of sustaining intellectual work in the university at a time when the economy was, and as it continues to be, in crisis and politics were subsumed under military rule. Differing understandings of my identity, and therefore my 'place' in the academy and the society at large, have been at play in shaping the possibilities of my contributing to developing feminist praxis and women's studies. The fact that work on gender and women's studies in Africa has often been carried out without necessarily being marked by feminist politics (Tsikata 2001a; Mama 1996a) highlights the need for more analytical work in this area (Pereira 2000).

Negotiating identities, whether determined by others or self-defined, has textured my experience in significant ways. As a Kenyan of Indian descent, married to a Nigerian, my self-identification as an African feminist has often been at odds with dominant definitions of myself as a 'Niger wife' (a foreign woman married to a Nigerian man), or even as a 'white' woman! In the northern Nigerian context of the early 1990s, women and men of Asian descent as well as those of European descent (expatriates) were equally referred to as 'white'. Coming from a background of anti-racist struggles in the United Kingdom, at a time when people of Asian descent involved in such struggles self-identified as 'black', including myself, I found this new categorisation astonishing, to say the least. In common parlance, to be an expatriate is 'to be white' and 'to have foreign exchange' (particularly US dollars).

I interpret this scenario as a manifestation of Nigeria's particular history and politics (see e.g., Hall 1980). The development of racialised hierarchies and divisions in Nigeria appears to be shaped by historical relations of domination brought about through colonialism and capitalism and sustained by prevailing global and local conditions of social and economic underdevelopment. Unlike those parts of the African continent where settler colonialism was a dominant feature of political history, Nigeria experienced indirect rule for the most part. In everyday interactions, race consciousness and racial hierarchies have not structured social relations in West African countries such as Nigeria and Ghana in as pervasive a manner as they do for example, in South Africa or, to a lesser extent, Kenya or Uganda.

In contemporary Nigeria, whilst the differences in colour are only partially reflected in language, this is not because such differences are not perceptible. It is because the significant feature, and the assumed common feature about racial groups such as Euro-Americans and Asians (collectively referred to as expatriates) in the Nigerian context is their association with foreign capital. The identification of class interests has not taken place along a singular dimension of race but across several. The continued significance of racialised hierarchies and consciousness reflects to a large extent, but not exclusively, the continued salience of foreign capital. Regional differences in the way in which such capital is deployed – whether through transnational oil companies in the Niger Delta or Lebanese and Indian factories and trade in Lagos and parts of the North, for example – are likely to be implicated in apparent regional differences in the manifestation of racialised consciousness.

The situation is complicated by the interplay of race and gender ideologies. My obvious difference from those around me on the grounds of race was further accentuated by my identification as a feminist. In my new setting, the dominant view of feminism was that it was 'un-African' and 'alien'. It is clear, however, that the epithet of 'alien' is quite selectively applied in the domain of knowledge production, practice and politics. The generalised acceptance (until relatively recently) of other 'alien' phenomena, such as 'modernisation', raises the question of what lies behind the widespread resistance to feminism. Changes in the dominant perceptions of feminism are slow to come about, even among activists clearly working to further gender equity. Yet such change is evident in the greater tendency to talk either in terms of African feminism or to use terms such as womanism (see Tsikata 1997).

Knowledge Production: The University

The scope for knowledge production in Nigerian universities is shaped by the broader social, political, economic and cultural context within which universities are located, as well as the conditions shaping the development of the university system itself (see Pereira 2007). Of the 45 years of flag independence in Nigeria, since 1966 military rule has prevailed for all but 15 years. One of the many consequences of prolonged military rule is the permeation and reinforcement of authoritarian and antidemocratic tendencies through the multiple levels and arenas of social relations in families, communities and institutions, including those of the state. Despite Nigeria's huge oil wealth, the vast majority of the citizenry are excluded from the possibilities of development as a result of poverty, corruption and the public debt burden. The Nigeria Human Development Report (UNDP 2001) estimates that 70 per cent of the population lives in poverty and 70 per cent of these people are female.

The expansion of universities across the African continent by the new nationalist regimes that came to power after independence during the 1960s, was driven by the notion that universities should serve the nation and participate in the country's development. However, economic crisis in the late 1970s and early 1980s restricted the possibilities of African governments maintaining investments in education. By the late 1980s and 1990s, economic and political crises had deepened in most African states, and universities were not exempt from their effects. The combined weight of structural adjustment programmes (SAPs); the excessive control of social actors and institutions that SAPs required for their implementation by the state; and the mismanagement, bureaucracy and corruption inherent in the running of state institutions and universities led to the demise of the university system in Nigeria as well as in other African countries (Sall 2002; Sawyerr 1998; Jega 1994). One of the consequences has been an exodus of academics out of universities to other sectors within the country or to universities outside (Bangura 1994).

The overall ethos in Nigerian universities since the onset of structural adjustment is hinted at in the prevailing attitudes towards staff members who retained a political and intellectual existence during this period. Among this group were a few women activists among the academic staff, who tended to be linked to international networks of feminists and travelled relatively frequently to meetings abroad. Their apparent autonomy, accentuated in some cases by their relative youth, was in stark contrast to the dependence of most university staff (male and female) on their meagre monthly wages. The immiseration of the middle class, in particular, under SAP has had serious implications for the capacity of university staff to cope with increasing cuts in their earning power.

In this context, women activists who travelled outside the country were the focus of considerable envy by the majority of their colleagues, who assumed that they were making vast sums of money (in US dollars). Also envied were those (predominantly male) academics who were able to sustain their intellectual existence through research and their links with international networks, which necessarily occasioned foreign travel. Those who inspired envy were intellectually and politically active; their activity necessarily rested on hard work and the existence of a track record. Increased productivity, however, did not give rise to accelerated promotions: the latter were time-bound[1] and very often delayed by institutional crises and setbacks.

Neither hard work nor the existence of a track record in itself was the *primary source* of envy on the part of the majority of academic staff. This was clear from the fact that the norm for most academic staff was to avoid doing more work than was necessary. The generalised lack of respect for intellectual effort was manifested, in some instances, by senior academic staff not turning up for their lectures or appearing late. Very little effort was put into devising alternative sources and strategies for teaching, despite the paucity of texts and documentation in general. Often, the very lack of resources was viewed as reason enough for not doing one's work. Research, it should be said, was barely contemplated by most academic staff. What fuelled the envy of individuals who travelled to foreign parts was the belief that such activity was financially lucrative.

The military takeover and running of Ahmadu Bello University from November 1995 exacerbated the erosion of intellectual autonomy and possibilities for meaningful scholarly work that had begun in the mid-1980s. By the end of 1997, I had left Ahmadu Bello University. One of the consequences of the destabilisation of the university system in Nigeria is that many former university lecturers – I count myself among them – now choose to work outside the system, since our experiences within have proved tremendously hostile to research and innovation in general. In this context, maintaining a profile of engagement in research and activism is difficult, not least because of the time required to raise funds for research and the competing claims on time that arise from activism. For many in this situation, consultancies, to the extent that they are available, become the mainstay of personal livelihoods.

---

1. Promotions took place on a three-yearly basis, assuming the Appointments and Promotions Committee was functional in the university.

Knowledge Production: Consultancies

The use of consultancies in the development field and by donor agencies has marked a shift in the ways in which different forms of work, including intellectual work, have come to be structured. Whilst relying on an individual's research capacity and experience, the payment of consultancies makes no contribution to the development or renewal of such capacity. At their core, consultancies embody the notion that work can easily be abstracted from its institutional base, production costs and the reproduction of labour. Payment is typically made for a minimal number of time segments (usually days) within which, it is conveniently assumed, all the work will be carried out.

The time-bounded character of consultancy contracts introduces particular challenges for the person commissioned, such as grappling with deadlines and the difficulties of delivering on time. For the agency commissioning the consultancy, the use of a restricted notion of time as the basis for payment facilitates the erasure of the material and less tangible resources needed to make that time productive. These include the physical, intellectual and social infrastructure provided by the consultant's workspace; the resources required to produce the concrete output of the consultancy; and the resources necessary to re/produce the intellectual as a person capable of working.

Whilst consultancies essentially constitute a mode of payment, the use of the term to cover often quite diverse forms of work highlights the homogenising effect of the casualisation of work and payment in this process of aggregation. Arguments favouring the uptake of consultancies by those who benefit from their deployment include flexibility in recruitment and the assignment of work tasks (see e.g., Salmi n.d.), rapidity of output and reduced costs. These are all characteristics of piece-work, which, for several years, has typically been carried out by female homeworkers in industrialised Western economies as well as in countries of the global South (see e.g., Allen and Wolkowitz 1986, 1987). The increasing use of consultancies by development agencies and funders marks an era in which knowledge-centred activity is being increasingly casualised, taking the form of *intellectual piece-work*, even as the global knowledge economy is being championed by the World Bank and other interest groups. Whilst researchers are relatively privileged categories of workers, they are not exempt from the processes involved in the informalisation of economies. The resulting restructuring of work is taking place at a time of economic restructuring more generally, in the context of economic crisis, histories of structural adjustment, globalisation and the rise of neoliberalism.

Networks

Against this backdrop, regeneration of the university system requires radical rethinking of the nature of universities as sites of knowledge production, as well as their relations with outside agencies. The content of that regeneration has varied, depending on the agenda for change and the interest groups involved. Manuh et al. (2002) point to the challenges posed to Ghanaian universities by the formation of new policy institutes, which would represent potential partners for universities if collaborative relations with them were to be developed. In this context, the *interdependence* of universities and networks of various kinds, as devices for creating and sustaining knowledge through teaching and research, has to be recognised (Court 2000). In many parts of Africa, networks, as knowledge environments, have come into being precisely because of the failure of university settings in this capacity (Prewitt 1998).

One such network is CODESRIA – the Council of Social Science Research in Africa. The formation of CODESRIA heralded the emergence of regional networking dedicated to the pursuit of knowledge from a pan-Africanist perspective, the aim being to advance struggles for intellectual autonomy as well as democratisation. Yet even within CODESRIA, struggles for intellectual autonomy continue, as manifested by the demands of feminist researchers involved in CODESRIA's activities since the 1980s and beyond (Imam et al. 1997; Pereira 2002). Feminist researchers have insisted that the knowledge produced through CODESRIA's activities should take account of the differential perspectives, experiences and positions of women as well as men. This effectively meant transforming the kind of knowledge that was produced as well as the processes of its production – a project that simultaneously involved intellectual as well as institutional transformation.

With regard to university systems, even if these were functional by conventional definitions of the term, this would neither guarantee gender equality in institutional practices nor an awareness of gender in intellectual content. The general need, expressed above, for scholars to create additional knowledge environments through networks is even more critical for researchers working in the field of gender and women's studies. Whilst work in this area has a long history in Nigeria, scholars active in gender and women's studies still face difficulties in having their work treated as worthy of academic attention or respect. The paucity of research funds, isolation of individual researchers and lack of institutionalisation of gender and women's studies were some of the key factors leading to the establishment of the Network for Women's Studies in Nigeria (NWSN) in January 1996 (Mama 1996b).

In reflecting on these experiences, I explore concepts such as autonomy and dependence, security and insecurity, in the personal, intellectual and financial domains, highlighting contradictions as well as the articulation and disconnection of these elements with one another. This has entailed exploring ways in which power operates in terms of structuring relations in the overlapping domains of personal autonomy, intellectual life and financial security. Intellectual autonomy is ultimately premised on a material base and a degree of personal autonomy. For me, it has also been important to have a critical understanding of the organisations with which I work, and to grapple with the meanings of 'network' and its connections to different kinds of institutions. Not least, all of this is intimately connected to how I understand the practice of feminism.

This chapter is presented in three parts. I begin by addressing the conditions shaping the formation of the Network for Women's Studies in Nigeria (NWSN) and issues concerning its sustainability. The second part of the paper explores the dynamics of gender politics in the politics of funding, highlighting the example of one funding agency's response to NWSN's proposal to carry out research on sexual harassment in Nigerian universities. In the third part of the paper, I reflect on the contours of feminist subjectivity, scholarship and activism that have shaped my praxis in Nigeria.

The Formation of the Network for Women's Studies in Nigeria (NWSN)

Formed in 1996, the Network for Women's Studies in Nigeria (NWSN) is an independent, multi-ethnic and multi-religious nationwide network of scholars engaged in teaching and research on gender and women's studies. Membership is constituted on an individual basis: most members are located in the academy and are women. The formation of NWSN as an independent, national network of scholars marked the creation of a space for building capacity for teaching and research in gender and women's studies, as well as for strengthening the institutionalisation of the field. The Network was inaugurated at a workshop held in Kaduna in January 1996, on the theme of Setting an Agenda for Gender and Women's Studies in Nigeria. The aim was to "set up a process through which we will indeed be able to set our own agenda for the future development of gender and women's studies locally, but also with some awareness of the regional and international contexts" (Mama 1996b:1). The founding Coordinator was Amina Mama, followed by myself, in the wake of her departure to South Africa in January 1999.

The Network's aims comprise:
- Promoting theory and research in gender and women's studies
- Networking among scholars, researchers and teachers of gender and women's studies
- Facilitating the institutionalisation of gender and women's studies in Nigerian higher education
- Curriculum development in gender and women's studies at various educational levels
- Promoting the inclusion of gender and women's studies in mainstream teaching curricula at all levels of education.

The philosophy underlying these aims points to the institutionalisation of gender and women's studies in universities as an important pivot for the other goals – teaching, research, the development of theory and the facilitation of networking among African women scholars in this field. Institutionalisation, as a process, formalises recognition of gender and women's studies as an intellectual field and is a precondition for support from the university administration in the form of space and resources for the various programmes to be carried out in gender and women's studies.

Whilst institutionalisation facilitates the realisation of goals in relation to teaching and research, this does not mean that such goals cannot be pursued without institutionalisation. However, a lack of institutional support compounds the various difficulties in furthering the development of gender and women's studies, with all its ramifications. The reality is that gender and women's studies in Nigeria and elsewhere in Africa have developed in the academy, at best, without institutional support and more often under conditions of active hostility (see Mama 1996a; Sow 1997; Phiri 2000).

The formation of NWSN, whilst acknowledging the significance of institutionalising gender and women's studies, simultaneously points to the imperative of creating an autonomous base in order to articulate a liberatory agenda for gender and women's studies in Nigeria (see Pereira 2003; Mama 1996a). It should be pointed out here that the argument for institutionalising gender and women's studies is not synonymous with that of 'mainstreaming' in the development literature. 'Mainstreaming' refers to the aim of integrating gender concerns in 'general' development projects, as opposed to carrying out women-specific projects: its pre-eminence marks a shift from WID (Women in Development) to GAD (Gender and Development) in development thinking. 'Mainstreaming' is particularly favoured by a number of funding agencies (Tarasher and Ford-Smith 1990) and UN agencies, and is a key feature of the Beijing Platform for Action (see Tsikata 2001b).

With regard to NWSN, there are two key features associated with the emphasis on institutionalising gender and women's studies that distinguish it from 'mainstreaming'. The first is the recognition of the significance of autonomous bases (i.e., the NWSN) to protect intellectual autonomy in gender and women's studies. Rather than institutionalisation and autonomy being treated as oppositional dimensions, they are recognised as both being necessary in order to serve different purposes in a holistic approach to gender and women's studies. The second key difference between the concepts of institutionalisation and 'mainstreaming' in this instance concerns their application. NWSN's uptake of the notion of institutionalisation is coupled with a political insistence on the need for social transformation within the academy and beyond. This is distinct from the general application of the term 'mainstreaming' to refer to reform within the existing institutional, economic and political order (see also Tsikata 2001b).

Members of NWSN are based in 17 institutions of higher education (universities), two independent research centres, five women-centred advocacy organisations and one pan-African women's research organisation. Within the 17 institutions of higher education, there are five existing centres of gender/women's studies. These are: a) Women's Research and Documentation Centre (WORDOC) at the University of Ibadan; b) Centre for Gender and Policy Studies, Obafemi Awolowo University, Ile-Ife; c) Women's Studies Unit, Institute of Education, University of Nigeria, Nsukka; d) Ahmadu Bello University Gender and Women's Studies Group; e) Documentation and Analysis of Women's and Gender Studies Unit, Nnamdi Azikiwe University, Awka. The Network currently has a total of 49 paid-up members out of the 126 persons on its registration list and is based in Abuja.

NWSN carries out its work through four committees: a) a Working Group, with responsibility for policy direction, meetings, membership and overall coordination of the network; b) Research and Publications Committee; c) Curriculum Development Committee; d) Organisational Strategies Committee, working on the institutionalisation of gender and women's studies. Up to January 2005, NWSN had no employed staff: the work was carried out by a core of seven active volunteers, who sometimes engaged others whilst discharging their responsibilities. The core body of volunteers was made up of office-holders and Convenors of Committees, including the National Coordinator.

NWSN was supported in its formative period (1996-99) by an innovative three-way link programme under the British Council Higher Education Links scheme. The programme linked NWSN and Ahmadu Bello University, Zaria with Liverpool University, UK. Exchange visits were carried out with a view to curriculum development and the setting-up of a documentation centre at Ahmadu Bello University, both of which were successfully achieved. Documentation acquired during the exchange visits was also made available to participants at NWSN training workshops, in the form of individual study packs and collections of readings on the theme of the visit, at established centres in the Network.

Since January 1996, four NWSN workshops have been held on the themes of concepts and methodologies (Pereira 1997); curriculum (Odejide and Isiugo-Abanihe 1999); gender and policy (all held at Obafemi Awolowo University, Ile-Ife 1998); and the gender politics of violence (held at Jerrotel, Jos 2002). Resource persons for NWSN training workshops have been drawn from higher education institutions in Ghana, Sierra Leone, South Africa and the UK. The cumulative impact of these workshops has been to facilitate participants' access to new and ongoing research, as well as to published work on gender and women's studies in Nigeria and elsewhere. The workshops have also provided a forum for debate and discussion with peers across Nigeria, the exchange of ideas and experience and possibilities for future collaboration.

To date, NWSN is the only network of its kind in Nigeria, developing critical understanding of the deployment of gender and power in a variety of public discourses. NWSN takes as its starting point the conditions of knowledge production in the context of prevailing gender relations and other relations of dominance. In the process, NWSN challenges existing notions of what constitutes knowledge, who can be said to be a 'knower' and the conditions under which knowledge might be more appropriately produced. In an era when such critical thinking and analysis are *not* supported more generally, the need for networks engaging in activities of this kind is correspondingly greater. The work that NWSN carries out has wide ranging implications not only for the character of knowledge that is produced, but also for the trajectories and scope of social change that are entailed.

Whilst the aims and activities of NWSN are laudable, the real challenge lies in its sustainability. In order to carry out its aims, a network needs a minimal structure and resources of its own. Providing an institutional space within the academy has proven difficult for a host of reasons: the hostility of university administrations to gender and women's studies; the reluctance of university administrations to grant autonomy to existing centres of gender and women's studies; the lack of time and energy on the part of women scholars to run a network in addition to enormous teaching loads and gendered divisions of labour in the household and community. This raises the question of what kind of institutional space can be created for the Network outside the academy and what resources can be drawn upon for this purpose.

The difficulties of sustaining NWSN beyond the first three years, in the absence of an institutional base, with no funding and poor communications, have been tremendous. From 1999 to 2002, there was a three-and-a-half-year hiatus in annual training workshops. During this time, and subsequently, the very existence of the Network was being questioned by members, given the absence of a system to keep members regularly informed about the Network and the difficulties in raising funds for NWSN's self-determined goals. The situation was somewhat alleviated when, in April 2002, the Network held a successful training workshop on The Gender Politics of Violence. The issue of sustainability was discussed openly at that workshop and I quote from the report that I presented there as National Coordinator:

> The departure of NWSN's first National Convenor had two major effects, in my opinion. The first of these was to change the funding dynamic faced by the Network, since the second National Convenor (myself) was both less well known in funding circles and had less experience raising funds. The second effect was to deprive the Network of an institutional base, which although not dedicated to NWSN, was still supportive of its work. This was the office of ABANTU for Development, in Kaduna, an office set up by the first NWSN National Convenor in her capacity as Director of Research for ABANTU for Development.[2]
>
> The first point has to some extent been reduced over the last few years, in terms of my becoming better known in certain funding circles. However, I think there is still a lot to be learned, both by myself and by members of NWSN, in terms of developing fund-raising strategies. The politics of funding is clearly murky territory. Perhaps this needs to be explored further, even

---

2. See www.abantunigeria.org for more information about the work of ABANTU for Development.

as we attempt to build capacity in fund raising. Moreover, effective fund raising takes considerable time and energy. The extent to which such work can be sustained by a single individual is debatable.

The second point, the lack of an institutional base, has had serious implications for the maintenance of the Network. Running a network, whatever its nature, requires certain administrative tasks to be carried out on a regular basis – registering members, tracking their contact addresses, collecting dues, calling upon members to engage in activities, keeping members informed of the network's activities, fund raising, sharing of information, organising events and so on. These activities need to be designated to known individuals and carried out effectively. Above all, members need to be able to communicate with one another for the network to continue to exist in real terms. I have not come across any network that can do all this without an organisation or institution to provide a secretariat for its work. A secretariat necessarily needs people to run it.[3]

Having an institutional base brings with it a number of advantages: the formalisation of work responsibilities by designated persons, remuneration for the work carried out by paid staff, space to house resources of the Network and a formal locus for members' communication with the coordinating body. Some of these features, however, may also introduce tensions. For example, remuneration for some but not for others may introduce a feeling of being short-changed on the part of those who are not paid. Staff, for their part, may not be as committed to the work as members would like them to be, particularly in a context where work on 'gender' or 'women' is attractive to many primarily as an avenue for job-seeking and upward mobility.

As for members' personal commitment, the discussions following the 2002 National Coordinator's Report made clear to those present that there was a need for such commitment and that this was a prerequisite to collective engagement. Both personal commitment and collective engagement were necessary for the Network to fulfil its aims. Tangible commitment from members was manifested through the payment of dues, voluntary contributions to NWSN and volunteering to take on administrative responsibilities. Nevertheless, the challenges faced in maintaining the existence of the Network remain considerable.

The question of how the Network and its activities are to be funded is no straightforward question. Many NGOs carry out their activities in areas

---

3. Pereira, C., 2002, "Network for Women's Studies in Nigeria – National Coordinator's report", April 2002, p. 1.

awash with donor funds (such as reproductive health, 'good governance' and so on). Only some of these organisations can be said to have had such issues on their agenda prior to the availability of large-scale donor funding. This is an indication of agendas being *shaped*, at the least, even if not always entirely *driven* by the availability of donor funds. It is not always the case, however, that paying the proverbial piper determines the tune that can be played. Yet the demands of survival and the lure of greater financial security for non-governmental organisations cannot be dismissed, given the larger context of economies sapped by structural adjustment and neoliberal policies.

NWSN may have retained its intellectual autonomy more than many organisations, but so far we have been in the unenviable situation of being autonomous without any modicum of financial security. Whilst it was true that NWSN was not bound by any donor-driven agenda, we had no funds to pursue our own agenda either. The problem was not simply one to be solved by writing a good proposal for which funds would subsequently be disbursed. Instead, the issues were more fundamentally political, as the following section demonstrates.

Gender Politics and the Politics of Funding

In December 2002, I was invited to become part of a collective research project on universities and the university system in Nigeria, referred to as Case Studies of Nigerian Universities. The project was facilitated by the Social Science Academy of Nigeria and funded by a consortium of four private US foundations. My major involvement was in carrying out a gender analysis of the university system. The research agenda of the consortium – reforms in the university system – provided a starting point for addressing larger questions relevant to my assignment, such as how gendered structures and processes at the contextual and systemic levels affect universities; ways in which the workings of the university system have contributed to bringing about the observed gender differentials; and women's contribution to policy issues in university education (Pereira 2007).

In the process of carrying out the research on gender and the university system, it had become clear to me that a recurring feature of the landscape of higher education was sexual harassment. Not only was this very widespread, but the subject was submerged and generally treated as a regrettable reality of universities but not something that could really be changed. It was certainly not thought of as a subject for research.

At the end of the above research project, in March 2002, I was invited by a (woman) programme officer of one of the funding agencies in the consortium to present a proposal for further research on gender and the university system. It seemed to me that the subject of sexual harassment and sexual violence could usefully be taken up by the Network for Women's Studies in Nigeria. The theme seemed particularly appropriate for research within a network, and given the theme of the Network's forthcoming workshop, The Gender Politics of Violence, NWSN seemed well placed to plan how to engage in such research. This we did in group work during the workshop and the discussions fed into the planning proposal for a research network to engage in research on sexual harassment and sexual violence in Nigerian universities.

The subsequent rejection of the proposal by the programme officer's (male) boss, apart from being unexpected and very disappointing, raised many issues for me. Before I go into the 'reasons' given for his rejection of the proposal, I quote extensively from the programme officer's email communication of the news to me, to highlight the considerations informing her view that sexual harassment and gender-based violence were important issues worth researching:

> As you can imagine, I was very disappointed by his decision, all the more so because I feel I've wasted your time since I invited the proposal from you. The fact that the network [NWSN] comprises researchers from seventeen Nigerian universities, plus a number of other institutions and organisations, gave me confidence that issues identified as priorities by the network represent some level of consensus across the system, certainly by those who are attuned to critical issues facing women. And the issue itself resonates even more strongly with me now – between reading the excellent gender analysis you did of the Nigerian university system, reviewing the results of my most recent visits to our university partners in Nigeria, listening carefully to the discussions at the international women's congress at Makerere, and discussing the issue further with colleagues in South Africa, the impact of sexual harassment and gender-based violence takes on special significance. The complexity and lack of context-specific understanding of the issue, the paucity of empirical work done on it in Africa, the lack of effective remedies in most countries around the world, and the fact that the mere mention of it puts so many people on the defensive combine to make it a highly appropriate issue for foundations to address. It might not affect all women in universities (although, as colleagues have pointed out, many women are so used to being harassed that they don't even identify such behaviour as aberrant), but clearly it contributes to the negative atmosphere that inhibits

women's advancement and, indeed, affects women's career decisions. Until universities contrive means of making women feel secure in their educational/professional environments, it is difficult to imagine that they will be able to achieve the goal of gender equality.[4]

According to the programme officer's boss,

> Sexual harassment, if recognized as a priority, should feature as one of the problems and impediments to recruitment, successful training and career progress of women in universities.[5]

This suggests that if sexual harassment could not be shown to constitute an 'impediment' to recruitment, training or career progress, then basically it did not constitute a problem at all. In other words, sexual harassment is significant only to the extent that it disrupts *efficiency*. Issues of *gender justice* or *women's security* do not figure here, a scenario that is familiar in prevailing Gender and Development (GAD) perspectives (Razavi and Miller 1995) and which is here manifested in its higher education version.

Returning to the NWSN proposal, there were two main 'reasons' given by the programme officer's boss (a former Vice Chancellor) for rejecting the proposal. The first concerned the timing of the proposal. Since the agency had just approved planning grants for partner Nigerian universities to identify priorities for funding, the proposal had come at the wrong time.

> Progress in [sic] this front will best be made if universities' leaders are convinced that sexual harassment needs to be dealt with, and if they are determined to main-stream [sic] adequate solutions alongside solutions to other impediments. Therefore, if a study is to be made, it must obtain the blessing at least of the VCs of the universities that [the agency] will support. I do not support an approach that puts VCs in the role of defining their priorities at the same time that in parallel we support research in one priority selected by other means.[6]

In other words, research priorities could only be appropriately defined by Vice Chancellors of universities! It is worth noting that this 'principle' was

---

4. Email message from programme officer to author, 20 August 2002. My insertion in square brackets.
5. Email message from programme officer's boss to programme officer, forwarded by the latter to the author on the boss's request. 20 August 2002 (original message 16 August 2002).
6. Ibid. My insertion in square brackets.

only applied when alternative priorities that subjected gendered power relations to scrutiny were defined by a women-centred network. The 'principle' was not even enunciated when the same funding agency was considering the possibility of supporting the Social Science Academy of Nigeria's (SSAN) proposal to carry out nationwide research on university students. In this instance, it was not a condition for the SSAN 'to obtain the blessing of Vice Chancellors' before potentially engaging in the research, nor was it even considered necessary that the Vice Chancellors should identify this research area as important before the agency could consider the proposal!

The second 'reason' given for the rejection of the NWSN proposal was that it narrowed down a larger problem.

> I would welcome research on all or on the main factors (impediments) to women's achievements, particularly if it yields a comprehensive strategy ... In my view it is misguided to single out one of the problems, even if this is the most serious impediment. And I don't know that for a fact. I have not seen what are the other and lesser impediments.[7]

The sub-text here is that even if sexual harassment and gender-based violence did constitute "the most serious impediment" to women's advancement in universities, this particular bureaucrat would not be prepared to fund research in the area. We should seriously question why funders should push for a theme to be identified, *a priori*, as "the most serious impediment" to anything before it merits research funding. This point is even more critical in those instances where the theme in question has barely been researched. We should also question why funders should try and impose upon researchers a particular version of causality that implies ranking of so-called 'causal factors' in a reductive and exclusivist manner. Bureaucratic modes of decision-making are no substitute for analytically nuanced or theoretically sophisticated modes of understanding.

In a postscript to his message to the programme officer, her boss stated that:

> It would help Charmaine and the Network that she works with if she wished to discuss with the VCs to ensure that sexual harassment will be properly addressed within the proposals that we will receive from the universities.

This statement suggests an almost wilful misunderstanding of the power relations within which universities, Vice Chancellors, donors and independ-

---

7. Ibid.

ent researchers (particularly women) are immersed. Vice Chancellors seeking to raise funds from donors will be keen to present their universities in as positive a light as possible, avoiding as far as possible any mention of subterranean violations such as gendered violence and sexual harassment. It is not clear why such highly placed officials should listen to (women) researchers outside their universities telling them to conduct research within their own universities on a sensitive and fraught issue, of which they are likely to have little understanding. The suggestion that such a scenario should even take place betrays the assumption that no expertise is required to conceptualise, plan or carry out such research – all that is necessary is to discuss the matter with Vice Chancellors "to ensure that sexual harassment will be properly addressed within the proposals".

In practice, some Vice Chancellors are themselves guilty of engaging in sexual harassment.[8] It is highly unlikely, to say the least, that sexual harassment will be prioritised for research in such instances. Quite apart from that, it should be emphasised that whenever the existence of gendered violence and sexual harassment in universities has been exposed, it has rarely been as a result of concerned initiatives by Vice Chancellors and others heading the academic hierarchy. Mamphela Ramphele's (1994) enlightened intervention at the University of Cape Town, where policy development began as far back as 1987, is one example of a (female) Vice Chancellor's exceptional practice proving the general rule. Initiatives on sexual harassment and gender-based violence have more often been the result of struggle and advocacy on the part of feminist researchers and activists within the academy, than by highly placed administrators.

The formation of the Network of Southern African Higher Educational Institutions Challenging Sexual Harassment and Sexual Violence (NETSH) in the 1990s is a noteworthy example of organising for change by researchers and activists (see Bennett 2002 and this volume), one that has inspired the NWSN's efforts in this area. Such initiatives have to be acknowledged and valorised, instead of being rendered invisible through ignorance or wilful misunderstanding. Clearly Vice Chancellors will be important for implementation efforts to succeed. However, such efforts have to rest on an appropriate understanding of the issues and the context – hence the need for research that is prepared to go against the grain of the status quo.

Overall, this experience raises serious questions about the gender politics

---

8. Personal communication, Ayesha Imam, December 2005.

of senior men in donor agencies, whilst reiterating the need to be aware of the politics surrounding the funding of research, particularly when the research engagement is collective and the choice of research area is sensitive. I am happy to say that the NWSN has since been successful in raising funds from elsewhere.

In 2003, the Nordic Africa Institute (NAI) kindly funded a planning/pilot study that formed the basis for writing and presenting a research proposal to SIDA, with a NAI programme officer in attendance as a demonstration of the institute's support. The proposal was for a three-year action research project on sexual harassment and sexual violence in Nigerian universities, and included the establishment of an office for NWSN. No doubt the willingness of the then-Director of NAI – a man who was familiar with the workings of SIDA – to support the proposal in subsequent discussions with the funding agency, played no small part in securing the grant. The success of the application enabled NWSN to open an office in February 2005 and start work on its first major programme.

In reflecting on the politics of funding, it seems to me that there are a number of issues that often converge in complicated ways, which those of us engaged in knowledge production need to be clear about. In their different ways, the issues I highlight all concern the critical arena of agenda setting. The first is about self-determination regarding African feminist agendas – intellectual and political. Organisations, networks, collectivities in short, need to determine their own needs, and within these, which elements are negotiable and which are non-negotiable. This underlines the significance for NWSN of engaging in the process of setting an agenda for gender and women's studies, a process that was initiated at the inaugural workshop (Mama 1996). Secondly, there are the agendas of donors. One has to study the funding sources and understand each of these very well, that is, on their own terms. What are their priorities, what programmes do they run, what language do they use? More importantly, what are the ideological assumptions underlying the issues as they present them and the determination of their funding priorities?

A third issue, probably the most insidious and difficult to resist in economically constrained circumstances, is the epistemic power accruing to donor agencies as a consequence of their economic power. The most visible manifestation of this convergence of power relations is the power that funders have to determine *what is worth knowing* – by targeting issues for which funding is available, by determining funding priorities and by regularly changing these priorities. The problem is compounded when funders go so far as to specify *who should be a knower* – not gender-sensitive women researchers but Vice Chancellors, as I showed earlier. That example also highlighted one funder's efforts to impose *appropriate modes of knowledge production* – a unilinear, reductive and exclusivist model of cause and effect as opposed to a more dynamic understanding of causality in which multiplicity and recursivity are key dimensions. 'The single, most important' cause or strategy, favoured by many such funders, is often less likely to be a significant feature on the agendas of politically conscious researchers and activists than a consideration of multiple, interlocking levels of power and its effects in their sphere of work.

One of the unfortunate consequences of the convergence of epistemic and economic power wielded by funders is that their practice (like that of dictators) is rarely subject to critique. Those who are most informed and able to provide this critique – the individuals and organisations seeking funds from such agencies – are generally unwilling to do so, either because of their economic dependence on such funds and/or their fear of jeopardising their chances of receiving the funds. But the absence of critique is unhealthy, especially for those who feel they least need it. The willingness to engage with dissenting views is a precondition not only for knowledge building but also for democratisation. Yet how many agencies, particularly those that champion both knowledge building and democratisation, are themselves able to engage with dissent or critique?

It seems to me that the pursuit of self-determined organisational agendas in the course of fund raising requires an engagement with the donor's own agenda as well as an understanding of, and healthy resistance to, the epistemic power wielded by the donor. Ultimately, I see the task of raising funds not as one of carrying out activities for which donor funds are available, but as one of deploying funders' priorities to serve the agenda of my organisation. This is only partly an intellectual task – writing proposals with an extensive literature review, incisive research questions, appropriate methodology and so on. The covert features of this task have more to do with the internal politics of the funding agency – who runs which programmes, how much power 'the boss' wields, who is willing to defend your proposal if the boss is not enthusiastic, the (lack of) internal democracy within funding agencies, including, perhaps even especially so, those that ostensibly strengthen 'democracy', 'transparency' and 'accountability'.

Feminist Subjectivity and Praxis

In this section, I continue a process that has been implicit in previous parts of this paper but which I make more explicit here. This is the process of reflecting on my consciousness of being a feminist – in other words, feminist subjectivity – and the implications that this has had for practice and ultimately, feminist politics. In doing so, I consider the relationships between ideas and action, between scholarship and activism. I use the term 'subjectivity' to refer to multiple sources of individuality and self-awareness (Henriques et al. 1994; Mama 1995), as opposed to the more rigid singularity of ascriptive characteristics (such as race *or* ethnicity *or* gender) generally involved in the fixing of 'identity' (Rowbotham 1994).

Once I had left Ahmadu Bello University, I had to think about how to refer to myself, since 'lecturer' or 'academic' was no longer available as a descriptive label. I resisted, and continue to resist, being called a 'consultant' mainly because I see consultancies as more accurately defining a form of payment than a type of work. These days I am more likely to call myself an 'independent researcher' or a 'scholar-activist', since these describe more appropriately both what I do and how I would like to see myself.

To contextualise this process, I begin by posing the question of what makes it possible for women to come together and engage in collective action in diverse feminist projects. The possibilities and ambiguities inherent in the very category 'women' are critical to an understanding of "the historical and the contemporary strains upon, and the alliances of, various kinds of feminism" (Riley 1992:121). What meanings have my academic colleagues given to my actions, and how did this differ from my feminist sisters' meanings, or mine? How does this configuration impinge on my activism? These are large questions, to which I attempt only to sketch the outlines here of a response.

In reflecting on the trajectory that has taken me along the path so far outlined, I am mindful of the first piece of research that I became engaged in, nine months after my arrival in Nigeria in 1993. This was an action research project on Women and Laws, carried out under the auspices of the international solidarity network Women Living Under Muslim Laws (WLUML). The project was part of a 26-country study addressing the practice of Muslim laws as they affected women. One of the overall aims of the research programme was to highlight the diversity of *Muslim laws*, contrary to those who argued for a singular, unchanging corpus of *Islamic law*. In the process, the difference between principles and practice was to be placed in the foreground, since this lacuna was very often denied and used against Muslim women. The project goals were elaborated not only by Muslim feminists but also by feminists from Christian, Jewish and secular backgrounds working collaboratively within the network.[9]

As head of the Archival Team, I was one of three team leaders, the other two being the heads of Field Research and Legal Research. Overall leadership of the project was provided by the national coordinator. Of the four of us, I was of Christian upbringing, the only non-Muslim. The particular incident I refer to here occurred in the run-up to the Dakar preparatory meeting in 1994, prior to the Fourth UN World Conference on Women in Beijing, 1995. The three team leaders and the national coordinator were to present a paper based on the Nigeria country research.

Whilst not initially raising the question of identity politics, my engagement in the Women and Laws project could not avoid this completely. The stage was set for such a scenario once I criticised the approach taken by the team leader who was to present the Nigeria country paper. The substance of my criticism concerned the conservative direction of her presentation – such as the continual use of the phrase 'Islamic law', which the Women and Laws project was intended to deconstruct. Moreover, the presentation she had prepared for the Dakar meeting was intended to outline the collective work of the Nigeria project but she did not appear to see the need for consultations with other team members during or after her preparation. This seemed to me to be inappropriate, given the collective nature of the work as well as the radical intent of this feminist project, and I communicated my views to her. As it happened, the other team leader and the national coordinator both agreed with me on the substance of my criticisms.

Although initially very positive towards me, the colleague that I had criticised subsequently began to pose the question of how or why I, as an 'outsider' (a non-Muslim woman), could 'speak for insiders' (Muslim women). Implicit in this approach were two assumptions. The first was that I did, in fact, attempt to 'speak for' Muslim women (in some undifferentiated sense), as opposed to my understanding of attempting to assert the project goals (as elaborated by a particular group of Muslim and non-Muslim feminists). The second assumption was that my Muslim colleague, or any Muslim woman, would indeed be better placed to 'speak for' all Muslim women, as opposed to speaking from the positioning of a Muslim woman.

---

9. See www.wluml.org for more information about the work of Women Living Under Muslim Laws.

The National Coordinator's response to this situation was that WLUML was constituted of Muslim as well as non-Muslim women. Although true, this response elided the power relations within this diversity. Since the focus of the network was Muslim laws, it was clear that Muslim women would be more likely to be the ones to assume power within the network, in the sense of assuming overall leadership and the like. I accepted this in principle but was also of the view that all members of the network should be able to exercise their critical faculties in the service of WLUML's political project.

The right to speak one's mind is generally accepted within WLUML, even if some individual members find it difficult to apply this in practice. In terms of priorities, the guiding principle in the network is that those most affected by Muslim laws are those who should define the priorities and strategies. Most of the time, these are Muslim women, whether or not they identify themselves as such. In a number of instances, however, the people most affected by Muslim laws are not only Muslims but members of other religious and cultural groups, as in the case of Pakistani Christians affected by blasphemy laws in their country.[10]

I should point out that my presence in the project team was the result of an invitation to join, not an application. One of the regional coordinators had first met me in the UK, prior to my arrival in Nigeria. At the least, this implies that those leading the project would have felt I had something to contribute to it, regardless of my religious identification. This contribution, I felt, was my feminist politics, my research capacity and experience and the likelihood that I would be willing to participate in the project. The fact that I was also physically located at Ahmadu Bello University, as were the national coordinator and the other two team leaders, would have made meetings more feasible and convenient.

The larger question that this experience raised for me concerned the character of solidarity. What was it about being a 'woman' that gave me any grounds for engagement? What was an appropriate balance, in this instance, between feminist politics, the capacity to do research and one's religious identification? Should 'identity' be a basis for political action, even among those ostensibly resisting identity politics? To what extent is it possible to avoid identity politics of some sort, in such a context? How far could one go, as someone represented as 'other', in any solidarity struggle? Where did all this leave women in Nigeria, in efforts to work across lines of division? These are ongoing questions – more useful in the process

---

10. Personal communication, Ayesha Imam, December 2005.

of being posed than in any attempt at permanent resolution (see Crosby 1992).

In another early experience, I recall the obstacles faced by the Ahmadu Bello University's Women's Studies Group (set up after the inaugural workshop of NWSN in January 1996) in our efforts to establish a Higher Education Link Programme on curriculum development in Women's Studies with Liverpool University, UK as well as the Network for Women's Studies in Nigeria. The possibility of a Link Programme had been offered to Ahmadu Bello University by the British Council for some time, but as a result of uninterest on the part of the university administration, the offer had never been taken up. Concerted efforts on the part of the Ahmadu Bello University Women's Studies Group included lobbying university authorities; meeting key players in the administration; and writing a proposal on developing a programme of Women's Studies within Ahmadu Bello University itself, on the basis of current taught courses across faculties and departments. Considerable time and energy was spent in this way.

Exchange visits between the UK and Nigeria were planned to take place yearly, over a period of three years. The Nigeria Coordinator of the Link Programme would be making the first visit to the UK to collect course material and to purchase texts for a proposed documentation centre in Women's Studies at Ahmadu Bello University. As the Nigeria Coordinator of the Link Programme (the choice of Coordinator being proposed by the Ahmadu Bello University Women's Studies Group), I soon found that this elicited all kinds of assertions on the part of male colleagues within the Sociology Department where I worked. The substance in each case concerned their greater competence (than mine) to take on the position of Coordinator. This was so despite their lack of involvement in initiating the process, coupled with a lack of connection to the Women's Studies Group that pursued the realisation of the Link Programme.

Taking the lead in this fiasco was my Head of Department, who despite an absence of feminist inclination, previous work in this area or even analytical competence, persisted in claiming that he was 'the right person' to coordinate the Link Programme. The arguments that he marshalled against me included the fact that I was a contract worker (not tenured) and that my degrees were in Psychology (not Sociology). Both of these features were known prior to that time, but had not previously constituted grounds for mobilising against me or not recruiting me. My greater visibility in the university was now beginning to raise hackles among some men – a 'Niger wife' was acceptable as long as she kept quiet but not when she acquired a voice of her own!

Ultimately, it was impatience with this kind of 'politricking' on the part of my Head of Department that led the Deputy Vice Chancellor (Academic) to sign the form establishing the Link Programme between Ahmadu Bello University and Liverpool University. The cumulative efforts of the Women's Studies Group had ultimately paid off, even if the triggering factor was not one we had anticipated. Despite all my Head of Department's efforts to usurp me as Coordinator, he did not succeed. In the end, I was recognised by the university administration as the Coordinator of the Link Programme. Shortly afterwards, my Head of Department came to the end of his tenure and was forced to step down, albeit very unwillingly. The Link Programme was very successful and a documentation unit housing the collection acquired through the programme was finally set up in the university's Institute for Human Development.

Concluding Remarks

The importance of setting agendas and clarity in doing so is multiplied when one works outside an institutional base. Having left Ahmadu Bello University at the end of 1997 and spending ten months out of the country after that, my return to Nigeria marked the beginning of life outside the university. Working without an institutional base has been difficult in many respects, not least in the lack of financial security that defines such a position. How then does one function with a modicum of such security in this unaligned, often indeterminate space?

The two main sources of funding that I relied on for my livelihood were funding from research projects and consultancies. The first of these has proved relatively sparse to date: in order to raise such funds, one has to have established a research record and this takes time. I have resisted entering into consultancies for short-term projects (sometimes as little as 10 days or so) that pose as 'research'. This is partly because the time-scale involved generally allows only a superficial treatment of the issues and I much prefer doing whatever work I do in-depth. In addition, the payment for this type of work is rarely commensurate with the hidden costs incurred, even if the project were to be carried out in the manner initially conceived.

This does not mean that I have not accepted any consultancies at all. However, these have tended to be for work I have carried out either in a training capacity – as a resource person for NGOs, occasionally donors – or some aspect of organisational work, often for donors. Most training workshops are constrained by their short timeframes. Despite this, I generally accept such offers because they afford an opportunity to create space for reflecting on goals, strategies and effects within the context of aiming for transformational practice as opposed to technical reform. The organisational work has also offered possibilities for engaging with donors in a critical examination of issues concerning gender equality in practice.

For a long time, this meant accepting an uneven and precarious financial existence (as an independent researcher and scholar-activist), coupled with a workload that appears always to increase rather than diminish. The rewards are a considerable degree of intellectual autonomy and personal satisfaction from recognition by women's organisations (and others) of the value of my work. Ultimately, the possibility of my engaging in scholar-activism in this way rested on the knowledge that my husband has 'a real job' (read, a paid job) and that I could count on financial support from him should I need it – a somewhat ambivalent position for me as a feminist who values women's economic independence! My financial situation improved considerably in January 2005 when the SIDA grant allowed me to be remunerated as the project coordinator of NWSN's action research on sexual harassment and sexual violence in Nigerian universities.

Ultimately, the fostering of intellectual autonomy is very much underwritten by the development of functional institutions, whether directly linked to knowledge production, as are universities, or indirectly, such as agencies in the state. The scope for gender and women's studies to grow in Nigeria will be largely shaped by the support it receives within and beyond the academy and other research institutions. Feminist activism has a large part to play in pushing male-dominated institutions, such as universities, to arrive at a position that makes possible the enhancement of gender and women's studies.

For me, feminist praxis has encompassed varying combinations of scholarship and activism. The formation of the Network for Women's Studies in Nigeria combines the imperative of creating an autonomous base at the same time as pursuing the institutionalisation of gender and women's studies, in order to further a feminist agenda for gender and women's studies in Nigeria. The Women and Laws project was born out of activism outside the academy, although the research itself was carried out by a non-institutionalised group whose leadership was based in the academy. The example of activism by the Ahmadu Bello University Women's Studies Group was necessarily based within the academy, in support of scholarship that ideally would be institutionalised in the university.

I have explored feminist subjectivity here through some of the ways in which discourses of identity were mobilised so as to fix boundaries around 'appropriate' modes of thought and action. It is the business of gender and women's studies, it seems to me, to interrupt, if not disrupt, and redefine such boundaries. Charting new paths for gender and women's studies is as much a political and institutional struggle as it is an intellectual one. In the process of crossing and recrossing boundaries of different kinds, where you end up reflects not only where the boundaries were drawn in the first place but also the synergies made possible by the companions in your struggles.

References

Allen, S. and C. Wolkowitz, 1986, "Homeworking and the Control of Women's Work", in Feminist Review (ed.), *Waged Work: A Reader*. London: Virago Press.

—, 1987, *Homeworking: Myths and Realities*. Houndmills, London: Macmillan Education.

Bangura, Y., 1994, *Intellectuals, Economic Reform and Social Change: Constraints and Opportunities in the Formation of a Nigerian Technocracy*. United Nations Research Institute for Social Development (UNRISD), Geneva Monograph Series 1/94.

Bennett, J., 2002, *Southern African Higher Educational Institutions Challenging Sexual Violence/Sexual Harassment: A Handbook of Resources*. Network of Southern African Higher Education Institutions Challenging Sexual Harassment and Sexual Violence. Cape Town: African Gender Institute.

Court, D., 2000, "The Interdependence of Universities and Networks in Africa", paper presented at the SSRC-AAU workshop on "Networks and African Universities: Towards Co-operation in Research and Training", Accra, 24-26 February 2000.

Crosby, C., 1992, "Dealing with Differences", in J. Butler and J. Scott (eds), *Feminists Theorize the Political*. London, New York: Routledge.

Hall, S., 1980, "Race, Articulation and Societies Structured in Dominance", in UNESCO (ed.), *Sociological Theories: Race and Colonialism*. Paris: UNESCO.

Henriques, J., W. Hollway, C. Urwin, C. Venn and V. Walkerdine, 1984, *Changing the Subject: Psychology, Social Regulation and Subjectivity*. London: Methuen.

Imam, A., A. Mama, and F. Sow (eds), 1997, *Engendering African Social Sciences*. CODESRIA, Dakar.

Jega, A., 1994, *Nigerian Academics Under Military Rule*. University of Stockholm Report No. 1994.3.

Mama, A., 1995, *Beyond the Masks: Race, Gender and Subjectivity.* London, New York: Routledge.

—, 1996a, "Women's Studies and Studies of Women in Africa During the 1990s", *CODESRIA Working Paper Series* 5/96.

— (ed.), 1996b, *Setting an Agenda for Gender and Women's Studies in Nigeria.* Report of the Network for Women's Studies in Nigeria No. 1. Tamaza, Zaria.

Manuh, T., J. Budu and S. Garba, 2002, *Change and Transformation in Ghana"s Public Universities: A Study of Experiences, Challenges and Opportunities.* Final report for the Case Studies of African Universities Project.

NHDR, 2001, *Human Development Report: Nigeria 2000/2001 Millennium Edition.* Lagos: United Nations Development Programme (UNDP).

Odejide, B. and I. Isiugo-Abanihe (eds), 1999, "Curriculum Workshop for Gender and Women's Studies in Nigeria", *Report of the Network for Women's Studies in Nigeria* 3.

Pereira, C. (ed.), 1997, *Concepts and Methods for Gender and Women's Studies in Nigeria.* Report of the Network for Women's Studies in Nigeria No. 2. Tamaza, Zaria

—, 2000, "Feminist Knowledge", *Seminar 490* (Issue on African Transitions), June, New Delhi, 77–85.

—, 2002, "Between Knowing and Imagining: What Space for Feminism in Scholarship on Africa?", *Feminist Africa* 1, 9-33.

—, 2003, "Locating Gender and Women's Studies in Nigeria: What Trajectories for the Future?" http://www.gwsafrica.org/knowledge/pereira.html

—, 2007, *Gender in the Making of the Nigerian University System.* James Currey, Oxford in association with the Partnership for Higher Education in Africa and Heinemann, Nigeria.

Phiri, I., 2000 "Gender and Academic Freedom in Malawi" In E. Sall (ed.) *Women in Academia: Gender Academic Freedom in Africa* CODESRIA, Dakar

Prewitt, K., 2000, *Networks in International Capacity Building: Cases from Sub-Saharan Africa.* Vol. 2 New York: Social Science Research Council.

Ramphele, M., 1994, "Challenging Sexual Harassment: Strategies within Tertiary Education". Welcome and Opening Address presented at Conference on Sexual Harassment in Southern African Tertiary Education, held at University of Cape Town and hosted by the Sexual Harassment Support and Prevention Service and the Equal Opportunity Research Project of UCT, 29th-30th October, 1994.

Razavi, S. and C. Miller, 1995, "From WID to GAD: Conceptual Shifts in the Women and Development Discourse" OP1, United Nations Research Institute for Social Development (UNRISD), Geneva.

Riley, D., 1992, "A Short History of Some Preoccupations", in J. Butler and J. Scott (eds), *Feminists Theorize the Political.* London, New York: Routledge.

Rowbotham, S., 1994, *Women in Movement: Feminism and Social Action.* London, New York: Routledge.

Sall, E., 2002, "The Social Sciences in Africa: A Tentative Regional Map and a Perspective on Trends, Issues, Capacities and Constraints", paper prepared for the Human Capital Committee of the Social Science Research Council, "Mapping Human Capital Globally".

Salmi, J., n.d., "Tertiary Education in the Twenty-First Century: Challenges and Opportunities" Mimeo.

Sawyerr, A., 1998, "Does Africa Really Need Her Universities?" *CODESRIA Bulletin* 3 & 4, 20-25.

Sow, F., 1997, "The Social Sciences in Africa and Gender Analysis", in A. Imam, A. Mama and F. Sow (eds), *Engendering African Social Sciences.* Dakar: CODESRIA.

Tarasher, S. and H. Ford-Smith, 1990, "Women and Funding", *Women in Action* 3 & 4, 36–41.

Tsikata, D., 1997, "Feminism and Feminist Theory", in C. Pereira (ed.), *Concepts and Methods for Gender and Women's Studies in Nigeria.* Report of the Network for Women's Studies in Nigeria No. 2. Tamaza, Zaria.

—, 2001a, "Introduction", in D. Tsikata (ed.), *Gender Training in Ghana: Politics, Issues and Tools.* ISSER/DAWS/TWN Accra: World Publishing Services.

—, 2001b, "The Politics of Policy Making: A Gender Perspective", in D. Tsikata (ed.), *Gender Training in Ghana: Politics, Issues and Tools.* ISSER/DAWS/TWN Accra: World Publishing Services.

CHAPTER FOUR

Advocacy for Women's Reproductive and Sexual Health and Rights in Africa
Between the Devil and the Deep Blue Sea

Adetoun Ilumoka

Introduction

Self-conscious women's health advocacy by women has grown tremendously in Africa since the 1980s, set within the context of the growth of the Women's Movement and feminism on the continent over the last 30 years and during the UN Decade for Women. The Women's Health Movement on the continent is thus still very young and in its formative stages, spearheaded by researchers, professionals and non-governmental organisations (NGOs). Now, as it grows in age and hopefully matures, may be a good moment for critical reappraisal.

This chapter reviews some of the activities of this budding movement in Nigeria and related international advocacy for women's reproductive and sexual rights, with particular reference to unwanted pregnancy, abortion and contraception. The chapter provides a critique of some of the processes of conceptualising and advocating for women's health, and of the imposition and development of an emphasis on rights discourse and strategy within the women's health movement. It highlights some of the dilemmas and challenges faced by feminists and women's health advocates in the Nigerian and African context in their efforts to articulate and shape a women's health agenda. The chapter concludes by making a case for the strengthening of local agendas and visions for women's health and for the building of movements and organisations to actualise those visions. However, in spite of the specific focus on Nigeria and the case studies adopted, this chapter represents a more general critique of the dominant discourse of rights in the modern world and the women's health movement, well beyond the glaring contradictions evident in the Nigerian and African context, and advocates the need for reconceptualisation.

Between 1988 and 1998, I was very actively involved in advocacy for women's health in Nigeria and globally and participated in many of the major local and international activities, workshops and conferences held during the period on issues of women's health, including those referred to in this paper. I also had the opportunity of exploring my deep personal interest in this subject through research projects and engagement with many researcher/activists and communities in Nigeria and elsewhere. This privileged engagement took place under the auspices of organisations such as Women In Nigeria (WIN) and the Empowerment and Action Research Centre, a NGO of which I was Executive Director between 1992 and 2002. It was facilitated mostly through grants made by a variety of donor agencies in Europe and North America. This account is thus at once a narrative of aspects of a specific life *herstory*, reflecting personal experiences and perceptions of activities and interactions within the international feminist and women's health movement, as well as a call for critical reappraisal in the quest for better futures. As we manoeuvre in the treacherous waters of 21st century global society, how shall we improve the ways in which we deal with the challenges we face? What lessons and strategies can we pass on to the next generation of women's health advocates? If this chapter succeeds in raising pertinent issues and stimulating open discussion on some of these questions, it will have served its intended purpose.

Advocacy for Reproductive Health and Rights by Nigerian Women

In the late 1980s and 1990s in Nigeria, there was a growing interest in, and visibility of, women's health issues. In that period, important alliances between the medical profession and women interested and seeking improvements in women's health were forged.[1] Gynaecologists (with a specialist interest in women's health issues) and other medical practitioners highlighted the health problems of women they encountered in their practices. Notable among these and of great concern to them were conditions related to pregnancy and childbirth, which resulted in high levels of maternal mortality and morbidity. Several research reports exist on the major causes of these phenomena, including anaemia, haemorrhage, sepsis, complications from

---

1. Much credit for encouraging and supporting these alliances in this initial period should go to the International Women's Health Coalition, a New York-based organisation dedicated to promoting the health and rights of women, with a focus on Africa, Asia and Latin America.

unsafe abortions, hypertensive diseases and obstructed labour (WHO 2002). The persistence and recurrence of these problems has led various doctors to investigate their underlying causes. Several of them pointed to the socioeconomic origins of women's health problems and recommended policies and a vigorous campaign to eradicate them. To quote a distinguished obstetrician/gynaecologist in Nigeria: "The point is that poverty, when combined with gross inequality, ranks as the major killer" (Harrison 1997). Following earlier international initiatives in Nairobi, the Safe Motherhood Campaign was launched in Nigeria in 1990 emphasising prevention of maternal mortality and morbidity (PMM) as well as management and cure. The launching spawned several local and international projects on PMM over the next decade. In the first section of the chapter, I will report and comment on three different instances of reproductive health advocacy in Nigeria regarding a) abortion, b) contraception and c) participation in international advocacy in the context of UN conferences.

Practice and Policy on Abortion in Nigeria

Unsafe abortion is ranked by various studies as a major cause of maternal mortality and morbidity in sub-Saharan Africa (Okonofua et al. 1991). Available evidence points to the fact that in cities and small towns in Nigeria unwanted pregnancies and attempts at terminating them are widespread among women of all ages and classes. Rapid urbanisation and the proliferation of Western-style education have changed attitudes towards marriage and the timing of childbearing. Girls are expelled from school or pressured to abandon or suspend their education when they fall pregnant. Women seek smaller families due to the pressures of work and the cost of living. Many of the initiation rites related to the advent of puberty, and forms of passing on knowledge and coping mechanisms between generations have been lost, changed or so significantly modified that they no longer fulfil their function. Healing traditions, knowledge and the availability of herbs are also being eroded in the process of modernisation and globalisation.

Abortions in Nigeria are performed by doctors, nurses as well as numerous other people professing various skills, ranging from attendants in chemist shops to hospital ward attendants, herbalists, 'traditional' practitioners and 'lay' people in the community. Many of the complications seen in hospitals are also the result of badly performed abortions by medical doctors (Oye-Adeniran et al. 2002). In part, this may be because some of the damage caused by other practitioners using non-surgical methods may not lead to emergency situations. For example, several surveys on induced abortion in Nigeria referred to in this paper report that popular methods of inducing abortion by women and young girls who cannot afford to see a doctor include drinking substances such as 'blue' (a very strong household cleaner popular in Nigeria), lime and potash as well as various herbal concoctions and drugs dispensed by workers in chemist shops and patent medicine stores. While these substances may do considerable harm and even permanent damage, which may not be immediately evident, they are less likely to result in the obvious physical damage to organs and prolonged bleeding that result from surgical intervention and lead to victims being rushed to hospital emergency departments for treatment. The use of crude sharp objects by women themselves, which could lead to similar emergencies, is not widely reported.

In many cases, young girls are accompanied or supported by girlfriends and boyfriends and occasionally parents or relatives in procuring abortions. Many women have the procedure performed with the support, financial and otherwise, of their male partners. Information available to them as well as how much they can afford have a significant bearing on the kinds of services different women have access to.

Induced abortion is a criminal offence in Nigeria except when performed to save the life of the woman.[2] These criminal laws were part of the package of colonial laws introduced to the country by the British. While the practice is surrounded by secrecy, the law does not appear to deter many practitioners, especially as it is rarely enforced. Several women interviewed at a government-owned general hospital in Ikorodu, a small town near Lagos, during a survey of Women's Perspectives on Family Planning and Population Policies in Nigeria in 1991, had no idea that abortions were illegal in the country and said they would simply ask their doctor to perform the procedure if they had an unwanted pregnancy.[3] For them, secrecy, or more accurately and from their perspective, *discretion,* was more a matter of decorum than morality or fear of the law. You simply did not broadcast your health problems and issues for all to hear. They were between you, close friends or family and the doctor or health practitioner. The fact that most

---

2. See S. 228, 229 and 297 of the Criminal Code, applicable in Southern Nigeria (1963). Cap 77, Laws of the Federation of Nigeria 1990; and S. 232, 233 and 235 of the Penal Code applicable in Northern Nigeria. Cap. 89, Laws of Northern Nigeria1963.
3. See report on in-depth interviews with women visiting the antenatal and post natal clinics in Ikorodu General Hospital, 1990 (Ilumoka and Simpson 1996).

of the women interviewed were in socially acceptable marriages or sexual unions is, of course, important in explaining their attitudes regarding the morality of abortion.

Although the law relating to abortion in Nigeria has its origins in the colonial period, there is no groundswell of opinion on the need to change it. In a small-scale study carried out among university students in Jos, Plateau State by Women in Nigeria (WIN) in 1989,[4] there was a considerable ambivalence concerning what policy should be on abortion. Most of the respondents who admitted to having terminated a pregnancy before were of the view that abortion should not be made legal or decriminalised. When asked what they thought should happen in cases of rape or severe congenital disorders, they took a different view: these could be exceptions. In two surveys carried out by the Empowerment and Action Research Centre between 1993 and 1998, women in a low income, high density area of Lagos expressed the view that abortion was wrong and that the law should not be changed to ease access for women (Ahonsi and Ilumkoka 1992). The earlier study carried out in Ikorodu referred to above did not yield significantly different results, except that low income women in Lagos were far more forthright in admitting to having had abortions and in talking about the high incidence of abortion in the city.

Advocacy for Abortion Rights in Nigeria

In 1989, the annual conference of the Society of Obstetricians and Gynaecologists of Nigeria (SOGON) focused on the problems of unwanted pregnancy and abortion in Nigeria as an aspect of maternal mortality and morbidity. A female researcher – Professor Mere Kisseka – in the Department of Sociology at the Ahmadu Bello University in Zaria, who was interested in women's health issues, obtained support to facilitate participation by a group of female researchers and activists in this conference to ensure that women's perspectives on the issue of unwanted pregnancy and abortion were heard and to promote advocacy by women on women's health issues. Thereafter, individual researchers and the women's organisations they were active in, such as WIN, were encouraged to undertake small projects towards under-

---

4. This was one of the first surveys conducted by a women's organisation on abortion in Nigeria and was funded by the International Women's Health Coalition (IWHC) and coordinated by myself and Lahadi Tseayo of the Deptartment of Sociology at the University of Jos.

standing women's perspectives on abortion and to work with doctors to advocate for and promote women-friendly interventions in health policy and health service provision. Since much of this support came from US-based foundations and women's organisations such as the Ford Foundation, the McArthur Foundation and the International Women's Health Coalition, the issue was often framed as one of 'reproductive rights' rather than simply as one of access to and changing policy on abortion, the terms in which the local struggles were initially spontaneously framed and understood.[5]

An attempt was also made in 1991-92 to change policy on abortion in Nigeria through the influence of the medical profession and SOGON. This included the formation of a coalition of women's health advocates and medical practitioners to pursue these goals. The coalition was named the Campaign Against Unwanted Pregnancy (CAUP) and I was a member of the group at its initiation. This strategy was based on a belief that women interested in improving the status and health of women (and who might better understand where the shoe pinches) had an important role to play, along with a medical profession largely represented by males, whose interest was professional but who were often better placed and organised to influence policy.

The Minister of Health at the time – Professor Olikoye Ransome-Kuti – was supportive of a change of policy and law to reduce maternal mortality and morbidity and to improve the health of women. He made public statements to this effect as a possible prelude to law reform. His statements triggered a heated debate in the newspapers and evoked a largely negative and vocal response.[6] The issue of changing laws on abortion in Nigeria was thus returned to the back burner. This backlash continued for several years and for the first time in Nigeria a large 'pro-life' conference, to take place in Eastern Nigeria, was advertised in popular daily newspapers in 1992.

In view of the widespread practice of abortion, the dearth of arrests and prosecutions for the offence, the generalised cooperation of male partners in procuring abortions and the reluctance of women to speak out or support policy and legal change on abortion, the question arises as to the basis of a campaign on reproductive rights of women or focused on changing laws. Did enough women believe in 'a woman's right to choose' to advocate for

---

5. My own paper presented at this workshop had its title changed by the editor to include the term "Reproductive Rights", to which I had no particular objection although I would not myself have used it.
6. See his statement clarifying his stance quoted in Okonofua and Ilumoka,1991.

it? It appears not. Against whom or what were abortion rights or the right to reproductive health being asserted? The state and most religious organisations turned a blind eye to the practice. The studies on this subject earlier referred to indicate that women seeking to terminate pregnancies were dying or suffering complications as a result of lack of information on, and access to best practices and procedures for procuring abortions; the incompetence of practitioners and exploitation by them; and lack of finances to have the procedure performed by a competent practitioner in a properly equipped facility. Simplification and control of technology and techniques thus appear to be key issues in abortion care in Nigeria, as well as mechanisms for passing on pertinent information to women, especially young girls. It is, however, difficult to determine the scope of the problem of mortality and morbidity resulting from induced abortion. In view of the alleged prevalence of the practice of abortion, the numbers of cases presented at medical facilities could be an indication that many women had the procedure performed safely, or that they suffered few visible complications. The reported cases of complications and death from abortion are a minute fraction of reported incidence, which is already low. This could of course also be due to the difficulty in diagnosing the causes of possible complications that surface years later, or to severe underreporting. Much research still needs to be done on this subject, although this does not preclude advocacy by concerned persons and groups for access to safe abortions. However, the question remains as to whether the effort to address the challenges around abortions was best expressed as a right in this context?

Whose interests would a change in the law really serve? It is noteworthy that the first attempt to introduce a bill decriminalising abortion was made in the National Assembly of Nigeria by a medical doctor in 1981, when the first Termination of Pregnancy Bill was introduced in the House of Representatives (Adi 1982). The later attempt in the 1990s was also centred on the support of doctors. It was assumed that criminalisation was the key obstacle to abortion and that decriminalisation would be a first step in improving services for women. The underlying presumption was of a state-centric medical and legal model. Whether basic and safe services rendered and controlled by a male-dominated medical profession was the only option and the ultimate goal, was not questioned. Certainly, decriminalisation of abortion would give doctors licence to practice without fear of prosecution. It has also been argued that it would create a more open and enabling environment for teaching appropriate procedures properly in medical schools (Oye-Adeniran 2002). This is an important argument when the procedures in question are specific to induced abortion as opposed to more generalised procedures such as dilation and curettage (D&C), which may be required in other situations, including cases of spontaneous abortions.

In a context where most people experience law and the state as alien and oppressive, and where women's influence on these institutions as well as their solidarity is very weak, the efficacy of a focus on law for achieving change in the interests of women at that time was highly questionable. Finding ways of establishing and strengthening women's solidarity and access to information and services on sexual health, contraception and abortion was more important.[7]

Advocacy for the Right to Contraception

Another factor canvassed by women's health advocates, particularly in Europe and the United States, as key to women's empowerment and improved health status is the right of access to contraception. The use of modern contraception by Nigerian women was rated as very low in the 1980s.[8] The Nigerian government, under pressure from international financial institutions and donor agencies in the 1980s, introduced a population policy and national family planning programme in 1988. Later in the 1980s and 1990s, international organisations and foundations supported women's groups and NGOs in Nigeria to advocate for the right to contraception, which, as in the case of abortion, was linked to reducing maternal mortality and morbidity. Women's groups and feminists from Europe and the United States joined in to support this advocacy. Yet what Nigerian women got as a result of advocacy for the right to contraception on their behalf, was an array of selected, imported contraceptive drugs and devices, and a concerted campaign to persuade them to use them, no matter what the discomfort. Between 1990 and 2000, contraception provided in most family planning clinics meant pills, IUDs, Depo Provera and later Norplant and Uniplant. There were no diaphragms, few spermicides, no Billings Method and few condoms until the HIV/AIDS pandemic was well under way. This advocacy for women's right to contraception generally fitted in well with the agenda and programmes of those canvassing population control through provision of efficient methods

---

7. And indeed some organisations, such as IPAS, focused on this in collaboration with members of the medical profession.

8. Contraceptive prevalence rates among married women in the mid-1980s to 1990 were estimated at 6–7%, and in 1999 at 8.6% by the Nigerian Demographic and Health Surveys 1990 and 1999.

of contraception to Nigerian women. All attention was focused on *women* and on *'efficient' methods* of contraception. Too little was directed towards gender inequalities and *male responsibility* for reproduction.

At first, in the late 1980s and in 1990, the contraceptive drugs and devices were provided free of charge, but gradually user fees were introduced and raised.[9] The continued importation and donation of heavily subsidised contraceptives raises important questions as to the motivation behind and sustainability of donor-driven and state-sanctioned and -sponsored family planning campaigns in the country. Just a few critical voices (from the Catholic Church, and, ironically, women's organisations) during this period opposed the population policy and the mode of executing the family planning programme by focusing on promoting acceptance of provider-dependent, long acting and invasive methods of modern contraception.

Who was claiming the right to contraception in Nigeria and in what context? Who or what was obstructing it? Is the State obliged to provide services? How and at what cost? These are some of the questions we can ask in reviewing a decade of activism. Advocacy for the right to contraception was again directed at the State. This time the greatest pressure to intervene with a policy and programmes came from international financial institutions, the foreign governments which controlled them and other donor organisations. They sought a reduction in population growth rates, which were considered too high. Women's NGOs and organisations advocated the right to contraception to meet the perceived 'unmet need' of women to control their fertility. The assertion that the State should have a policy and provide services was ironical at a time when the State was being pressurised by the same international financial institutions to reduce its involvement in health and education under Structural Adjustment Programmes (SAPs). One may conclude that these institutions were not seeking or advocating the right of women to contraceptives, but the *duty and responsibility of women to use contraceptives*. Yet many women's organisations and NGOs unquestioningly thought the strategies for these two goals could, and did, coincide.

Advocating the right to contraception for women in Nigeria at that time within the framework of the existing state-sponsored family planning programme, without a thorough examination and critique of it, thus legitimised foreign-led, state programmes of population control, not necessarily

---

9. For example, in the Ikorodu General Hospital and at the PPFN Clinic in Lagos, between 1989 and 1992 there was no charge for any of the contraceptives provided, except condoms.

beneficial to women and sometimes injurious to their health; a medical model that is based on chemicals, drugs and modern manufactured devices; a model of fertility regulation programmes that is not sustainable in view of its dependence on imported drugs and devices; and a model that did little to promote gender equity and male responsibility in sexual relations. No information was provided on natural fertility regulation or female barrier methods (such as the diaphragm) in most family planning clinics and there was no policy on or research into, or development of, traditional methods or the promotion of local production of contraceptives.

Participation in International Advocacy

These attempts to influence state policy in Nigeria on different fronts took place in the eight years preceding the UN's International Conference on Population and Development (ICPD) held in Cairo in 1994. In the preparatory conferences leading up to the ICPD and during the ICPD itself, NGOs working on women's issues and health sought to influence the language in the Platform of Action for the conference. In particular, they sought the reformulation of concepts of reproductive and sexual rights. Coalitions and networks of women's NGOs were built and an attempt made to arrive at a minimum agenda in the form of a Women's Declaration on Population Policies. These women's groups sought to lobby national delegations as well as to present alternative views and perspectives at the parallel NGO Forum at the Conference. They were successful in broadening the debate at the Cairo conference and placing women's health and gender equity on the agenda as well as raising awareness around the world on these issues and the UN policy-making process.

Debates on the right to abortion and sexual orientation were the most controversial issues at the conference and the women's caucus did not succeed in having them included in the way some groups wanted. However, a great deal of time was spent trying to secure the inclusion of these issues in the Platform of Action and unsafe abortion and complications from abortion as women's health issues *did* get a mention in the compromise that emerged.

Some African women participated in these processes either as members of their country's delegations and/or as key members of independent NGOs participating in the parallel forum. A notable feature of much of that participation was that it was facilitated by Northern-based NGOs in the US and Europe. Understandably, as these NGOs were seeking to build coalitions of like-minded persons and organisations to advance their agendas, this process of selection had a significant impact on the pattern of representation from the region at those conferences. This holds true for many prior and subsequent UN conferences and other international meetings, and its implications for the nature and quality of African women's organising and advocacy at the national and regional levels, as well as for women's advocacy at the international level is far-reaching. Nonetheless, the experience of participating in these meetings and strategising to influence national and international policy was significant for all the women who were there, including the African women. The discomfort of many of the African women participants at the NGO Forums for the Preparatory Committee meetings and the ICPD itself, with advocacy for abortion rights threatening to dominate discussions, was ignored, glossed over or even labelled as anti-feminist by many Northern colleagues. Yet, as far as many of these women were concerned, there were more fundamental and pressing issues on the women's health agenda in Africa than the right to abortion. The universalising tendencies of powerful Northern women's lobbies with access to the UN and greater resources were evident in the ICPD process, and in much of the visible work done and produced internationally, including research into laws of different countries, campaigns for reform and campaigns at the level of the UN on reproductive and sexual rights. The resistance to and stifling of alternative views and perspectives until they are deemed acceptable by these powerful lobbies does much to influence and weaken national- and regional-level advocacy in Africa, as there is a general reluctance to differ with those who control funding or the allocation of resources.

These international meetings in the 1990s and women's participation in them marked an important point in the development of a discourse on women's health and reproductive rights, which has rapidly gained currency internationally. The pressures on African women to adopt a rights discourse in their advocacy for better health, conditions of living and gender equality and equity and their responses illustrate the politics of knowledge creation, transmission and agenda setting in the modern world and the challenges and dilemmas that arise in the quest to define appropriate and relevant health agendas by African women in the region, and to advocate for their implementation. This paper argues that rights discourse, as demonstrated in patterns of advocacy for reproductive rights, far from being a universal and unqualified human good, requires scrutiny and that, like any other, the field of human rights, women's rights and reproductive rights is an arena of struggle. These struggles must be waged with a clear vision and clearly defined substantive goals, as well as the adoption of appropriate organisational forms and vehicles for the transmission of those goals.

Rights Advocacy and Law Reform: Some Critical Questions

The claim of rights has historically been a response to threatened or actual violation, and an attempt to define a new legitimacy. Such claims are usually made by self-conscious and relatively empowered groups within societies. Many individuals and groups throughout history and in all parts of the world have made claims to entitlement which may be interpreted as rights claims. Their success is dependent on the flexibility of the system in which these claims are made and the balance of power between contending forces.

The modern discourse on rights presumes that rights are pre-declared and universal, recognisable as such by all and enforceable by or against the state. The source of these rights is either presumed to be 'natural' or derived from a social consensus. These rights, when asserted or violated, are adjudicated upon by neutral tribunals, such as courts, applying objective principles and procedures. Their enforcement is, however, sometimes problematic where the State or other organ of enforcement is itself the violator[10] or has no power to enforce. The extensive body of international human rights declarations and conventions is an attempt to articulate a chronicle of rights and principles which represent universally acceptable standards of behaviour and guarantees of human dignity.

This dominant modern notion and strategy of claiming rights is closely linked to Western liberal democratic conceptions of positive law and the State, on which it depends for enforcement, even though it appeals to the idea of natural law in proclaiming universal and inherent rights. Critiques abound of this Western liberal concept of rights as pre-declared, objective and universal entitlements.[11] These include its emphasis on individuals as free autonomous bearers of rights, which tend to be exclusive and paradoxically lead to the articulation of competing rights, such as foetal rights and father's rights in the abortion debate. The way in which responsibility, which is the other side of the coin of rights, is often de-emphasised has also been

---

10. Which is why there is a concern about the independence (supposed to be a guarantee of neutrality and objectivity) of the judiciaries and judicial officers who are called upon to enforce rights in courts and tribunals.
11. See, for example, Elizabeth Kingdom,1991 and Mutua, 2002.

criticised.[12] Expressions of rights as immutable values and principles, universal and applicable to all persons equally, can be a powerful means of imposing specific value systems of the powerful on other interest groups. Thus decontextualised, they tend to obscure the real social relations and contexts, which render them meaningless to some groups, due to their lack of participation in setting standards as well as their lack of access to conditions precedent to the fulfilment of specific articulated rights. For example, what does the legal right to abortion confer on a woman who cannot afford the cost of procuring one within a system of privatised healthcare? Furthermore, universalist conceptions of rights and their enforcement through the due process of law which is implied can neutralise the claims of relatively weak groups seeking fundamental change by defining the acceptable parameters of the discourse of change and transformation. This is why actions of some groups and social movements claiming entitlement to livelihoods and resource control through armed struggle or occupation of land and installations, such as in the Niger Delta oil-producing areas of Nigeria, are not usually described as human rights struggles unless and until they involve a court action or are framed in the particular language of legal claims. An adversarial enforcement and adjudicatory system usually associated with legal claims to rights also tends to aggravate rather than resolve conflict by pitting these bearers of rights against one another to determine which rights should have priority.

The articulation of human rights, particularly at the international level, is an attempt to establish minimum entitlements for all persons and to set standards of behaviour for the humane treatment of persons. However, the catalogue of human rights ranges from general principles such as equality, non-discrimination, fairness, prohibition of cruelty, arbitrary taking of life and detention or restraint, to specific provision of certain conditions and benefits considered essential to human life, such as shelter and education. This catalogue is constantly expanding and one can frame virtually any claim in the language of rights today. It is this attempt to go beyond general principles to detailed stipulation of entitlements and to universalise them that fragments and decontextualises rights, rendering them meaningless until activated in specific struggles or contexts. These struggles and contexts represent sites of political contestation over the meaning of rights, through which that meaning and the priority or value accorded to the rights claimed are established in concrete terms.

---

12. See initiatives for a Universal Declaration of Human Responsibilities facilitated by UNESCO in 1997, and a later one by the InterAction Council in the same year.

In Europe and North America in the 1960s, women were confronted with State institutions that effectively monopolised policy making and enforcement and regulated provision of medical services. The Church also had tremendous influence on definitions of legitimacy expressed in state policy. The women's campaign against unwanted pregnancy and for access to services for termination of pregnancy was therefore focused on changing the law or passing new laws legitimating generalised access to abortion services on the grounds that it was a woman's right to choose whether or not to carry a pregnancy to term. European and American women's claims of abortion rights made sense in the context of stiff opposition from Church and State and within the framework of a thoroughly medicalised healthcare delivery system monopolised by doctors and men and often reflecting male values. They were also adopting the legal model and language of the State, which had become pervasive, to fight the State. However, even in these contexts, as African-American women's groups have pointed out, the right to abortion as initially expressed by white, middle class women was not *their* biggest problem or priority: they were more concerned about the conditions necessary to exercise that right freely, including information, the choice of whether or not to have an abortion in the face of coercive population control policies, access to properly equipped facilities and the financial resources to pay for the procedure. Legal choice is no guarantee of access, although, where the State has effective control of services, it can be one of the conditions necessary for it (Bond 2001).

Where the State does not effectively monopolise policy making and enforcement or provide or regulate most medical services, and there is no strong, direct opposition to women seeking abortions from the State, as in the Nigerian example, women were not inclined to frame their quest for abortion services in terms of rights. The source of major restrictions on access was not so clearly identifiable with institutions of religion and State as to trigger that response. That women want access to technology and to simple safe methods of contraception and abortion controlled by them is evident from the complaints they have about the attitudes of some doctors towards women seeking abortions, and the popularity of self-help methods, which involve the ingestion of herbs and other substances, some of which are ineffective or harmful. Whilst actively seeking access to abortion services when the need arose, many women didn't see it as a *right* to be asserted negatively or positively in relation to the state or any specific institutions or groups perceived to be the major source of obstruction or provision. Within the Nigerian context, therefore, the assertion of women's rights to abortion and advocacy for decriminalisation had little resonance.

Furthermore, in the struggle for abortion rights, anyone or group can claim rights – the woman, her male partner claiming paternity, the foetus or groups acting on its behalf. The abortion rights struggle is thus a classic example of the clash of rights and a movement struggling to establish a new legitimacy. The quest for law reform and the claim of rights for women as individuals or a group by women's health advocates does not address the broader context of unwanted pregnancy and what women want. Why are contraception and childbearing and rearing viewed as problems in specific instances and what is the nature of male and social responsibility for them? Is termination of unwanted pregnancies a coping mechanism with which many women are uncomfortable? Do abortion rights advocates sometimes seem to focus on abortion as a solution for unwanted pregnancy, insisting on generalised access and neglecting the issue of why the pregnancy is unwanted? Access to safe abortion services reduces but does not solve the problem of women's vulnerability to exploitation and ill health, especially where repeated abortions are used by women as an alternative to contraception. There are also other factors contributing to the high incidence of unwanted pregnancy and impeding access to abortion services, not just legal and moral barriers. These include knowledge of and access to safe technologies for contraception and abortion, as well as attitudes towards sexual relations and contraception and decision-making processes and power in sexual relations.

The women called upon to support advocacy for abortion rights who appeared ambivalent or undecided both locally and at the UN-level may be seen as expressing a real discomfort. The idea of being either for or against abortion rights represents typically Western rational and linear thinking. These African women were neither entirely for nor entirely against abortion (and one may question why they should be forced to take such polarised positions). They constantly sought to situate the act of terminating an unwanted pregnancy in a specific context, rather than viewing it in abstract terms, and did not see blanket legislation for or against it as a solution or priority. In the same vein, access to contraception may be an important issue for women, but they may not necessarily frame it as a right, especially when they do not identify an active agent obstructing access. They want greater participation in decision making in the family and for men to take or share responsibility for contraception (Ahonsi and Ilumoka 1997). Establishing women's legal right to contraception does not necessarily establish choice, or the choices that women want, and may work against them, placing extra responsibilities on their shoulders.

Between the Devil and the Deep Blue Sea: Dilemmas in Agenda Setting for Women's Health in Nigeria Today

In Nigeria, as in many parts of Africa, healthcare became a major concern of the post-colonial state in the 1960s and 1970s. This was expressed in state policies and development plans. Medical professionals trained in the Western allopathic[13] tradition from colonial times have dominated policy making (but not necessarily healthcare delivery). Access to modern medical facilities is limited in many areas. The introduction of SAPs in the 1980s has led to the reduction in the scope and efficacy of state health programmes and facilities in many countries. The state cannot achieve full coverage of its territory in terms of its adopted model of healthcare and yet continues to dominate agenda setting on health, occasionally giving some women's health advocates and other civil society organisations space to participate. However, individual women and professional groups traditionally concerned with healthcare, such as herbalists, traditional birth attendants and other classes of healers, continue to play an important role in service delivery in Nigeria. Their marginalisation in official agenda setting and allocation of resources has not prevented them from doing their work, but it has affected the transmission of knowledge and skills and the internal development and regulation of their healing practices.[14] Increasing commodification of all aspects of life and commercialisation of this system of healthcare has led many untrained and 'quack' practitioners to profess various healing skills. With the gradual withdrawal of the state from healthcare in a period of major economic and social transformations which are impoverishing the majority of people, much of the population in the country is left to the mercy of a chaotic private sector, including the remnants of a traditional healthcare delivery system whose development has been stunted in many instances. In response, many people revert to self-help or religious institutions for succour. This is the situation in relation to abortion services and many other health services in Nigeria and women are by far the largest group of users of these services. Their individual isolated actions are no longer an adequate re-

---

13. A tradition that tends to fragment the analysis and treatment of disease and has created specialisations in science and medicine accordingly, as opposed to more holistic traditions that see inextricable linkages between things.
14. Missionary activity and education sometimes sought to delegitimise and degrade these practices. Regulation of practices that might have been achieved within specified hierarchies in village communities or groups of communities have been weakened over time.

sponse to larger-scale state and corporate interests and interventions. Familiar, small community based groupings and modes of organising are often no longer effective in new social and economic circumstances. Organised and conscious women's health advocacy is thus becoming an important component of local and global governance. What then affects the forms it takes? What can we learn from 15 years of advocacy focused on women's health and reproductive rights in Nigeria?

Nigerian women have in the last century adopted various modes of organising and advocating for social change favourable to them, reflecting differing bases of solidarity and differing agendas. Their organisational bases have included trade, religious and community-based groups; women's wings of political and professional associations; associations focusing on gender roles and power relations; and most recently, a host of professionalised NGOs engaged in advocacy of various kinds. These organisations have provided a site for women to interact and influence policy and practices affecting them.

Agendas for women's health and wellbeing in Nigeria today continue to be developed and influenced largely by Western educated medical professionals (mainly men), bureaucrats and donor agencies, whether bilateral, multilateral or private, who have the resources to influence policy and directly intervene in healthcare provision. Women's health advocates from other countries and at the local level are struggling to influence some of these donor agencies and bureaucrats, as described in the earlier discussion of UN-level activities before and during the Cairo and Beijing conferences which produced various inputs on women's perspectives on population policies and family planning programmes. The problem is that in this process, whether inadvertently or not, they are often reproducing hegemonic processes and discourses which reduce their ability to propose a viable alternative to the policies and systems they oppose, and which threaten the interests, perceptions, expression and way of life of large groups of women on whose behalf they are advocating change.

This chapter focuses on the example of reproductive rights, a term and concept which, until about ten years ago, was rarely used by Nigerian women spontaneously, irrespective of their occupation, level of education or social class. However, because of its increasing use in international forums, it is gaining currency, irrespective of their understanding of it and preferences. The dilemma of those who use it, mainly those engaged in advocacy for women's empowerment through NGOs and intergovernmental agencies, is that they are often adopting meanings and strategies of reproductive rights which have little resonance among the majority of people they interact with. Faced with this situation, the response of most of these people and organisations has been to embark on or support 'human rights education' programmes to teach people their rights and how to advocate for them. The very concept of rights that underlies these efforts is one of rights as fixed, pre-declared principles, especially those contained in UN conventions, waiting to be put into effect against or by the State through specific legal procedures. People's own spontaneous claims of entitlement and methods of enforcing them – their very contribution to defining values in their environment– are thus ignored, delegitimised or weakened. Yet it is this alternative rights discourse and the way in which it might (or might not) interface with the dominant rights discourse that deserves close attention, if the enforcement of rights is to be sustainable.

In several forums in Nigeria in which I have participated, well known women leaders have defended their advocacy for reproductive rights and adolescent sexual rights by reference to the provisions of the Platforms of Action of the ICPD and Beijing conferences, not to their own or their groups' convictions or the desire for and importance of these issues to Nigerian women. It is not my intention to criticise international-level advocacy and collaborations by women's groups, which can be an extremely important means of information-sharing and lobbying for policy change. I am simply arguing that local and national level advocacy is vital and should feed into the international level. Such advocacy, therefore, needs to be strengthened and leaders of movements should consult and build stronger constituencies through information-sharing and discussion processes that enable more women and men to articulate their opinions and positions on issues of importance to them. The articulation of Nigerian women's perspectives on many so-called women's issues is still extremely weak, reduced in many instances to reciting 'politically correct' language from donor agencies and women's organisations in other countries. Advocacy for women's rights in this context is thus in danger of becoming a sterile process alienated from the desires and struggles of real people. Much of the women's health and rights movement has not yet taken ownership of the discourse it is engaged in and questions should be asked about why this is so and why they engage in the discourse.

I pose this as a challenge to all women's health advocates, including myself. In our work at the Empowerment and Action Research Centre in Nigeria between 1992 and 2002, in the area of reproductive and women's health, it was clear that the health priorities of low income urban and rural women were the following: work to guarantee a means of livelihood, food, clean water, shelter, education and access to health services. This was repeatedly and spontaneously stated in many group discussions that took place over a period of seven years. Attempts to ask participants to focus on *reproductive* health in discussions of their needs and priorities still yielded answers such as access to good food; clean water; antenatal, obstetric care and postnatal services; treatment of malaria and general check-ups.[15] These women simply did not conceive of reproductive health as separate from the other aspects of health that daily confront them. Contraception and abortion were never mentioned, although *when these issues were raised by facilitators* some of the women who participated in these discussions said that they would appreciate better information and services.[16] In a sense, therefore, these women have defined their priority reproductive health issues as access to food, clean water, shelter, work, education and health services, including antenatal and obstetric care and care of their children. They do not define contraception and abortion as rights or as priorities. To frame these things as rights and to reprioritise them in terms of what we perceive to be specifically reproductive health issues, is to appropriate their voices – as often Western and local feminists do – by imposing a different framework on them and redefining their role and identity as women and social actresses (rather than as victims). Non- literate and low-income women often feel compelled to accept or acquiesce in these redefinitions because of disparities in power and control over resources by more powerful groups.

By the same token, some African women's health advocates working at the international level, who respect and seek to represent honestly the experiences and perceptions of the groups of women they interact and work with at the local level and to maintain their commitment to the process of building relevant, people-centred, gender-sensitive agendas and programmes – these women's health advocates face similar dilemmas. Confronted by a) national institutions and governments that are insensitive to and nonchalant about research and about gender inequality and women's health b) bilateral and multilateral donor agencies that also often view African and 'Third World' women as statistics and a means to an end such as population

---

15. EMPARC Forums on Peoples' Perspectives on Population Policies and Family Planning Programmes in Nigeria 1995 and Forums on the Feasibility of Community Health Insurance in Nigeria 2000.
16. With abortion there is usually general discomfort expressed with having to terminate a pregnancy (See Ahonsi and Ilumoka 1997).

control or control of HIV/AIDS; c) processes of corporate concentration and globalisation that impoverish them; and d) male-dominated organisations that exclude or marginalise them, these women's health advocates look to like-minded women and organisations within international movements for support. Unfortunately, here also, dominant power relations are often reproduced, and their 'friends' appropriate their voices, stifling dissent.

At the women's caucuses at the ICPD in Cairo 1994 and the preparatory meetings which preceded it, as well as other international meetings on women's health, it was almost taboo to express disagreement or discomfort with abortion rights and reproductive rights as they were being touted. The response was often a "*What!* you don't support reproductive rights for women? Then what the heck are you doing here?", which sometimes effectively silenced dissent and further exploration into precisely what was meant by reproductive rights, and what the differing perspectives on them might be. The magic words 'reproductive rights' brought forth donor funding for projects professing to be focused on promoting women's rights, whilst any critique and reservation was viewed with suspicion. When some women raised the issue of developing a Nigerian Women's Agenda to feed into post-Beijing processes rather than a post-Beijing agenda that took the Beijing Conference Platform of Action as the starting point and point of reference, this was resisted on the grounds that it might alienate funders of post-Beijing activities. This fear of not fitting into funding priorities or of losing funding by articulating an alternative emphasis or process is rife among Nigerian and African NGOs and is evidence of the weakness of their roots and structure, as well as some intellectual laziness and opportunism. There are, however, tremendous disparities in decision making power regarding resource allocation between donor agencies and their local 'partners', and these partners are subjected to everyday pressures of making a living that cannot be discounted. As a result of these trends, the dominant discourse on reproductive rights expanded its ambit with minor challenges for awhile, imposing the experiences and strategies of specific groups as universal.

Thus, caught between the devil and the deep blue sea, many Nigerian women and groups are forced to reassess and shift their alliances and strategies constantly. The result has been the weakening or changing of local agendas and even disintegration of some major organisations. In their own multifarious ways, women are learning to swim in the deep blue sea, but it can be exhausting. The challenge to African women health advocates is how to equip themselves and the next generation to survive these turbulent waters and make it to shore in better physical, mental and spiritual health.

The Challenges Ahead for the Women's Health Movement

As earlier noted, major changes in economic, political and social organisation have taken place in communities in Nigeria over the past two centuries, which are reflected in the healthcare delivery system, with the introduction of a radically different system based on a Western allopathic tradition with a different worldview and personnel seeking to dominate an existing one. As a result, the exchange of knowledge between these two systems has been very limited.[17] New social contexts, such as arrangements for education and systems of production and earning a livelihood, have thrown up new health issues or increased the incidence of old ones, rendering old ways of solving them inappropriate and new ways inaccessible. The examples of abortion and contraception discussed in this chapter are illustrative of this. Changing social circumstances and modes of organisation and regulation have increased the incidence of pregnancies that are experienced as unwanted, making access to methods contraception and of inducing abortion an issue for many more women and families. Methods of safely inducing abortion, which may have been known to a few specialists or older women, did not become public knowledge available to be passed on. People are thus left to find solutions to what they have identified as a problem in the new system of medical care, which has inadequate coverage, or through innovations and self-help of various kinds. The vulnerability of women due to their biology and of specific groups of women, such as the low income and the young, in this transition is what makes women's health advocacy in its modern forms necessary and desirable. Understanding this context, identifying problems and developing strategies to tackle them is, however, crucial to that advocacy.

Various organisations and networks in Nigeria have for many decades been engaged in activities to promote women's health and improvements in their lives. A characteristic of these organisations until fairly recently was that they were voluntary associations, some of which employed a very small administrative staff.[18]

In Nigeria, one of the main voluntary membership organisations, which emerged in the 1980s and focused on issues of gender equality and equity, was WIN. WIN was founded by a group of women and men committed

---

17. The interaction between the two systems is becoming increasingly limited and difficult as there are very few people alive who still understand and have access to both, and the 'traditional' systems have been transformed significantly in this transition.
18. Such as the National Council of Women's Societies, which is a large umbrella organisation.

to deepening understanding and analyses of the situation of women in Nigeria and strategies to improve it. The organisation was essentially funded by members' dues and services in kind, which were occasionally supplemented by funds and facilities raised by members locally from well wishers and supporters, government institutions and corporate organisations. Ironically, the infusion of larger grants from foreign funders[19] to support specific projects as well as general overhead costs showed up the weaknesses in the organisational structure and damaged the solidarity of members. With members drawn from a wide range of professional, social and class backgrounds, without a strong enough vision and basis for solidarity or clear and established policies on funding and accounting procedures, and with deliberate subversion by male members and leaders in their own personal interest, the organisation was too weak and young to withstand the manipulations of the various interest groups.

What organisations like WIN represented was a space for sharing experiences, building solidarity, carrying out advocacy and political campaigns – in short, building a movement. The importance, independence and power of voluntary membership organisations with a broad and committed constituency in lobbying for social change needs to be appreciated, and such groupings need to be actively promoted. Women's health advocates organising for change in policy and women's health status need to develop such groupings and a strong local agenda in response to the realities of the societies in which they live in order to mobilise increasing support over time.

With the burdens placed on women by SAPs in the 1990s, women's organisations were weakened as their members had too little time and not enough resources to organise beyond the purely local level and around occupations.[20] The proliferation in this period of new NGOs engaged in specific projects ranging from research and advocacy to service delivery was the result of the infusion of foreign donor funding into the country and actually further weakened the few voluntary organisations that existed, such as WIN. Much of the conscious women's health advocacy in the past 15 years has been conducted largely through these NGOs, which have acquired some influence with governments.

Many of them are small, drawing on the active commitment and energy of one or two founders to grow. They are dependent on donor funding,

---

19. Notably the Ford Foundation and the MacArthur Foundation in the early 1990s.
20. Such as trading, e.g., market women's associations, and other professional women's associations, such as the Medical Women's Association.

much of which comes from foreign donors and occasionally national governments, intergovernmental agencies and private individuals and corporations. Too often, these sources of funding are not sufficient, stable or long term. As a result, organisations compete for meagre resources and the handling of such support can and does subvert their agendas at an early stage of their development, creating frictions within and between them. Their quest for survival may thus become paramount, making them vulnerable to donor manipulation. The organisations with a potential to survive the vagaries of funding and to enforce administrative rules and procedures are social movements organised as membership associations whose members have a primary means of livelihood that is not dependent on the organisation. As they also have a large membership, they tend to be more effective as lobby groups in policy making.

Yet NGOs are being promoted as the new agents of development in Africa. It is noteworthy that most of them are viewed as *'implementation partners'* of intergovernmental agencies, donor agencies and governments. This nomenclature suggests that their task is not to define the agenda for action but to implement pre-defined agendas. As a result, most funding to these organisations is for projects already defined as relevant or as priorities, and dissent is not viewed favourably. Relatively few resources are invested in research and agenda setting, and institution building over the long term is also rarely funded to any significant degree. This discussion on the importance of building solidarity groups and institutions to influence policy in Africa has highlighted the importance of advancing democratic governance in the continent. Many of the dilemmas experienced by individual women's health advocates and small NGOs can be viewed as challenges for institution building and reform – an important aspect of democratic governance. The debates on the nature and future of the State in Africa are very pertinent here. The current drive towards privatisation, which is also reflected in organisational forms, is disturbing and can only lead to fragmentation and a weakening of the position of African nations and groups in the world today. It does not solve the problem of corruption nor does it promote efficiency. This is evident in the NGO sector. Weakening or abandoning the State and social movements is not the answer.

Two processes are key to strengthening African women's efforts at organising in the face of the onslaught of global capital,[21] growing patriarchal

---

21. This happens while corporations are increasingly influencing and determining the direction of public policy.

power and the universalising tendencies of some powerful Northern women's groups: a) developing clear visions and agendas, and b) demanding an allocation of resources and decentralisation of power to facilitate their empowerment. The forms of organising are thus only significant insofar as they advance or weaken these processes. I am suggesting that these times and our experience over the past two decades demand innovative issue-based partnerships and a revitalisation of social movements, rather than competition between social movements and NGOs. Furthermore, a different attitude to resource mobilisation and to accountability for those resources is required. In the struggles for women's health described in this chapter, attempts by some Northern women's groups and donor agencies to stifle alternative views and a failure on the part of women's health advocates from Nigeria and other parts of Africa to insist on developing local agendas and framing priorities in terms meaningful to them, is a result of a global concentration of resources and centralisation of decision making power which goes largely unchallenged and unaddressed.

Strengthening advocacy for women's health requires more intensive mobilisation of critical masses of women;[22] creating opportunities for expression of interests and priorities; sharing experiences; probing for causes and roots of problems and the formulation of agendas for change and development. In this process, agendas reflecting the needs, desires and priorities of the majority of women as well as specific groups of women will be developed. Stronger alliances and institutions to lobby for and defend these interests also need to be built. It is a process that must begin from where people are, in order to carry them along and exchange experiences to build common ground. It cannot and should not railroad them into moving in directions dictated by powerful groups or they will be dragged along in the tide, clinging to whatever bits of driftwood were doled out by these interest groups, and arrive at their destinations disoriented and alienated. Yet, in this situation, unable to participate energetically or enthusiastically in specific advocacy activities, the people are blamed once again for ineffective action.

Conclusion

This chapter has sought to examine the process of developing agendas for research and activism in the African context, taking as an example recent

---

22. I am not suggesting one critical mass of women in a monolithic organisation, but critical masses of women in various organisations and interest groups reflecting similar perspectives and goals.

developments in advocacy for women's reproductive and sexual rights in Nigeria. It has focused in particular on the way in which foreign donor agencies and activist groups have influenced the process both locally and internationally, and the impact their assistance has had on policies and practices affecting women's health. It has argued that African women need space to define relevant and contextualised women's health agendas – space which they have been unable to claim fully and utilise because of the attraction of donor funds for agendas defined in other contexts. African women also need to contribute to the implementation of what they have defined. They are already labouring under tremendous pressure in difficult economic and political environments. Their allies should not compound that pressure. Part of their struggle should be to call for a release of pressure, and not to submit to the delegitimation of their experience and the experiences of other women in their communities. This is a political struggle and it has only just begun. The strategy of empowerment which it involves can be subverted by 'rights fundamentalism' – an insistence on a specific discourse of rights made universal as the only way. As was evident in some of the organising for the Cairo conference, in the process of universalising their experiences to gain international recognition for and assist their local battles, Northern women's groups and donor agencies sometimes inadvertently stifle the emergence of strong solidarity movements and relevant agendas in the South, thus assisting the hegemonic project of Northern states and corporations. Although my focus is on the experiences of many Nigerian and African women's health advocates and groups, the issues raised are, of course, general issues of domination through centralisation and misuse of power, recognisable in many parts of the world.

I have been very active between 1989 and 2003 in some of the processes of advocacy for women's health described in this paper. This review of my personal experience and the experiences of several colleagues has been ongoing for many years and is not meant as a condemnation of our activities nor those of our partners. I salute my colleagues in Nigeria and elsewhere in Africa who work under such difficult circumstances and have sacrificed so much to engage in these struggles. I salute our friends and partners all over the world who have supported us morally and financially for many years. It is responses to critical evaluation, ours and theirs, that determines our good faith and capacity to improve our contributions in the future. As activists, as we seek to reshape our societies for the future, we should constantly ask ourselves certain questions: do we have a clear vision, do our strategies and tactics contradict our vision and goals, are our agendas and programmes sustainable, whose or what interests do we serve? We owe it to ourselves and to the women with whom we profess solidarity to bear witness to our times, to learn from our mistakes and to refresh our visions. I hope that this is one contribution to that process of empowering ourselves, finding our voices and facing our challenges.

References

Adi, I.E., 1982, "The Question of Abortion", *Nigerian Current Law Review* 191–204.

Ahonsi, B. and A. Ilumoka, 1997, *Nigerian Women's Family Planning Experiences and Perspectives: Insights from Metropolitan Lagos.* Monograph Series 2. Lagos: Empowerment and Action Research Centre.

Bond, T., 2001, "Barriers between Black Women and the Reproductive Rights Movement", *Political Environments* Issue No. 8:1–5.

Ilumoka, A. and A. Simpson, 1996, *Women's Perspectives on Birth Control in Nigeria.* Working Paper Series No. 1. Lagos: Empowerment and Action Research Centre.

Harrison, K., 1997, "Materna; Mortality in Nigeria: The Real Issues", *African Journal of Reproductive Health* 1(1):8.

Kingdom, E., 1991, *What's Wrong With Rights: Problems for a Feminist Politics of Law.* Edinburgh: Edinburgh University Press.

Mutua, M., 2002, *Human Rights – A Political and Cultural Critique.* Philadelphia: University of Pennsylvania Press.

Okonofua, F. et al., 1991, "Assessing the Prevalence and Determinants of Unwanted Pregnancy and Induced Abortion in Nigeria", *Studies in Family Planning* 30(1):67–77.

Okonofua, F. and T. Ilumoka, 1991, "Prevention of Morbidity and Mortality from Induced and Unsafe Abortion in Nigeria", *Critical Issues in Reproductive Health* 1991, 9. New York: Population Council.

Oye-Adeniran et al., 2002, "Complications of Unsafe Abortion: A Case Study and the Need for Abortion Law Reform in Nigeria", *Reproductive Health Matters* 10(19):18–21.

Republic of Nigeria, 1963, *Criminal Code.* Lagos: Nigeria.

WHO, 2002, *Making Pregnancy Safer; Nigeria Country Report.* Washington DC: WHO.

CHAPTER FIVE

Critical Feminism in Mozambique
Situated in the Context of our Experience as Women, Academics and Activists

Isabel Maria Casimiro and Ximena Andrade

Introduction

In Mozambique, studies on social relationships between women and men have been developing since the mid-1980s and became established in the 1990s. The Centre of African Studies (Centro de Estudos Africanos, CEA) at Eduardo Mondlane University (Universidade Eduardo Mondlane, UEM) has been responsible for making this new field of study more visible and also for conducting research on women from a feminist and gender perspective. In particular, the practice of action-research was created, giving a special dynamic to gender studies in Mozambique. This has had a significant influence on the UEM curricula; the integration of gender issues into tertiary course subjects; the mobilisation of women to join otherwise predominantly male courses;[1] the emergence, development and support of women's associations and the women's movement in Mozambique; the modification and making of public policies and the alteration and formulation of non-discriminatory legislation.

An early focus of gender studies at the CEA was gaining information about the lives of women in Mozambique before colonial intervention and the impact of colonialism on the division of labour between women and men and on access to and control and sharing of resources and power. In this context also, the role of women in the anti-colonial resistance and na-

---

1. Here we refer to the courses in history and linguistics at the Institute of Anthropology and to the geography course in the UEM Faculty of Arts. We also refer to certain parts of the courses given at UFICS (Social Sciences Training and Research Unit) and to the recent experiences with the Master of Education programme at UEM and with the Women and Engineering project in the Engineering Faculty at UEM.

tionalist movements, and their contribution to the armed struggle for national liberation led by FRELIMO[2] were researched. In the course of this work, we realised that the study of social relations between women and men, between women and between men, that is to say, the social relations of gender, was a category with great analytical potential.

The research-action experiences of the CEA and the networks with which we have worked have demonstrated the usefulness of this analytical category for understanding the roots of discrimination against women; the ways in which the female and the male are produced and reproduced; how the domestic spatial-temporal dimension and the spatial-temporal dimensions of production, the marketplace, community, citizenship and the world have been constructed in Mozambique, from the colonial period through to the 21st century (Santos 2000:254). This construction of the male and the female relates to the context of capitalist relations that coexist with and are reproduced alongside precapitalist socioeconomic relations, which are a reality in significant parts of the country and for large parts of the population.

Issues of Epistemology

Our empirical work gradually required deeper epistemological analysis in order to provide an understanding of the reality that surrounds us, to reconstruct concepts and methodologies and to re-conceptualise our scientific paradigms, in short, to generate knowledge – not just facts to be worked on by others outside our country. In the following we discuss some important issues of epistemology at the intersection of gender and development work.

Between the 1960s and 1980s, human and social sciences underwent a major transformation due to the changes in the world situation, which coincided with the resurgence of the feminist movement in the 1960s. This phase of the feminist movement took shape at a historical moment of great ideological upheaval, when the need became evident to rethink the prevailing paradigms so as to better understand the world in order to change it. Women, who felt a need to know, understand and make visible their lives, forced social and human sciences to review their conceptualisations, which were often based on implicit androcentricity. Fields of knowledge such as history, anthropology, psychology, psychoanalysis, philosophy and linguis-

---

2. FRELIMO: Mozambique Liberation Front (Frente da Libertação de Moçambique).

tics underwent great epistemological change, finally satisfying at least some of the feminist concerns. By conceptualising the themes of society, culture and the individual in new ways, these disciplines came to address relationships and differences, male and female, power and hierarchy and uncertainty. This is where our contribution to reflection on gender is situated (Pérotin-Dumon 2000).

The generation of knowledge by different streams of feminism represents an epistemological breakthrough, perhaps the most important of the last 40 years of social science (Harding 1988), inasmuch as it upset the androcentric harmony of wisdom – social, scientific and political – secured by the dominant scientific paradigm. It provoked, as Julieta Kirkwood puts it, challenge, insolence, boldness, liberty and disorder (1986), allowing the blindfold of oppression to be removed and bringing insights in closer touch with the real world.

As a concept, gender implies a series of dimensions of power relationships expressed symbolically in body language, in the representation of the male and the female, as a constitutive element of identities and subjectivities, in micro/macro articulation and in practices. 'Gender' also reveals how male domination is inscribed in language, in things and objects, in spaces, in mental structures, in the way we perceive others, and it is inscribed in the way that the body itself is used, under certain conditions being a basis for female subordination (Corrêa 2000).

The validity of the category 'gender' has often been questioned: whether this is not just another category imported and assimilated in the context of 'development', along with other concepts foreign to our African reality. Very often too, people confuse 'gender' with 'women'. Paradoxically, the concept of 'gender', which was used by psychologists and adopted by feminists in the 1960s and 1970s to get away from the biological references of the word 'sex', is often used as a synonym for sex:

> Sex is a biological term, gender is used in psychology and in relation to cultural processes. It might be thought that these two words are simply two ways of considering the same difference and that if, for example, a person is of the female sex, then they automatically belong to the corresponding gender (the female, in this case). But in fact this is not so. Being a man or a woman, a boy or a girl, is as much about dressing, gestures, actions, social network and personality as the genital organs of each of them. (Oakley 1972)

As Simone de Beauvoir says, "One is not born, but rather becomes, a woman". Furthermore, it is important to keep in mind that the use of the concept of sex in biology refers exclusively to the reproductive aspect of human beings (in the male and female couple) and is independent of sexuality and the practice of sexuality, which is something human beings acquire. It is equally important to keep in mind that nowadays human reproduction is separated more and more from its natural biological dimension, being incorporated in the techno-social framework of the engineering of human reproduction.

Despite the fact that a lot of disagreement and, in particular, ignorance, devaluation and cooption still surrounds the concept of gender, it did gain strength and today it is considered a *sine qua non* for international donor support of projects or activities. The first Mozambican government to be elected in multiparty elections proposed in 1994, with regard to youth, women and families, "to introduce the concept of gender in the design, analysis and definition of national development policies and strategies" (Programa Nacional do Governo 1994, 60). After the Beijing Action Platform was approved in 1995, the Mozambican Government drafted a Post-Beijing Action Platform, which specifically mentions policies with a gender focus, and it initiated Gender Focal Points in almost all of its ministries.

However, as with other potentially emancipating concepts, the use of this concept entered the territory of political and academic wars, wars over spaces, capital and power. The result was the devaluation of its analytical content and its ability to transform oppressive and unequal realities, since the concept was coopted by power, which is *always* intelligently opportunistic. The question remains how to put gender policy into practice without redefining the entire agenda for development. In most countries, what has happened is that policies have been given new terminological clothing, with no changes in terms of different power relations, either within countries or between countries and international donor organisations.

One risk is the neutralisation of the term 'gender' by using it in a way that strips it of its revolutionary content: gender ends up as a descriptive category for statistical information about men and women and is often understood as a synonym for women (even academics at our university have said, "we already have gender at UEM", referring to the presence of women in the institution). Another risk is attached to the concept of empowerment. What is power and what are we talking about when we refer to power? There is a simplification – power is resources; resources are power. But the other dimensions? Symbolic power? These are not considered, and discourse on the propounded equality is kept within the parameters of the existing power model (Corrêa 2000). Nevertheless, the concept of gender has made it possible to visualise the inequality of women and discrimination against them, above all in the public sphere. Thus, the concept has allowed for institutional recognition of inequality and discrimination against women, despite the abovementioned risks and shortcomings.

In the academic field, feminist studies have reached an important phase through highly relevant theoretical analyses (Corrêa 2000). There have been changes in terms of theory, methodology and action, and there have been advancements on epistemological levels within the framework of critical feminism. Furthermore, the critical and activist contribution of the feminist movement to the creation and advancement of knowledge about sexuality has been significant.

Creation of knowledge in the academic field has not been isolated from the feminist women's movement in the field of action: various forms of collaboration but also tensions have been generated. These tensions still exist. Some feminists maintain that the ideology of activism in the movement should not hamper the critical debate of the academic world, hence the suggestion to maintain a distance in critical solidarity between academic feminism and the activist movement. This is not only in order to support activism in itself, but also to allow for better theoretical development, with the aim of better capturing the reality. The idea would be to further intelligent collaboration and solidarity towards a common goal.

The Institutional History of Gender Studies in Mozambique

In 1985, UEM together with the UNESCO Human Rights and Peace Division promoted a seminar entitled 'Women and National Reconstruction in Mozambique'. Various governmental and non-governmental institutions and socio-professional organisations conducting work and/or research on women in Mozambique participated. This seminar was a follow-up to a series of studies and seminars organised by UNESCO on the participation of women in national liberation struggles and their role and activities in recently independent states in Africa.[3]

One of the proposals emerging from this seminar indicated the need for UEM and other institutions to organise themselves and use their capacity for research and training of and about women, thereby contributing to their greater involvement in the development of the country. This seminar was

---

3. In 1983 the CEA/UEM History Workshop was represented at a UNESCO-organised encounter in Bissau on the participation of women in armed struggle. One of the authors of this chapter presented a paper written by the History Workshop.

also concerned with the coordination of the different projects and research activities on women in Mozambique. It was found that research work did exist that could greatly improve the understanding of the situation of women, but that this work was unknown to institutions and socio-professional associations.

After this first assessment of the work conducted in this area, CEA (which, through its History Workshop had been conducting research on the participation of women in the armed struggle for national liberation) initiated internal debate and debate with other institutions. The aim of this collective reflection was to find ideas for the development of research work that focused on women as the object of study.

In 1989, plans began to emerge for what would later become the Nucleus for Women's Studies (Núcleo de Estudos da Mulher, NEM) at CEA. During that year, CEA sought to incorporate people interested in working in this field of research. Two female students from the Superior Pedagogic Institute (ISP) were recruited and contacts were established with OMM (Mozambican Women's Organisation), UGC (Maputo General Cooperatives Union), AMODEFA (Mozambican Association for Development of the Family), DNDR (National Directorate of Rural Development), the Ministries of Justice, Education, Labour and Health and the National Directorate of Statistics, in order to coordinate and plan joint activities.

NEM was created in 1989. It embarked on a series of tasks, among which an important one was to coordinate at national level the Mozambican sub-projects of the regional Women and Law in Southern Africa research trust, the first being The Legal Situation of Women in Mozambique and Maintenance Rights. In addition, the newly-created nucleus set out to draft an annotated bibliography on women and development in Mozambique and, in this context, to train two students in women and gender issues and computerised data organisation. From the start, it was considered important to establish contacts with governmental and non-governmental organisations and with Mozambican, regional and international social organisations. NEM also embarked on other research projects and consultancies in accordance with its general objectives.

By 1991, the debate arising from the inquiries into the bases of discrimination against women and the increasing inclusion of the concept of gender as a systematic category to explain the elements that make up this discrimination, led to the research unit being given a name more in keeping with the ideas of the debate. Thus, the unit was renamed the Department of Women and Gender Studies (Departamento de Estudo da Mulher e Género, DE-

MEG) and it became a point of reference for those studying or working in this field and others.

Aspects of the Work of DEMEG

The activities of DEMEG were organised around six dimensions of research-action, taking into consideration the fact that all the professionals involved were university teachers. This implied that a gender perspective was incorporated into the subjects being taught by these professionals. The following is a description of each of the six dimensions, with selected examples of activities and research.

1. Institutional organisation of DEMEG

At the beginning of the 1990s, the Ford Foundation – which had been supporting CEA research work since its inception – agreed to support DEMEG, leaving it to the department's researchers to decide what activities to carry out. At this juncture, we thought that the institutional development of the department should involve a bibliographical database, and people were trained to develop this resource.

The freedom of decision granted by the Ford Foundation seems to be linked to historical factors: on the one hand, in the early 1990s Women and Development programmes were at their height and donor agencies supported activities related to this topic. On the other, in the case of the Ford Foundation, the subject of women has been one of its concerns since its inception. In Mozambique, DEMEG was the first point of reference for gender-related studies from a feminist perspective.

2. Participation in national, regional and international research projects and related consultancies

The cases here are many and we highlight only some examples.

Research at a national level: Women and Autarchies, funded by NORAD (Norwegian Agency for Development Cooperation), 1998. With the first municipal elections in Mozambique in 1998, NORAD asked CEA to conduct research into the participation of women in the electoral process, as voters and candidates for municipal posts.

The research had two phases. During the first phase, from April to June 1998, we surveyed the autarchic legislation, documentation on civic education, the press and the programmes of groups and political parties running for election. We also reviewed all written literature on electoral processes in Mozambique, thereby constructing a model for analyses. In all municipalities, there were at least two rallies organised by one of the groups or parties. This phase was concluded with a set of interviews with election candidates. In the second phase of fieldwork, interviews were conducted with all presidents of municipal councils and assemblies and with assembly members and councillors.

Some of the difficulties encountered with NORAD in this process should be pointed out. First, NORAD objected to the observation tools that the CEA proposed as part of the theoretical-analytical research framework. In the face of this objection, and because of the fact that in any research proposal there is a close relationship between the theoretical-analytical framework and data collection tools, our position was that either the proposal should be maintained or else another team would have to be found that would follow NORAD's guidelines. As a consequence, our research proposal was accepted in its original form.

There were also problems due to delays in the disbursement of funds, which forced the leadership of CEA to advance funds for work in the provinces. Because of the characteristics of the research and the need to accompany the electoral process as a whole, the delay in disbursement by NORAD placed constraints on the preparation and work of the teams in the northern provinces of Cabo Delgado and Nampula, the central province of Sofala and in the city and province of Maputo. As a result, part of the beginning of the electoral process was not covered.

However, it should be noted that in terms of the theoretical and methodological conception of the research, and as a result of our initial struggle with NORAD, the CEA team obtained total freedom to design, conduct and develop the research. The perspective used in this work followed the feminist theory of difference linked to discourse on equality only in relation to the exercise of human rights. In this sense, the power relationships between women and men were at the centre of the debate, and we struggled to identify women's subordination without any notion of essentialism.

Research at a regional level: Women and Law in Southern Africa, Women and Law in Southern Africa Research Trust (WLSA), funded by DANIDA (Danish International Development Agency. From the inception of this regional comparative project, the research teams in the six (later expanded to seven) Southern African countries have had the freedom to select their topics, the theoretical perspective and the methodologies used, with regard both to analytical tools and to data collection. This was (and is) in fact a regional research project, funded by donor money. It was/is not linked to consultancies.

We want to emphasise the fact that it was as part of the research conducted under this project that we acquired our information, our knowledge and our experience of feminist theory. It was in this project that we became feminists, learning that knowledge and the feminist position is recreated and developed day by day. The category of gender, which had been created in the context of feminism, was taken up and developed by the research teams involved in WLSA Mozambique, and feminist thought and sensitivity were being incorporated step by step. In this process, our contribution to feminist thought and also the development of non-traditional methodologies was very important. We in the Mozambican WLSA team learnt a lot through the regional collaboration, and meetings with feminist researchers in neighbouring countries were of great importance. (For further discussion of the WLSA project, see below).

Research at international level: Profile of Urban Environmental Management in Intermediate Cities: Public Policies and Local Dynamics: A Study of Beira City. International project with the participation of Bolivia and Pakistan and the support of the Swiss Research Fund, 1994–95.

This was a research project whose results were to be applied immediately in the context of the Programme for the Reform of Local Institutions (PROL), Environmental and Urban Management component, through its Programme Officer in Beira. The research work was conducted in collaboration with students from the UEM and the Catholic University of Beira, and in collaboration with local institutions. However, the Swiss Research Fund did not disburse the amount forecast for the immediate application of the results, a fact which almost jeopardised the work that had already been programmed with PROL, the Catholic University and the local institutions of the city of Beira. This work only became possible because of the support provided by the Dutch Embassy.

Consultancies – example: Base line study for the Kulhuvuka Project – 'Corridor of Hope'. Study requested by the Community Development Foundation (FDC, a Mozambican NGO set up by Graça Machel), Maputo, July 2002. This was the second phase of a consultancy in the framework of FDC's 'Corridor of Hope' programmes. The Kulhuvuka Project is a programme on

HIV/AIDS covering the four southern provinces of the country and extending also to South African territory within the Rand mining area. Within the objectives established by FDC, we succeeded in negotiating a theoretical conception and a methodology which we considered best suited to the time limits established for the consultancy (three months). The aim was to give the consultancy a research character, to the extent that the data collection methods were essentially qualitative. The methodology pursued consisted of a literature review, semi-structured interviews with target groups established by FDC, data recording and a review of the recorded data on the prevalence of HIV/AIDS. In this way, what started out as a mere consultancy ended up as research – not full-scale research, but still research.

3. Training inside and outside UEM

From the start of DEMEG and the development of research within this department, several different departments and faculties at UEM have requested courses on gender relations. This has involved teamwork among various teachers and researchers associated with DEMEG for the purpose of debating which courses were to be taught, as well as teaching methods. Courses outside UEM have also been held. Because of the heterogeneity and different educational levels of the participants, these courses have been organised in terms of group work, without, however, losing the academic character of the UEM courses.

4. Activities and Seminars for theoretical reflection on Human Rights, Feminism and Gender Relations

During 2000, two seminars were organised. At the first seminar, in August, Sonea Corrêa from DAWN (Development Alternatives with Women for a New Era) was the facilitator, and the starting point for the debates was the Inventory of Studies and Research conducted in the Area of Women and Gender by UEM during the last 25 years. Various themes from research projects, carried out or in progress, by researchers of the CEA, UEM and other institutions or associations were discussed. The topics were many and included on a more general level sexual and reproductive health and rights, gender and power, women and armed conflict and feminism and women's organisations. Among more specific research projects the following were discussed: Local Dynamics in Peasant Associations in Manhiça District, Lobolo (brideprice), Power and Control over Resources – Land and Domestic Violence.

During the second seminar, held in November, facilitated by Signe Arnfred, of the Nordic Africa Institute, Uppsala, issues related to the work of several state associations and institutions and their connection with research conducted by UEM were discussed. The relationship between research results and the programmes of these associations was analysed, as were issues of power at all levels, women's movements, feminist movements and feminist theories and development assistance. In each case, this work was undertaken with a gender perspective, and investigated power relationships between the associations, the state and donor agencies.

Participants in these seminars were, in addition to researchers from CEA and UEM, people from local NGOs, some ministries and a few FRELIMO members of parliament . The seminars provided important opportunities for meeting, networking and sharing experiences related to issues of gender between researchers, activists and politicians.

5. Activism: Contribution to the creation of national women's associations and active participation in national, regional and international women's associations

Activism has always been given high priority at DEMEG. Most if not all the researchers connected to the department are also activists. For example, DEMEG researchers contributed to the creation of important Mozambican women's NGOs, such as MULEIDE (Women, Law and Development in Mozambique), NUMMA (Nucleus for Women and the Environment), and Fórum Mulher, an umbrella organisation for women's NGOs in Mozambique. DEMEG researchers also participated in working groups on Women in Development (WID Committee/ Grupo de Coordenação Mulher no Desenvolvimento [Co-ordination Group for Women in Development])[4] and in the organising of Mozambique's participation in the international campaign, '16 Days of activism for non-violence against women', from 25 November to 10 December. This has been done every year since 1995. In 2003, researchers of CEA, WLSA Mozambique and women's organisations participated in the deliberations of African women on the occasion of the African Union summit held in Maputo in June 2003, at the request of Graça

---

4. The WID Committee was composed of WID Programme Officers of international and United Nations organisations working in Mozambique. Grupo Coordenação Mulher no Desenvolvimento became Fórum Mulher in 1993. CEA, through DEMEG, was elected to Fórum's Board of Directors for 1993–2000.

Machel of FDC. WLSA represented Southern Africa at the PRECOM of Women held one week before the summit. In 2005, CEA and WLSA Mozambique participated in the Fórum Mulher working group to draft a proposal for the Law against Acts of Domestic Violence.

6. Lobby work in relation to the Mozambican state

Of note among its activities is DEMEG's participation in the debate on the draft Family Law, which was approved by the Assembly of the Republic in 2003. It should be highlighted that the Family Law, which was ultimately passed, actually contains the main points suggested by the various women's organisations promoting women's rights, namely minimum age of marriage; elimination of the legal concept of a male head of the family and the husband's power to fix the family's residence; recognition of traditional and religious marriages, provided that they have been registered, while preserving the established principles of civil marriages; rejection of legal recognition of polygamous unions; and acceptance that, after one year of cohabitation in a de facto union, on its dissolution property is divided according to the rules applicable to marriage in community of property; recognition of a wife's right to pursue any commercial activity autonomously.

Gender researchers/activists from DEMEG and other women's organisations participated vigorously in the debates leading up to the approval of the draft Family Law, in the process repeatedly providing the Minister of Justice with arguments and background material. This was an example of successful lobby work, testifying to the political commitment and the researcher/activist identity of DEMEG researchers.

Important Lessons from WLSA Mozambique

One of the projects that contributed greatly to the development of gender studies in CEA has been the WLSA Project – Women and Law in Southern Africa – which operated out of the CEA from 1990 to 2002.[5] This Research-Action project led to the creation of networks of researchers from higher/tertiary teaching establishments, state institutions, the justice sector and the associations that were emerging. In this way, it got researchers and university students interested in studying the problem of women using a gender focus, also mobilising other sectors of society to promote women's human rights.

---

5. In 2002, WLSA Mozambique established itself outside the university.

This project was one of the first research projects on women and the law in Africa with a gender focus. Its conception began at a meeting held in 1988 in Nyanga, Zimbabwe, in which academic women and men, members of NGOs and activists from various Southern African countries participated. At this seminar, reports on the legal situation of women in the different countries were presented and an evaluation was made of the research conducted in the region, the research methodologies and perspectives and the challenges for the future. As a result of this first encounter, priority themes were drawn up, a regional comparative research effort was designed on the basis of common problems, and various ways of approaching possible donors were proposed. Starting in 1990, six countries, namely, Botswana, Lesotho, Mozambique, Swaziland, Zambia and Zimbabwe, undertook a regional comparative project on Women and Maintenance in Southern Africa. South Africa and Namibia, which had participated in the preparatory encounter, could not take part due to the international sanctions in place against the apartheid regime. Malawi became part of WLSA in 1996.

When the Mozambican team became involved in the WLSA project, it was aware of the challenges it would face. While it is true that CEA had accumulated enviable scientific capital over its 15 years of research and teaching, it should be remembered that this was a new phase in its history. There were some old guard researchers, who had helped to create the centre, but most were recent recruits who had just finished their studies. There had not yet been any research in the legal scientific field, studies on women and gender had barely begun at the NEM, soon to be transformed into DEMEG, and few people showed an interest in being involved in this new scientific challenge, since gender and legal issues had not yet entered the struggle for space in the academic field, in activism in various organisations and at the level of state power structures. The NGO movement was young, since the constitution that recognised freedom of association had been passed by the then People's Assembly only in November 1990. The NGOs in the field were AMODEFA (Mozambican Association for Development of the Family), created in November 1989, and ACTIVA (Mozambican Association of Entrepreneurial and Executive Women), formalised in December 1990. OMM, created in 1973 by FRELIMO, was the only nationwide women's organisation.

Fieldwork for the first WLSA project was conducted under extremely difficult conditions, since Mozambique was still immersed in a war of destabilisation (until 1992, when the Rome Accord was signed between the Mozambique Government and Renamo), which displaced some five million people (one-third of the population) and left one million refugees in neighbouring countries. For security reasons, it was not possible to stay in the areas of study, so teams were forced to travel there every day after class, at one o'clock in the afternoon, to return before half past four.[6] In neighbourhoods in Maputo's peri-urban belt, it was also necessary to work during weekends, which created problems for respondents because of their involvement in various income-generating activities, as well as social, family and community-related tasks. Thus, the destabilisation factor was an impediment to our broadening the area of study during the first phase of the WLSA project in 1990-92. It was only in the second phase, in 1992, that we were able to extend the areas of study to the northern province of Nampula, where fieldwork conditions had been difficult before the General Peace Accord signed in Rome in October that year.

A further challenge was the legal system in force in the other five countries and the use of English as the language of communication, thought and report writing, which called for added efforts on the part of the Mozambican team. The Mozambican team had to produce reports in two languages, while keeping to the same time limits as those applicable to the other countries. These conditions forced us to acquire an understanding of the legal systems of the other WLSA countries and to implement a 'translation' policy for the purposes of comparison among the different legal systems in force in Southern African countries.

We can say that, despite all the challenges, throughout all these years of intense work on the WLSA Regional Project the Mozambican team has been committed not only to meeting the deadlines for producing reports in Portuguese and English, but also to meeting the epistemological challenge. We are here talking about the concepts and methodologies of research-action, of contributions within a feminist and gender perspective and to the development of a truly interdisciplinary effort, not only through the involvement of researchers from different fields, but also in the endeavours to make this study trans-disciplinary.

Since early 2002, WLSA Mozambique has operated outside CEA and became legalised as an independent association at the end of that year. Still, however, WLSA maintains the research relationship it has with CEA and with UEM.

---

6. The spatial areas of study were the capital city, Maputo, and Boane district, about 30 km away.

Gender Studies as Spaces for Identity Construction

Since the mid-1980s in Mozambique, our research with a feminist focus on women, taking gender as an important analytical category, has made us face many questions and few certainties. Each new task takes us from pain to pleasure, but it is always part of an ongoing challenge: with colleagues, we study and debate theories and methodologies, the new concepts which enable us to understand and to describe what we perceive. From all of this emerges a new awareness and practices, which are ultimately expressions of the citizenship of women.

We asked ourselves to what extent the prevailing analytical categories in the field of science, which shaped our training, actually enable us to understand the social realities around us? For this reason, we opted for a feminist epistemology, which is being constantly developed and which has, since the 1980s, provided a new model, a holistic paradigm which also takes into consideration the subjective desires of women and men. This paradigm must be constructed in constant dialogue with human beings, with their subjective desires and personal freedoms, desires which in the present situation are much contaminated by the patriarchal imagination and are not conducive to real transformation (León 2003). The professional experience accumulated over the years, in constant dialogue with scientific work undertaken elsewhere and in combination with our own experience and the context to which we belong, has allowed us to construct ways of seeing these realities.

Our research work has been guided by a critical feminist perspective, which incorporates elements of Marxist, nationalist and post-structuralist feminism (Mbilinyi 1992). This perspective is closest to the so-called 'Third Wave' of feminism, that is, the feminist theories of difference (León 2000), reconstructed in such a way as to draw on feminist theories of equality, but only in the context of human rights and based on respect for difference. One of these critical perspectives was developed in the 1980s by Third World feminists in a way that contributed to the conceptions being developed in the First World, which was dominant in feminist studies at the time. The perspective stems from the different experiences of various groups of women in the political struggles in their respective countries. Its focus is on social relations of gender, class, race, ethnicity and imperialist relations. It is located in a neo-colonised country, within the framework of the capitalist world-system and it takes an anti-imperialist stand.

The perspective is based on situated knowledge, which reflects our lives, our individual and collective ways of being and of doing analysis. It is a perspective marked by our family education, as well as political, cultural and social experience as women, academics, members of political parties and civil associations, as mothers and as wives. The perspective is marked also by our participation in the previously mentioned WLSA research project.[7]

When we research and record research results, we are also recording our national and political history, including our history as feminist women. We are thus recording a very recent history, a history experienced through the pains and joys of day-to-day life, in a process of personal and temporal 'engagement' and 'distancing' as researchers. It is a day-to-day experience that is sometimes marked by discomfort, by the need to be inside the goings-on, to live them, confront them and influence them, but also by the conviction that we are operating in contexts that escape conventional analyses. The Mozambican reality forces us constantly to reflect on and find ways to interpret the diverse ways of being and thinking, other forms of rationality and ways in which they appear through lifestyles and ways of talking, through actions and strategies, which are interlinked and intermingled and which sometimes elude our understanding. But we must maintain this reflection and interpretation without slipping into easy analysis, that is by fitting those other forms of rationality neatly into preconceived concepts and discourses, and without sliding into justification and paternalism. And we must not let ourselves fall into a hierarchical classification and a devaluation of these forms of rationality and understanding in relation to knowledge that is considered scientific, thus relegating them to a category of '*other*' knowledge (Santos 2000, 2002; Casimiro 1999).

What we are referring to are "theoretical traditions and social science methodologies" and "different cultures and forms of interaction between culture and knowledge, as well as between scientific knowledge and non-scientific knowledge" (Santos 2002:238). We are talking about "struggles, initiatives, alternative movements, many of them local, often in remote parts of the world and so perhaps easy to discredit as irrelevant or too fragile or localised to offer a credible alternative to capitalism" (Santos 2002:238). It should be highlighted that many of the experiences that we analyse are those of women in our countries, women who in terms of the prevailing economic and cultural model are considered to be on the periphery of the world system, outside modernity. These are experiences which, to be understood and interpreted, require different vantage points as well as "epistemological and democratic imagination, in order to construct new and multiple

---

7. Cf., WLSA publications 1992, 1994, 1998, 2000a, 2000b.

conceptions of social emancipation on top of the ruins of the automatic social emancipation of the modern project" (Santos 2002:273–4).

This fragmented experience, with its diverse identities that are often contradictory and in conflict with one another, represents a rich source for our feminist vision (Harding 1987; Mbilinyi 1992; Mulinari 1995). This is work that seeks to incorporate historical analysis and is multi- and interdisciplinary and multi-dimensional, inter-relational in its analysis of economic, political, cultural and psychological aspects. In epistemological and methodological terms, this perspective seeks to combine the subjective and objective aspects and to consider the processes of fieldwork and of writing and recording as being parts of and the culminationof the research process (Harding 1987; Stanley 1993; Mulinari 1995; Amadiume 1987 and 1997; WLSA 1998).

We believe that a feminist researcher, committed to analysing social relations with a view to transforming society/societies, is not a neutral subject. Each one of us has her own ways of being and analysing what surrounds us. The authors of this article are teachers at UEM, working in the CEA (Isabel) and the Department of Geography in the Arts Faculty (Ximena). We are members of women's associations – WLSA Mozambique, Fórum Mulher and MULEIDE. We have both participated in the creation of women's associations. We are militants in political parties. Isabel was a member of the Assembly of the republic on the Frelimo Party bench from 1994 to 1999, following the first multiparty elections in Mozambique. We took part in the World Social Forum because we believe that "another world is possible". We are associated with research networks and regional and international feminist organisations. Therefore, when we analyse the world around us we are aware of the manner in which we do it and also of the fact that we are researching subjects who have their own views and their own diverse ways of interpreting them, and that our education and training and the binary systems of analysis based on Western rationality do not always enable us to understand and interpret those views and ways. We are also tempted, when confronted with the injustices we witness in the course of our research, to take measures, to contribute to change, to 'help people to help themselves'. We are academics and activists. But we are also women, mothers, wives, sisters and aunts. To put it another way, we carry with us in our daily lives a multiplicity of identities that are fundamental to our work as feminists.

The theoretical and analytical perspective we have described was constructed – and is continuously under construction – based on the experiences, desires, interests, needs and resistances of different groups of women, characterised by their diverse classes, races/ethnicities, rural/urban origins, status, training, religion, sexual orientation as significant indicators in relation to the hypotheses presented. These experiences of the diverse groups take into account that women do not make up a homogenous group and that their existence is multifaceted. As social actors bearing a multiplicity of identities, which are not totally fixed and where words and practice are sometimes contradictory, we feel that we as academics and activists can appear not as invisible, anonymous, authoritative voices, but as real, historically shaped subjects, with lives, positions, desires and concrete and specific interests in the significance of identities and in the functions and roles performed. In this perspective, the deconstruction and construction of primary identities are seen as necessary conditions for understanding the complexity of social relations, which gives us a better understanding of the multiplicity of relationships of domination and subordination in which we women are involved, so that we can perceive the feminist struggle in a plural way, where the principles of liberty and equality can be applied (Harding 1987; Mouffe 1999; Castells 1999). In this way, our history and our experience as academics and activists shape the results of our analyses and are part of the empirical evidence, either in favour of or against the recommendations emerging from our research results (Harding 1987; Mouffe 1999).

The feminist perspective of gender that we endorse is based on an analysis of social relations between women and men, between women and between men, which allows us to study the way female and male identities are constructed, socially and relationally, recognising that the social nature of hierarchy in gender relations is fundamental for conceiving transformations, and denying that social differences between women and men are given by nature. The constructions of femininity and masculinity are interrelated with the variables of race/ethnicity, class, rural/urban origin, training and status, as already mentioned. The sharing of power, knowledge and competence in different spheres of society is under continuous renegotiation, giving rise to resistance and opposition, but also to acceptance or entrance into spaces in the established order at different moments and in different spatial contexts. This is all connected to the search for an identity of a feminist project that accomplishes radical changes for an alternative world that is truly human for women and men.

References

Amadiume, Ifi, 1987, *Male Daughters, Female Husbands*. London: Zed Books.
—, 1997, *Reinventing Africa. Matriarchy, Religion and Culture*. London: Zed Books.
Beauvoir, Simone de, 1960, *O Segundo Sexo. Fatos e Mitos*. São Paulo: Difusão Europeia do Livro.
Casimiro, Isabel, 1999, '*Paz na Terra, Guerra em Casa'. Feminismo e Organizações de Mulheres em Moçambique*. Dissertation written for Masters degree in Sociology, Faculty of Economics, University of Coimbra, pp. 304.
Castells, Manuel, 1999, *O Poder da Identidade. A Era da Informação: Economia, Sociedade e Cultura* Vol. 2, Paz e Terra, 3ª edição, São Paulo.
Correa, Sônea, 2000, "*Epistemlogia Feminista*", seminar conducted by Sônea Corrêa, organised by Programa Mulher, DEMEG, CEA, UEM, Maputo.
Governo de Mocambique, 1994, *Programa Nacional do Governo 1994*. Imprensa Comercial de Indico.
Harding, Sandra, 1987, *Feminism and Methodology*. Indiana: Indiana University Press.
Kirkwood, Julieta, 1986, *Ser politico en Chile. Las feminists y los partidos*. Facultad Latinoamericana de Cierncias Sociales. Santiago, Chile.
León, Victoria Sendon de, 2000, "Qué es el Feminismo de la Diferencia?", *Mujeres en Red*, http://www.nodo50.org/mujeresred/vitoria_sendon-feminismo_de_ la_diferencia.html 31-10-2000@t, 16 pp.
—, 2003, "Respuesta Feminista a la Globalización", Revista *MUJER SALUD*/Red de Salud de las Mujeres LatinoAmericanas y del Caribe RSMLAC, pp. 55–66.
Mbilinyi, Marjorie, 1992, "Research Methodologies in Gender Issues", in Ruth Meena (ed.), *Gender in Southern Africa – Conceptual and Theoretical Issues*. Harare: SAPES BOOKS, pp. 31–70.
Mouffe, Chantal, 1999, *El retorno de lo politico*. Buenos Aires: Ediciones Paidós.
Mulinari, Diana, 1995, "Third World Women and Discourses of Domination", in Signe Arnfred (ed.), *Issues of Methodology and Epistemology in Postcolonial Studies*. International Development Studies, Roskilde University, Occasional Paper No. 15, Roskilde, pp. 31–55.
Oakley, Ann, 1972, *Sex, Gender and Society*. New York: Harper and Row.
Pérotin-Dumon, Anne, 2000, *El Género en la Historia*, Instituto de Historia, Pontificia Católica de Chile. Available at http://www.hist.puc.cl/historia/genero
Santos, Boaventura S., 1994, *Pela Mão de Alice – O Social e o Político na Pós-Modernidade*. Porto: Edições Afrontamento.
—, 2000, *A crítica da razão indolente: contra o desperdício da experiência [Para um novo senso comum. A ciência, o direito e a política na transição paradigmática*, Volume I]. Porto: Edições Afrontamento.

—, 2002, "Para uma sociologia das ausências e uma sociologia das emergências", *Revista Crítica de Ciências Sociais* 63, Outubro 2002:237–280. Centro de Estudos Sociais, Faculdade de Economia, Universidade de Coimbra, Coimbra.

Stanley, Liz (ed.), 1993, *Feminist Praxis, Research, Theory and Epistemology in Feminist Sociology*. London and New York: Routledge.

WLSA, 1992, *Direito a Alimentos e a Mulher em Moçambique: estudo de caso da região sul*, DEMEG, CEA, UEM, Maputo.

—, 1994, *Direito à Sucessão e Herança: Moçambique*, DEMEG, CEA, UEM, Maputo.

—, 1998, *Famílias em Contextos de Mudanças em Moçambique*, DEMEG, CEA, UEM, Maputo.

—, 2000a, *A Ilusão da Transparência na Administração da Justiça*, DEMEG, CEA, UEM, Imprensa Universitária, Maputo.

—, 2000b, (Ximena Andrade, Conceição Osório e João Carlos Trindade) *Direitos Humanos das Mulheres em Quatro Tópicos* – Revisão da Literatura, DEMEG, CEA, UEM, Livraria Universitária, Maputo (versão em língua inglesa, 2001).

CHAPTER SIX

Disappearing Dodos?[1]
Reflections on Women and Academic Freedom Based on Experiences in Ghana and the United States

Nancy Lundgren and Mansah Prah

Introduction

Our motivation in writing this paper stems from our personal experiences as women in academia. In our work as university teachers, we have both often gone through situations that have left us with feelings of anger, helplessness, vulnerability and sometimes humiliation. While it can be argued that everyone goes through such experiences at one time or other in the work set-

---

1. The Dodo was a bird that was first sighted by European sailors on the island of Mauritius at the end of the 16th century. It was a species unknown to them. By the year 1681, about 80 years after it had first been sighted, the last Dodo had died. The bird had become extinct. According to some accounts, the primary causes of extinction were the destruction of the forest (which cut off the Dodo's food supply), and the introduction by the sailors of cats, rats and pigs among other animals, which destroyed Dodo nests. Other accounts suggest additionally that having been isolated by their island location from contact with humanity, the Dodo greeted the newcomers with child-like innocence. Furthermore, its wings were disproportionately heavy, preventing the bird from flying. Because it could not fly, it was vulnerable to predators. The sailors mistook the gentle spirit of the Dodo and its lack of fear of the new predators as stupidity. They dubbed the bird "Dodo" (meaning something akin to simpleton in the Portuguese tongue). Many Dodos were killed by the human visitors, and those that survived had to face the introduced animals, the dogs and pigs, which soon became feral when introduced to the Mauritian ecosystem. (Sources: www.davidreilly.com/dodo/Background to The tragedy of the Dodo (1598–1681).htm; www.amnh.org/dodo.htm). We think the example of the Dodo's extinction presents an apt image of the situation of many female academics, who experience the academy as a male-dominated system that does not necessarily operate in the interests of women. Many either learn to adapt to the situation in one way or the other, or leave the academy. The number of women academics who attempt to fight and transform the system is small. Just as the environment for the Dodo was not supportive, the environment in the academy, we argue, does not allow women academics to flourish.

ting, we know that some of these occurrences are linked to issues of power and gender.[2] Many organisations, including universities, are gendered in the sense that they are dominated by male values and interests, which permeate relationships between women and men. Writing about these issues is for us a cathartic act: we need to write in order to overcome our pain.

Every so often, we have sat and discussed our impressions and feelings after Faculty Board or Academic Board meetings, or attempted to make sense of our own actions and reactions, and have been keenly aware of the constraints and pressures that we face as women, overworked, carrying all sorts of domestic burdens and responsibilities in addition to our teaching, research and the constant search for consultancies in order to make ends meet. The fact that we have positioned ourselves as 'feminists' also makes us particularly sensitive and critical about situations that others might not even consider to be of significance. In our rambling conversations about academic life, we have come to recognise the fact that academic freedom is gendered. The opportunities and spaces available to women and men to carry out their work unfettered are not equal: just taking into consideration women's reproductive roles makes that clear. But the issue is rather more complex, for there are other constraints beyond the issue of having to carry out more reproductive roles than men.

In this chapter, we argue that the patriarchal structure of the academy creates a climate that inhibits women academics from developing their full potential and calls into question the basis of academic freedom. This also means that the kind of knowledge that is produced, the type of ideas that are allowed to flourish, are limited or one-sided. We further argue that if knowledge is truncated, is inhibited by patriarchal values, a society's ability to define itself is limited. Therefore, the transformative potential of knowledge, the creative, the imaginative, can get lost, as is noted by Charmaine Pereira (2002). We are concerned about the implications and the future of doing research from a gender analytical perspective within a climate that tends

---

2. We are acutely aware of the difficult, complex nature of a paper that deals with the gendered nature of organisations. It is easy to be branded 'angry' or 'emotional' when one writes a paper that deals with gender-based interaction. Was the male colleague's action a consequence of his general attitude towards women or was it due to other factors, such as one's own politics, ability or demeanour? Is the workplace in question such that it is possible to view a colleague without 'seeing' his or her gender? In discussing this problem, Sandra Acker (1994:16) mentions the need to see both the 'forest and the trees', the patriarchal structures and the everyday forms of maintenance and control. In this paper, we try to see both.

to take the position that it is women who should do the gender research (Imam 1988; Imam and Mama 1994:85). We also wonder about our role as women 'gender experts' and consultants for international organisations and NGOs, and what sort of limits to independent thinking on gender issues the research reports we produce for them pose.

We realise that there is also a psychosocial aspect of the academic freedom of women scholars that has often been ignored. By this, we refer to the ability to express oneself, orally and in writing, with confidence and the ability to challenge the limits of one's mind without being self- conscious or self-censoring. We think that in general (due to socialisation and cultural factors), women cannot develop intellectual self-confidence as easily as men do. This limits women as individuals, and also restricts their contribution to knowledge. Ultimately, this impacts the transformative capacity of our scholarly work, particularly that which is gender analytical. We hope that by writing and reflecting on our experiences we will transcend the pain and rise to insights that will be useful in taking us to levels that will lead to liberating research and the transformation of gender relations in the academy.

Personal Experiences

In this section, each of us takes it in turn to describe and reflect on ways in which the issues we take up in this chapter have affected us personally in our work as academics. This is the practical, played-out reality of the theoretical issues we discuss in this chapter. We have felt these constraints, dilemmas and challenges, each of us in slightly different ways. Ultimately, however, we feel that our experiences are remarkably similar, as they are to the experiences of other women inside and outside Africa.

Personal Reflections: Mansah

I would like to begin my personal account by locating it within the broader framework of the patriarchal structures which characterise the university at which I teach in Ghana. The 2003 calendar of the university where both of us work presents a variety of collages depicting all the Registrars, Vice Chancellors, Pro-Vice Chancellors and Chairs of the University Council since the university's inception 40 years ago. *Only one woman appears in the calendar.*[3]

---

3. It may be of interest to note that the 2004 calendar still had no woman in it. Now, in 2005, after some of us women made a lot of complaints to the 'authorities', the calendar has pictures of women, including the authors of this paper!

The authorities have unwittingly produced a graphic presentation of the gendered nature of the top university administration over the years. The woman in question was a chair of the University Council for only a year.

I have often wondered how the designers of the calendar were able to publish it in the form they did without feeling constrained by a sense of political correctness, at least. The only page of the calendar that does not depict an official of the university features the *Asantehene* (the Ashanti king). I discussed this with a friend, a respected male senior colleague. His first reaction was, "Is it wrong?" When I explained my position to him, he grew quiet. He had been silenced by the reality.

Looking back now, I realise that I must have been extremely naïve when I joined the university, fresh from a graduate school in Germany with a PhD. I had just graduated *magna cum laude* from the University of Frankfurt. It was my first 'real' job, my first foray into the working world as a full time worker. Prior to my appointment as a lecturer at the university, I had done odd jobs in Germany – cleaning jobs, dishwashing, babysitting, translating and typing. In all these positions, I was an underdog, and being black did not help very much. These had been jobs that did not 'command respect', and I was very excited at the prospect of coming back home to a socially responsible and respectable position. I was young, energetic, idealistic and I had no family responsibilities. I was ready to contribute my quota to the development of my country, and happy to leave the difficult life in Germany, with its racism and other frustrations. I was the only woman in my department. I was not even particularly gender sensitive at the time. Being the only woman did not disturb me in any way. I was self-confident and did not think twice about my minority status. The only thing that disturbed me at the time was that there was no restroom for women in the building in which the department was housed. It may sound strange, but I did not know what was expected of me in order that I survive as a lecturer. I had no idea that I had to publish papers. No one told me anything. I had no mentor.

After the initial euphoria, I settled down to a routine. But I was very bored and felt that I was not doing as much as I could do. I went straight to the vice chancellor and told him my problem. I went to see him because he seemed an open and approachable person to me. My reasoning at that time was, "Well, he employed me and so if there are any problems I should tell him". He responded by asking me to represent the university on a board that was servicing one of the ministries. In retrospect, I think I should first have informed my Head of Department about my frustrations. I cannot state the point at which my problems in the department began: perhaps they started around the time I committed that *faux pas*. It happened simply because I did not have a very clear idea of Ghanaian conventions and how to go about such things. I had left the country at the age of 18 and returned at the age of 30, and there were very many things about adult life in Ghana that I did not know and had to learn over the years. I had been put on probation for two years. I worked hard, did my best. At the end of the probation I was summoned for an interview, a normal procedure at the time, and met a panel of men, senior colleagues. At the interview the vice chancellor invited me to comment on my experience so far at the university. I told him that it would be useful if the authorities could find a way of making more use of younger colleagues like me. I said this without malice, I was simply being honest and open. I noticed that my comment had not gone down well with some of the colleagues who took me on. I calmly answered their questions and my appointment was confirmed. But those colleagues, who had not been happy with my remarks, stopped greeting me, I noticed. Looking back, I realise that I probably had unwittingly taken a position that was politically dangerous, little did I know that tensions were rising around the vice chancellor and that some colleagues would eventually vote against him. I was in my own little world, adjusting to my new life and frustrated with my job. I began looking elsewhere for greener pastures. I was unmarried and felt free to go away. I took a leave of absence and went to Lesotho and then later to the US on a Fulbright grant. In Lesotho, I was assigned several courses and gained a lot more experience there than I had done in Ghana.

I returned to Ghana after three years, married and pregnant with my second child. I began to have more problems from then on, and started to link them with gender issues much later. What were the problems? I cannot remember all of them but I clearly recall an argument with my boss and telling him I was a free spirit whom he could not always rely on for support. Then, shortly after I returned, there was one semester in which no student registered for any of my courses (I did not teach any core courses). My head of department called me and asked why I had no students. I told him I did not know. I wasn't particularly bothered by it because I thought it would give me more time to take care of the baby I had had about four months earlier. I naïvely assumed that the students had not registered because they did not know me, after all, I had been away for three years. I had taught for one semester before my confinement. I did not attach any significance to it and happily stayed home that semester. I will explain how this was used against me later.

When I came up for renewal of my contract, I had a rude shock. It turned out that I had been earmarked for dismissal. The assessment of my performance as a university lecturer was very negative. A short letter addressed to me summarised my assessment. My research was of poor quality, my relations with students and colleagues were not cordial and I was not an effective teacher. I had applied for a six-year contract: instead I was given a two-year contract and asked to improve within those two years. It is important to note that I did not see the assessment (written in 1993) until the year 2000, when I had access to my file only because I became the head of the department. It is still not the practice at the university for teaching staff to see assessments written by their senior colleagues. Below are excerpts from the assessment of my performance in the Department of Sociology: "Her teaching style and efficiency need to be improved, for students continue to complain about her performance; some would even avoid her course rather than encounter her intolerance and displeasure…"

I had no idea that students had felt threatened by my teaching. No one had ever drawn my attention to that. I must say though, that because I teach gender-related subjects, the discussions were sometimes contentious. This was the first time in the department that gender-related courses such as gender and sexuality were taught from a feminist perspective. I had never had reason to think that my students felt intimidated in my classes. On my research, the assessment was as follows:

> There is no record to guide one in assessing quality of her research. Indeed I am not aware of any research conducted by her. She has however indicated in her application letter for renewal of contract that she has three publications (two forth-coming). The one article i.e. "Women and Education" which has been presented for this exercise reads more like a state-of-the-art report on women and education which raises a number of questions as to whether after six years of teaching and in spite of her claim to be a specialist in women and development she is only now beginning to take interest in research in the field. One expects a little more than this after six years of academic career in Ghana, Southern Africa and the USA.

I must state here that this senior colleague knew at the time that I was working on an edited volume of readings on gender studies. About eight months earlier, I had applied for a small grant to complete the work. The same colleague who had written the negative assessment had at the time been the Chair of the Research and Conferences Committee, the body responsible for approving such grants. My proposal was sent back to me with the suggestion that I should correct some mistakes. I had supposedly misspelled the names of a number of writers I had cited. I wrote back, indicating that I had not made any such mistakes. I never received a reply. In a letter that I had written to him just about three weeks before he wrote the assessment, I had given him the title of a paper I had worked on and sent out for publication. That paper was clearly based on research. It is not usual for department heads to personally assess and comment on already published papers: the paper he critiqued above had already appeared in a publication of refereed conference proceedings. The assessment continued thus:

> Her relationship with students needs to be improved considerably. As indicated ... there are complaints to the effect that she is intolerant to dissenting views in class. She is also unfriendly and haughty towards students. Her relations with faculty members can at best be described as dual. She appears friendly to some when she is in good mood (sic) and hostile to others. Her contribution to the work of the Department is not very impressive. She tends to give excuses to avoid extra commitments in the Department. She has therefore made very little impact on the development of the Department.

He had never discussed any of these points with me. These specific comments about the quality of my teaching and research must have somehow circulated because, many years later, someone told me that I had been the subject of a conversation he had heard in Accra, the capital, around that period. The people involved had mentioned that they had heard that I was up to no good and that I should not even have been employed as a university lecturer. In retrospect, I now think that the fact that no one registered for my courses that semester was significant. Unfortunately, I had had absolutely no idea about what had transpired and still do not know.

My relations with some of the senior colleagues became frosty. One of them told me at a meeting of the department that I was too junior to supervise graduate theses. Meanwhile, other departments had been using me as a graduate thesis supervisor. Since I was learning fast, I accepted the decision and decided not to tell them that I was already doing what they thought I could not do. I continued to give off my best to my students. But the climate in the department grew colder for me. My personal relations with some of the most influential senior colleagues (all of them men) deteriorated so much that we hardly spoke to each other. I had become a pariah. I hardly stayed in my office. Immediately after lectures I would go home. I never lingered in my office. Eventually I felt I had to let the vice chancellor know about my situation. The senior colleague and I were invited to the vice chancellor's office. The man's main complaints were that I was haughty and disrespectful. I remember him saying that I tended to snap at him. Nothing was said about the quality of my work. I wore dark glasses throughout this meeting, because I was fighting tears the whole time. All the vice chancellor could say at the end was that we should consider each other as brother and sister. I should see the man as a younger sister would an elder brother, while he should view me as a little sister. I was very disappointed at the outcome of the meeting. As soon as the colleague left, I burst into tears. I think I was hysterical. The tears did not stop flowing and the Vice Chancellor was visibly upset. The whole chain of events affected me so powerfully that I wept intermittently for about three weeks afterwards.

After this incident, my family stepped in with advice. I was counselled to set myself some concrete targets in my career and work towards them. I decided to work at publishing more papers and moving up the ladder. I was never engaged in any projects in the department, neither did I bother to demand to be. I must say that I submitted almost twice as many papers as required for my promotion to the rank of senior lecturer because I was afraid that the application could be rejected. For the next four years, I would apply for two-year contracts each time. I could no longer bear any more rejections, and my self-confidence was at its lowest. There are two other incidents that I would like to share as vignettes.

Vignette 1

A US foundation contacts the university with a request about women's needs. A committee is quickly set up. The chair is a woman, an administrator. There are four members including the chair. I am one of the members of this committee. The committee is made up of two men, two women. At one of our meetings, a male colleague says, "You know, the Vice Chancellor put me on this committee as a control mechanism, so as to tone down the report".

Vignette 2

(This incident took place shortly after I attained professorial status). The university is celebrating an important event, it is a festive occasion. After the main event, I move towards the hall where a reception will be held. The hall is close to the library, and I see one of the librarians standing on the veranda. As I am a little early I go and have a brief chat with him, to while away the time. He offers to show me a new state-of-the art computer laboratory that has been set up in the library basement. We move towards the basement together. Just as we enter the entrance of the basement, we bump into a group of dignitaries – the Vice President of Ghana, some ministers of state and top executives of the university. I am on the right hand side of the librarian and am physically closest to the group. The Vice President smiles and stretches his hand out to greet me. I do not know the Vice President, I have never met him. I give him a handshake. All this takes place within a few seconds. In shaking the Vice President's hand, I momentarily obstruct one of the top university executives. His demeanour shows that I am in his way and he wants to move on. He does not acknowledge my presence otherwise. He kind of sweeps me aside and I quickly move out of the way and move on with the librarian. I did not in any way want to cause any trouble. I am left with a great feeling of shame and humiliation. I wonder, "Would the top university executive have treated a senior male colleague in the same manner?"

The events regarding my unfortunate assessment and subsequent award of a two year contract I described earlier occurred during the 1993-94 academic year. Up to about 2002, I could not talk about them without feeling tears in my eyes. But I have moved on, not wanting to disappear like the Dodo did, and am now an Associate Professor, one of three women of this rank at the university. I was an Acting Head of Department between 2000 and 2003, became a substantive Head in 2004, and was recently elected Vice Dean of the Faculty of Social Sciences. I think I am generally a little less naïve than I used to be, but I do not think I have the carefree self-confidence of ten years ago. If anything, I have lost that spontaneous, unselfconscious self-assurance over the years. I feel I have to watch every step and think before I speak. I am not free to produce knowledge without any vestige of self-censorship. Many women face similar problems. It is, therefore, not surprising that a women's group has been formed here on campus with the principle aim of supporting each other's research. This group holds seminars for its members to 'air' their research in an atmosphere free from the opprobrium of the male academy. I would like to point out that such support groups are important as vehicles through which women can draw strength, even as they resist and fight the 'malestream'. Teaching Gender and Women's Studies is also for me an important means of navigating and resisting the 'malestream', in the sense that I know (and hope) that through this action younger generations will be sensitised and that the road towards transformation and change is being carved out.

Personal Reflections: Nancy

I am currently teaching at a university in Ghana. Previously, I had tenure at an elite, private liberal arts college in America. While the circumstances were quite different, the patriarchal environment is alive and healthy in both places and functions in many of the same ways. The university I taught at in America is very small, with a long, distinguished and radical tradition. It discourages hierarchy, espouses equality and encourages students to be 'empowered'. We call everyone by their first names (no professor here), have small discussion group-type classes, don't have exams and don't have grades. Students are encouraged to express themselves in their own way with guidance from their professors.

Discrimination, on any basis, is actively proscribed at this university. It prides itself on its attention to issues of 'race', class, gender and sexual orientation. When I came to the campus in 1987, the women had just won a Women's Studies major after a protracted struggle, and the campus was still stinging from its aftermath. Tensions were somewhat high and sensitivities palpable. The women were on a bit of a high. I seemed to be golden, because I was a feminist, radical enough politically, but small, young, friendly and not too scary. I was also a good academic, an anthropologist, not too mushy, with a political economic focus. The combination seemed to fit perfectly with the group that was mainly responsible for my hire, comprising the social science cluster, consisting of economists, political scientists, sociologists and faculty from business studies. I was the only anthropologist and the only woman.

The honeymoon did not last long. Soon, I was embroiled in the intense politics only possible in such a small, closed, self-conscious community. Soon I would learn what their 'liberal' commitment to equity really meant. I was to learn about the racist, sexist academy. I had a good buddy. She was hired at the same time. She was an African American social psychologist. She was big and loud and funny and smart. Soon it became obvious that she and I were very popular among our students. Our classes began to grow. Anthropology began to grow. We got our heads together and dreamed about new programmes, new ways to teach, new ways to approach issues having to do with 'race', class and gender, new ways to combine social psychology and anthropology.

But she was black and I was white and she was nearly the only black faculty member. Although she was sympathetic to feminist issues, the other feminists, mostly white, had not been too sensitive to issues of 'colour'. Her teaching load began to increase. Female 'black' students flocked to her for advice and counsel on all manner of things. My load also began to increase. I was a sympathetic female in an all-male department. Anthropology came out of the closet, where it had nearly died before, and became a place for the exploration of issues of relevance to this young eager population. The students were happy, we were happy. We thought we were doing our jobs. We thought we were supposed to work hard, teach well, engage in our own scholarship and we would be rewarded.

We were wrong. We got too many students with too many needs. We worked late into the night, trying to be fair and trying to reach them all. We were sent all the 'people of colour' and problem children. We kept long hours in the office, listening to problems and trying to encourage our students. We were put on several committees. All the committees needed a 'person of colour' and/or a woman. But no one listened to what we said, and we spent long agonising hours trying to figure out what was going on and why nothing seemed to change and why we remained seemingly invisible, despite our earnest and brilliant contributions.

Soon there were strong rumblings from below. There were things being said about us. Our courses were soft, we heard, that is why so many students took them. We were not rigorous enough, that is why we had so many students. The men were rigorous, that is why they only had five or six students. Most students could not live up to their standards. There are standards to keep, you know. Some of the students began to come into the classes with disdainful attitudes. My theories were passé, they had been told, old, out of style. My friend was not theoretical enough. We both were somewhat questionable as academics. Maybe we don't know our stuff. Maybe we just wanted to entertain.

At first, we didn't know what was going on. We kept plugging on. We were so overburdened and working so hard that at first we didn't see anything coming. But gradually it began to emerge. Students, and even other faculty, had been drawn in. They began to tell us what was being said. The 'big men', the ones who were rigorous, the ones who had the latest theories and most sophisticated views, took aside choice bright students and young willing faculty and shared with the unsuspecting students the sentiments about us described above, our supposed weaknesses. They wanted to steer their courses, to guide them into the realm of knowledge and academic excellence that was their due and which we, presumably, were not competent enough to do.

The departments were very small and disciplines even smaller. There were only two or three very good students for each discipline. In the social sciences, the 'rigour boys' liked to capture these two or three students and groom them for graduate school. They groomed them for the best graduate schools in America and then had them as trophies on their shelves. To have helped a student gain admission into the University of Chicago – well – that was a coup.

Before long, many of those students drifted into my office. They were distressed because they were taken on by one of these 'boys' and then they had to do what they were told. Paradigmatic wars, rigour wars, political correctness wars, gender wars, were only some of the possibilities for divisions. Somewhere in your career you had to 'declare' yourself, and if you didn't declare correctly, it might mean an end to possibilities for graduate school, fellowships or other career-related opportunities. At one point, three of the most recent favourites approached me in my office. They didn't know what to do. They didn't want to take a particular line in their senior project work, but if they didn't they could not work with certain people. Usually these kinds of problems surface at the graduate level, but because of the size and the expectations of this school (among other things), they developed here. The three students, two young men and one young woman, started working with me at the onset of this underground assault on my friend, myself and another female member of the psychology faculty. They completed their studies under my tutelage but not without a great deal of anguish and expenditure of emotional energy.

When I began working with the three students, it seemed to turn the tide and the more subtle forms of discrimination gave way to broader and more obvious ones. Then they began to squeeze us out of important committees and to attack women's studies and other agendas for equality. Of course we didn't really know all this was going on to the extent that it was. It was difficult for me to register that people would deliberately undermine you in these ways. I was especially disinclined to think that they would also use students. I naïvely thought that if I did a good job, got lots of students and served the university well, I would be recognised, appreciated and promoted. But gradually, certain students began to say things. Then one of our female colleagues who had been taken in as one of 'the boys' came to a women's studies meeting in tears, and narrated some of the terrible things being said about us three women behind our backs and to students. She said she could not even repeat some of it, it was so terrible and mean spirited, but she said enough for us to get the idea.

In the meantime, there were sexual harassment issues as well. Everyone knew that certain of the male faculty had relations with female students.

We had a policy against it, but it was largely ignored. Female students complained to us about the issue. We took the matter to the dean of students, but often the women themselves would change their minds or the complaint would be dropped in some other way. Some of the students complained that if a faculty member was seductive, it would mean that your work was no good, just your body. Some complained that if they were *not* chosen, they would not be appraised fairly and that the chosen ones got preferential treatment. One of the main 'rigour boys' was said to have been found under a desk at night with a student. He himself bragged about it. We went to the president. That was a mistake. He tried to appear to take the matter seriously, but it was clear to us all that, in general, his attitude had been, well, it is a bad thing, but, then, boys will be boys.

However, the female students got together and devised a sexual harassment policy in the aftermath of a series of sexual harassment issues on the campus. They stopped classes, interrupted meetings and became quite vocal on the issue. The few of us women who dared, who had been known to speak out, supported them in late night meetings, discussion groups, drafting sessions, etc. Tensions were heightened. The camps became more entrenched. We were accused of succumbing to the 'political correctness' politics of the day, watering down the academic environment and distracting the students from more critical intellectual pursuits. We were accused of divisionary activities on the campus and of fomenting discontent.

So we dissipate our energies, we fight the battles we see as necessary or we become invisible and try to ignore the climate. Whichever road we take, however, we are not able to clearly and fully develop our own research agendas. All of our talent, our training, our creative energies, go into holding on. It goes into meetings and counselling and preparing for students and, most of all, it goes into fending off patriarchy. It goes into trying to feel adequate, trying to feel competent, when all around you tells you that you are not. It goes into fighting endless subtle and not so subtle battles. It goes into activism, sometimes. But not much goes into research, writing, thinking, creating. This happens in America. It also happens in Africa. It takes remarkably similar paths.

Women and Academic Freedom: Issues and Debates

We have used our own experiences to make more vivid our argument that women, regardless of geographical location, are affected negatively in the academy in four broad ways. For heuristic purposes, we have used categories which are not, however, to be seen as mutually exclusive or static. They are: (1) economic discrimination, (2) socio-psychological and intellectual barriers, (3) cultural pressures, (4) disciplinary discrimination. These groupings combine to create what has often been referred to as the 'chilly climate' for women in academia and a work environment hostile to their personal and professional participation and development. Ultimately, the chilly climate affects a woman's scholarly work, her professional life, her personal life, as well as her ability to make a living. It will also hamper her ability to contribute to the creation of knowledge and the dissemination of information in the classroom. It may even threaten her survival. So, like our proverbial Dodo bird, her wings will become too heavy. She will be carrying too heavy a load and, unable to fly, she will fall to the ground. Unable to fulfil her function as an academic, as a scholar, as a researcher and activist, she may, like the Dodo bird, become extinct and with her extinction female knowledge may be threatened.

When the Dodo bird became extinct, an entire species was lost to humanity forever. When in the course of history we lost thousands of cultures, peoples became extinct, their uniqueness and vitality forever missing from our collective human repertoire. If a people lose their ability to dream, to imagine, to define themselves, they lose their selves, their identity. Although the academy is not the only place for such definition, such creative imagining, in the 21st century industrial world it certainly plays a role. The extent of that role is hotly debated, but the fact that institutions of higher learning are responsible for the creation and dissemination of knowledge by and about the human condition cannot be disputed. The academy is meant to be a place where the outer limits of our being are explored. It is a place where we challenge and critique ourselves and each other, where we provide intellectual leadership in the understanding of the complexities, curiosities and dilemmas of our increasingly complex world.

We used to have priests, chiefs, local philosophers and elders to guide us and to help us understand ourselves. Today, we still have the elders and the chiefs, but we also have a specialised class of thinkers, the academics, whose job it is to provide intellectual guidance to the people. They have a responsibility to their societies to provide their people with as much data about the physical and social universe as is humanly possible, and a mandate to be open, critical and honest in this task. They have a directive from the people and a responsibility to these same people. They create knowledge and imagine possibilities. They help to define who we are, where we have been and the possibilities in us.

Academics, of course, are not pure and the academy is not free. But to the extent to which it can be free and pure, it must be. We no longer can rely solely on our Gods, elders or chiefs for our identity. We need more specialised guidance. We have colonised and been colonised. Some of us have been destroyed as a way of life and as a people. We need to keep our bearings and define ourselves in the midst of chaos, calamity, upheaval, globalisation and the desire of others to define us. According to Mamadou Diouf (1994:233), intellectual pursuit needs an atmosphere of liberty, " a radical refusal to be tied to existing realities", a critical stance. Intellectuals, says Gramsci, are to have a critical consciousness, a reflexive self-awareness (Diouf 1994). In the midst of cultural hegemony, the people sometimes get lost. They lose the ability to be critical, to reflect on their realities. The job of the intellectual is to help the people to achieve the ideological independence that they alone cannot achieve. These intellectuals cannot, therefore, be a part of the ruling elite, they cannot represent special interests, they must be free.

The academy in Africa is plagued, it is under siege. It is plagued by poverty, poor wages, donor-controlled research, the aftermath of colonial domination, structural adjustment, internal censorship and tensions and a patriarchal infrastructure. Salaries in state universities are low and research is inadequately supported (Bennett 2003; Imam and Mama 1994; Hagan 1994; Tamale and Oloka- Onyango 1997; Zeleza 2003; Manuh 2002; Pereira 2003). These manifestations of what Sylvia Tamale and Joseph Oloka-Onyango (1997) call "third stage colonialism" emasculate intellectuals, draining their energies and seriously compromising their ability to create the emancipatory knowledge that it is their mandate to provide.

Since the academy is by its nature unfriendly to women, as our paper seeks to demonstrate, the above constraints have a particularly poignant effect on them. This is the case in the US and also in Ghana. In the first place, there is the economic issue. We are all aware of the monetary factors affecting the lives of women academics everywhere. These factors have to do with women being clustered at the lower end of the academic ladder and few women being in top administrative positions, which implies that women generally have lower salaries and experience structural promotion limitations. All of these circumstances place them at the lowest end of an already low pay scale. So they suffer *economic discrimination.*

In the second place, there is the psychosocial issue. The female academic suffers psychosocially from the intellectually limiting effects of the 'malestreaming' that is part of academic life (Pereira 2002). Subtle, and sometimes not so subtle, messages conveying to her that she does not belong, that what she does is not valid, that she is not 'one of us' sap her energy, stifle her creativity, limit her intellectual horizons. She is gradually made to understand that she should watch what she says, she should not be too 'strident', too 'bitchy' (Tamale and Oloka-Onyango 1997). She becomes invisible in meetings, her voice is never heard, her views are not engaged, they are simply ignored (Prah 2002). Therefore, we suggest that women academics also encounter *psychosocial and intellectual barriers*.

In the third place, the female academic suffers from *cultural pressures* defining her as a 'mother', 'wife', domestic worker. She is drained of time and energy as she tries to fit her intellectual life around her reproductive duties, duties that are undervalued, unpaid and often unrecognised.

Women's studies, hardly recognised in most African universities (Imam and Mama 1994), are universally considered to be a frivolous, politically driven, men-hating, semi-serious, pseudo-discipline. Women's issues are hardly considered serious and women as a subject matter hardly worth the investment. So another issue for many women academics is that they are also subject to *disciplinary discrimination*. It does not take much imagination to see how this disciplinary chauvinism affects one's free pursuit of one's academic and intellectual interests. But another aspect of this issue is that women are seldom free to explore a topic, research an idea, free from the politics of being 'a woman'. She is never just a scientist studying a scientific problem so as to find a scientific solution. She is always a '*woman* scientist', a '*woman* scholar', usually undertaking '*women's*' research for purely women's interests. Just as in the North, a person of African descent is rarely free to pursue 'pure' science, without the watchful eye of the dominant 'white' eye, defining her or him and his or her research as *African*-American or *Afro*-German. Never can she be simply an anthropologist or physicist, but an *African*-something scientist. Women (as other oppressed groups) never have the luxury of neutral, non-political work. They cannot give free vent to their imaginative, inquisitive, trained research minds, as they dodge, precariously, the mines carefully hidden in their fields. Being a woman in the academy *is always* political.

Challenges for Women

For women, the above issues have a unique and more profound resonance. The ways in which women have experienced these constraints, as human beings as well as scholars, have been thoroughly debated by many scholars (Imam 1988; Mama 1996; Bennett 2002; Pereira 2002; Imam and Mama 1994; Tamale and Oloka-Onyango 1997; Hagan 1994; Lorde 1984; hooks

1994; Zeleza 2002). There is no need to retread this already elegantly trod ground. Nevertheless, in order to frame our argument, we will point out the major themes of that discussion.

Funding Problems

As Charmaine Pereira tells us, knowledge production should be about transformation. It is about challenging what 'is'. Knowledge production in Africa is ideally about the "…quest for African societies free of all forms of violence and social injustice…" (Pereira 2002:2). Feminist research should be about ending the oppression of women. For this to happen, it is not a project of simply adding women on. It is a matter of transformation. Good scholarship is the creation of transformative knowledge.

Because women are usually at the bottom of the economic ladder, because they are few in number and strength and because they suffer many forms of discrimination, they are even more economically vulnerable than their already vulnerable colleagues. The social conditions in Africa, including water problems, transportation difficulties, heightened domestic responsibilities, the inevitable scramble for money, affect all scholars, making them vulnerable, but weigh most heavily on women. Therefore, their research is often of necessity predicated on outside donor funding, resulting in the 'consultancy syndrome' (Imam and Mama 1994). While this affords them crucial financial resources, it also has its obvious constraints. Research contracted by donor agencies obviously comes with the political agendas implicit in the way the research questions are constructed. Agencies are not looking to create new knowledge, to transform knowledge: they are looking for validation of their expensive social programmes. While the political agendas of funders may be congruent with those of the researcher, they also might not be. The much-needed freedom to imagine, to critique, to reach the outer limits of our imagination, urged on us by Charmaine Pereira (2002) and others, is perhaps possible, but unlikely, within the constraints of the demands of foreign agendas. As we were admonished so long ago by Audre Lorde (1984), the master's tools will never dismantle the master's house.

Chilly Climate for Women

Takyiwaa Manuh (2002) argues that though the African academy has been making efforts, it has yet to eradicate the problems facing female faculty, staff and students. The academic environment in higher education continues to be largely unfriendly towards women. This 'unfriendliness' takes many forms, with which all of us are familiar. Perhaps the most obvious form is what, for lack of a better term, we can call the patriarchal structure of the academy, which leads to what Pereira (2002) calls 'malestreaming'. This goes back to Enlightenment thinking and the dualism in Western analytical thought that divides knowledge into disciplines and 'knowing' into a particular style. It is a way of gaining knowledge that keeps the intellectual and personal apart in neat separate categories. Knowledge that is 'scientific', 'objective', 'technical', 'real' is privileged whereas social science research, and especially feminist research, is considered to be 'soft', 'peripheral', 'frivolous', 'easy', 'unmanly', 'nonessential' (Pereira 2002; Tamale and Oloka-Onyango 1997; Imam 1994; Zeleza 2002).

In this patriarchal system, there is institutionalised 'trivialisation of women's experiences' and a conflation of the term 'person' and the word 'man' that leads to a staggering indifference to calls for research which acknowledges the power of gender. Funding agencies, for the most part, allocate funds for research that is quantitative and policy oriented, not theoretical and innovative. Currently, most research funding in Africa comes from outside Africa. As we know, whoever pays the piper, calls the tune and, in this case, the tune is mostly policy-oriented, applied research tied to specific projects (Imam 1994). The funding of research projects is not only economically critical for women, but it also serves the purpose of validating the already well entrenched patriarchal norms and values and provides validation and credibility to men and male projects, and further marginalises women and 'soft' projects

The 'malestreaming' and disciplinary divisions and ultimate chauvinism, however, do not do damage only to women and women-focused research. As many have argued, they also jeopardise the whole academic/intellectual project. Ayesha Imam (1994:85) tells us that "the evidence demonstrates that 'gender blindness' is not only discriminatory and politically backward, but scientifically inaccurate and unobjective". It does not allow for the transformative power of knowledge to have free reign, thus jeopardising all forms of knowledge and all knowledge makers, male and female. Pereira (2002:2) again reminds us that "feminism is as much about transforming what goes on in the minds and hearts of women and men as it is about realising rights and justice". She goes on further to say that she is not just interested in knowledge, but what it means to "know" and what it means for the 'malestream' "not to know". Education should be about preparing to help with the emancipation of individuals and society from oppression and subjugation. But we know that the educational environment in Africa, as also in the countries of the North, is "designed to ensure the maintenance of the status quo". This means, among other things, the institutionalisation of a patriarchal consciousness and values (Tamale and Oloka-Onyango 1997:24).

Corporatisation

The most recent form that male, Western, Enlightenment, positivist thinking has taken is in the full-scale corporatisation of the academy. This is true in the North and is filtering to the South. As Paul Zeleza (2002:4) tells us, the new corporate model of running universities reinforces authoritarian and masculine management styles. He says, "as learning becomes increasingly valued for its instrumental value and more emphasis is put on the scientific, technical and professional fields, the humanities and even the social sciences become further marginalized". At a time when feminist scholarship is expanding, humanistic knowledge (where feminist paradigms, pedagogy and praxis are lodged) as a whole is becoming devalued. Universities are increasingly adopting the corporate model of business management, with its discourse of accountability, entrepreneurship and technology. Zeleza further observes that the university is changing. Its motor is ICTs, it is driven by transnational firms and it is fuelled by the neoliberal discourse. While they talk about globalisation, he says that what they really mean is the ideological dominance of neoliberalism. There is a dominant Eurocentric and andocentric globalising process taking place that could be transformed through feminist teaching and research. But increasingly the academy is gendered and critical of the production of feminist knowledge (Zeleza 2002). This trend makes sense, however, to Tamale and Oloka-Onyango (1997), who argue that it is in the interests of the patriarchal academy not to conscientise the masses.

The Personal is Political: Psycho-Social Issues

In an environment faced with both external and internal constraints, the survival of academic freedom, as well as the survival of the academic, both male and female, is difficult. It is painfully obvious, however, that the constraints women feel in this basically foreign hostile battlefield are frequently debilitating. Along with the more obvious structural constraints, however, are the more subtle ones that drain a woman's energy, challenge her competence, inhibit her creative intellectual work, wear down her soul and seriously call into question her academic freedom. As with any oppressed 'minority', women in the academy suffer from certain stresses not necessarily experienced by the appreciated majority. We will briefly review this well-trod ground to remind ourselves of these stresses.

It is a basic condition in the academy that women are not equal to men. This inequality is in number, as well as in attitude (Prah 2002). Women are often so few, especially at the higher levels that they often are the one representative of their department or committee (Bennett 2002; Tamale and Oloka-Onyango 1997). On some committees and in some departments, there may be none at all, as women are clustered more heavily in certain female designated fields. Women have to work twice as hard to legitimise their authority, as the entire environment is dominated by patriarchal beliefs and values and they are described as 'bitches' and subject to persecution if they point this out (Tamale and Oloka-Onyango 1997). There are several ways in which women are excluded and they face many challenges. Tamale and Oloka-Onyango (1997) tell us that the most powerful tool of exclusion is the dominance of patriarchal values, as we have suggested previously. These values inherently exclude women as they subscribe to the view that men are by nature inclined more towards higher brain functioning, reasoning, logic and other attributes that are valued in the academy. It is the view that men are in general superior to women, except, possibly, in the areas of home management and childcare, which are women's supposed natural specialties. So by definition, women are not at home in the academy. It is a place for men. The woman in the academy is, like our legendary bird, a Dodo.

Women scholars in the academy face a number of exclusionary and obstructionist aspects of the work place such as limited access to the upper levels of the organisation (deans, administrators, presidents, vice chancellors) and exclusion from 'old boys' networks. This exclusion affects their ability to be political within and outside the organisation, to lobby for jobs and funding and to share information about their fields as well as about the organisation. The gender-neutral language used seems to exclude her and she is subject to various forms of sexual harassment (Bennett 2002; Tamale and Oloka-Onyango 1997). Tamale and Oloka- Onyango (1997) have found in their work that sexual harassment is so common in the academy that, at least in African universities, it is seen as normal. This harassment takes many forms, from outright sexual propositions to suggesting sex in exchange for grades or job promotion to making degrading jokes or comments referring to females.

Women become exhausted from having to navigate this treacherous terrain and use up important energy in struggle. Their creative imaginations are all too often focused on ways to survive at the expense of their intellectual development. While the academy provides support and satisfaction for its male members, it tends to undermine women, causing them to question themselves, to doubt themselves and to censor themselves. They become more timid when their views are dismissed or derided as frivolous or unscientific. They fear to speak out when they are afraid of being labelled as a 'feminist' or 'man hater' or 'bitch'. They have more difficulty asserting themselves when it comes to committee work or research or funding opportunities.

All of this serves to undermine a woman scholar's sense of herself as a scholar and as a human being. It severely limits her freedom as an academic, intellectually and economically, and it chains her creative imagination. The female academic is virtually walking around with chains around her feet all the time. The fact that she is able to get around at all is a miracle. Chapters like this one are part of the female academic's resistance, an element of the process of navigating the issues and taking action to shake off the chains.

The Contemporary Situation in Africa

In this present time referred to as 'third stage colonialism' we are told that independent scholarship, gender scholarship, is in trouble. The gender strategy in Africa is highly influenced by bodies like the World Bank, which emasculates intellectuals as it emphasises effects rather than root causes (Tamale and Oloka-Onyango 1997; Manuh 2002). States are supposed to support research and higher education but, in the present reality of structural adjustment programmes and outside control, it does not happen. Therefore, donors have to step in. Donors, thus to a large extent dictate research topics and research strategies. Since the mid-1990s, Sylvia Tamale and Joseph Oloka-Onyango go on to say (1997:26), gender has been popular, it has been the 'flavour of the month'. But if we are to listen to Charmaine Pereira (2002) and agree that feminist knowledge is not about adding to progressive knowledge, but about transforming and invigorating it, then we have to ask how, in the present donor-dominated environment, a liberatory agenda is possible? In the first place, says Claude Ake (Pereira 2001), the development paradigm that is frequently used tends to have a negative view of the people who are the targets of this 'development' and their culture. The paradigm itself does not accept the people it is 'developing' on their own terms. Its point of departure is not what is, but what ought to be. Amina Mama agrees when she says that "the drain of quality scholars into consultancy work, rather than into independent intellectual production, affects gender research and women's studies as profoundly as it does in other areas" (1996:29).

Financing and institutional support of African scholarship has been identified already as a serious constraint on academic freedom and uncensored scholarly work. Traditionally, says Paul Zeleza (2003), Women's Studies in the South was focused less on the theoretically driven issues that often dominated work in the North, but more on 'practical' issues, hence the Women In Development (WID), Women And Development, (WAD) and ultimately the Gender And Development (GAD) frameworks. This trend suggests how gender teaching and research is increasingly dominated by market-driven and instrumental imperatives. There is considerable emphasis on gender training models, with technocratic, formulaic and atomised notions of 'gender' eroding a sense of complex human process.

The concern over the marginalisation of women in development projects was not officially a concern until women began to make it an issue and it became institutionalised as WID (Mama 1997). With the WID programme, women were to be added to the development agenda in an effort to address the 'woman' challenge. Thus, governments could use women to further their own agendas. Out of this, government-supported agencies emerged, including ministries of women and development, and programmes were funded for women's projects. Donor agencies, such as USAID, could readily 'add on' women to their projects and money was in the system for women. In this way, the field of 'women's studies' was easily coopted, its radical potential diffused.

Nevertheless, with all of the above constraints for women, not the least of which is financial, it is easy to see how women scholars in Africa are an almost inevitable part of their own cooption when they of necessity participate in donor-sponsored research. Of course, we cannot assume that donor-driven research cannot be good research. All research has an author and all authors have their own agendas. To take us back to Claude Ake (1994), the creation of knowledge in the modern (or postmodern) industrial state, is not, nor has it ever been, free. The academy is not free and there is, therefore, no such thing as academic freedom. Research in line with the interest of world capitalism has more chance of some kind of freedom, but for those of us on the margins, what chance have we? Our only hope is to continue to talk about it, to continue to question ourselves, to continue to challenge ourselves, to continue to hack away at our chains.

Despite the challenges, there have been many successful activist, liberatory, theoretically-grounded projects carried out by women across Africa. There have been activists who have worked on legislation improving the lives of women, programmes to educate and challenge women, as well as significant research and advocacy in the area of domestic violence. A growing number of African women now understand that the teaching of Gender and Women's Studies is itself an important political action that is necessary if attitudes are to be changed. A good example of this is a project coordinated by the African Gender Institute based in Cape Town, South Africa, which has facilitated networking of Gender and Women's Studies teachers across the continent, and the development of teaching and learning resources to assist the teaching of Gender and Women's Studies in Africa (see www.gwsafrica.org).

Reflections on Donor-funded Research and Academic Freedom – The Case of Ghana

Academic freedom has an added twist in Ghana and that is that donor-funded research opportunities are available in an environment where salaries are generally low and other income-generating opportunities for the academic are few. Of course, most research is funded and the funding source can influence the questions asked, the methodology and even the conclusions arrived at. However, we want to argue that when the funding source is explicitly political and where the environment of the funder and the recipient is one of structural inequality, the problem is exacerbated. It is exacerbated in ways that call into question the tenets of academic freedom. This is especially true when the researcher is a woman and where the research interests have to do with gender. Our experience supports many problems already outlined by the scholars already cited (Pereira 2003; Tamale and Oloka-Onyango 1997; Bennett 2002; Zeleza 2003; Mafeje 1994; Imam 1994, and others).

At our university in Ghana, the climate is not chilly, but cold. Here, there is not the rhetoric of equity, the liberal embracing of 'difference' as a topic, as it had been in Nancy's American university. Therefore, the whole issue of doing gender-based research in a free academic space is shrouded in what we suppose we should call a 'conspiracy of silence'. There are no female activist students monitoring the classrooms, and the few women faculty members do not yet have a clear vehicle or language for their suffering, although the presence of a women's support group has been a beginning towards providing such a vehicle. There were no female professors when Nancy arrived in 1996. Now there are two besides her, one being the second author of this chapter. Therefore, at meetings of senior faculty, there sometimes is only one woman present. Sometimes we are accompanied by one or two of our more junior female colleagues, but generally we are barely noticed. We have been conscious of keeping low profiles.

At our university in Ghana, the battle has just begun. There haven't even been enough women to push a feminist agenda and there are not enough feminists – only a few of us. And the climate is much the same as it had been for Nancy at her American university. The issues are the same, they have just been more successfully submerged in the murky academic waters. Nevertheless, from the point of view of Nancy, an American working in a Ghanaian university, there are also some pressures on African women in the academy that are unique compared to the situation in the US. One particular challenge is the one connected to donor-funded research. As a senior faculty member, Nancy is periodically asked to review files of those coming up for promotion. In this process, it has struck her that much of the professional work of the women she has reviewed has been in the form of donor-related research. She has been regularly surprised at the amount of this type of work that is presented as a part of academic scholarship and the relative ease with which this is considered to be non-controversial. All scholarship, by both women and men, is affected by this issue. But it is particularly relevant to women because they are vulnerable in all of the other ways. Add to this the pressure to publish, the limited funds available for research, limited time and resources, and the rationale for engaging in funder-driven research is obvious. As Boafo and Aryeetey (1990:44) have said, "The inadequacy of internal sources of funding has made it quite attractive for Ghanaian researchers to accept research contracts or collaborative research offers from external sources".

What does it mean for the African academic when most of the work done is of the training/technical, policy-oriented or outside-funded type referred to by Paul Zeleza (2002)? What does it mean, for example, that out of 23 publications, ten are technical reports, out of the remaining 13, nine are commissioned reports from outside funds and two are training oriented? Or, as in another case, out of another 23, four are technical reports and eight are the results from outside funded projects? The numbers, however, do not really get at the other issues, which have to do with how we do research, what are our goals and for whom and what are we doing it. Theoretical research, critical, questioning, challenging research, should go hand in hand with practical, policy-driven research agendas. However, when the research is funded by an organisation, the organisation will steer the direction of the research. As Boafo and Aryeetey (1990) also recognise, not only the direction of the research will often be affected, but also the interpretation of the research findings.

When it comes to consultancies, it would not be wrong to suggest, from our experience, that they follow a hierarchical pattern. Consultancies tend to 'trickle down' to the regions from the capital, unless they originate in the regions. Donors tend to look for consultants who are close by, so that colleagues in Accra have the first option, so to say. Academics outside the capital may cost more due to payment of travel allowances, and so such people get to be approached often only when those in the capital are unavailable. We also argue that women are usually not the consultants of choice, unless their expertise is needed in the area of women's and gender issues. An experience of Mansah's presented here in vignette form provides an illustration.

Vignette 3

A colleague from Accra, a 'professional consultant', phoned me one day and asked if I could introduce a 'gender perspective' into a road impact assessment he was doing. He would need the work within 12 days, could I assist? I would be paid $1,000 for the trouble. Without asking many questions (the prospect of the money was like adrenalin), I dashed down to Accra and he gave me literature and a couple of diskettes containing data collected from women who lived and worked alongside the road. He showed me the format for the report and paid me the money. I returned to my university outside Accra and set to work. I was able to produce a report using the material I had, but at certain points I needed information about the context, and I went back to Accra on two occasions to seek clarification on some points. It became obvious that my friend had been to the field only a couple of times, and that the data had been collected by others. He could not answer all my questions, was under pressure to deliver his report soon and needed my input quickly. So in the end he advised me to just get along as best as I could and finish the work. I had already accepted part of the money so I completed my report and handed it in. I felt very guilty, though. What kind of 'research' had I done? I thought I had as good as prostituted myself, allowed myself to be used. I had not helped the women in any way, for sure. This bleak scenario shows one of the dilemmas that poorly paid academics can be faced with. Where one's geographical location is outside the centre, as in this case, the tendency is to jump at whatever comes up, particularly when one is not often offered consultancies as a woman except when it has to do with gender issues. In this particular case, the gender analysis was used cosmetically, and the actual women involved might have been short changed. This example also shows the necessity for reflection on what one is embarking on when one accepts consultancies.

The neoliberal and male agenda currently in fashion with the IMF, World Bank and USAID, along with many NGOs, cannot help but influence research topics and research findings. Their paradigm is modernisation theory with neoclassical economic theory as its underpinnings. Their methods, therefore, are heavily quantitative, depending mostly on survey questionnaires for data collection. Radical transformative research questioning the underlying assumptions of patriarchy is obviously not on the agenda of most donor organisations. Their research agendas tend to fall within the range of topics that facilitate 'development'. Development, from the modernisation perspective, means full participation within the global capitalist economy. Thus, issues such as participatory development, entrepreneurship, savings and loan schemes, sustainable development projects and women's 'empowerment' schemes have priority. These are all within a context of concepts of democracy, free market economies and rule of law.

All of these concepts sound good, we all want them – who can argue with them? But we also know that they underlie the dominant neoliberal, neoclassically driven agenda. This agenda appears to be accepted uncritically as a given. However, it needs to be challenged. It needs particularly to be challenged in Africa where, as Claude Ake (Pereira 2002) has said, the underlying assumptions of this development model take, as a starting point, a negative view of people in the capitalist periphery. It is a model whose premises are the same colonial ones that allowed for the capitalist core to flourish in the first place. It is an imperialist model that starts with Europe and ends in the capitalist periphery. It is a model that says that people in the periphery are responsible for their own underdevelopment. It is not a model that includes such critiques as those of Fanon (1967), Rodney (1981), Amin (1976), Mies (1999), Wallerstein (1980), Ake (1994), Magubane (1979), Frank (1978), to name a few who propose a different analysis of development. It is a model that says that 'Third World' peoples are underdeveloped because they do not follow the rule of law (they are lawless?), they are backward and 'traditional' and refuse to embrace modern ideas and techniques. It says that they are superstitious, follow false Gods and engage in troubling, wasteful ceremonies. It says that they do not know how to use the land, manage money or organise themselves to work productively. They do not know the value of time, how to save it and not waste it and they do not know the value of investment and saving, all concepts essential to capitalist market behaviour.

This is all old ground. But it is important to remind ourselves that there is a potent set of assumptions underlying the contemporary modernisation rhetoric that drives research agendas, along with development projects and aid. These assumptions are not particularly useful for those in the capitalist 'periphery', and especially not for women. At the very least, they need to be challenged. But in our experience with these research projects, there is little room for such challenge. There is little room for the imaginative, transformative, original, critical research that should be the central and core feature of feminist research.

The fact that women are forced into these research projects, due to economic and academic constraints, places in serious jeopardy the concept of academic freedom. Where is academic freedom if our work is commissioned and funded by our former colonial masters, masters who are imperialist and patriarchal in essence? This may sound harsh, but it is a harsh reality. If academic freedom goes the way of the Dodo, if it becomes extinct, what happens to the academy? What happens to imagination, to creativity? What happens to the ability of a people to define their own reality, to interpret and to analyse and to critique. What happens to our ability to form a new reality for the oppressed of the world, for the women of the world?

As women academics, we owe it to ourselves, and we owe it to our sisters, to keep our eyes open, to not allow ourselves to die. Our colleagues, our funders, our helpers, would like to see us flounder. We are contentious, we are contrary, we are potentially dangerous. They would like to see that our wings are too heavy for our bodies and that we, therefore, will not be able to fly. But we must fly. If we don't fly, we will become extinct.

Conclusion

The two narratives of personal experiences have some similarities. The 'honeymoon' period, the difficulties, self-censorship and an attempt at resolution of the situation. Both narratives reflect on the difficulties in determining the structures of patriarchal maintenance and control. Even though we are different, one of us being American, and one of us Ghanaian, there are common threads in our experience as women in the patriarchal academy. Our experiences are but two examples of what others have so vividly expressed (see, for example, Tamale and Oloka-Onyango 1997; Manuh 2002; Peirera 2002; Zeleza 2002; Bennett 2002; Imam and Mama 1994; Acker 1994; Lorde 1984).

Both of us, in reviewing our experiences in the past and now, have pondered the subjectivities of our situations. How far could our problems have resulted from our own personal demeanours or politics? Despite the fact that this is difficult to determine, both examples demonstrate what has been brought to light by other women, that there are real issues of sexism in the academy. The exercise of our academic freedom is seriously impaired by the fact that we are women. These are not just personal issues, though, they impact the entire project of the creation of knowledge. Such issues curtail our imaginative, transformative intellectual powers, thus limiting the imagination of the academy and, ultimately, a people.

In conclusion we are saying that we have struggled and we have sweated. We have survived. We have not left the academy. But for all of us who have survived, how many of us have not? Many of the women in academic life have not made it. They have not been able to live through the chilly climate. We do not want to become extinct like our Dodo friend. We would like to preserve our lives and the life of academic freedom.

How, then, can we transcend these experiences, move on and in doing so support those who are still struggling and will continue to struggle after us. According to a Dagaare proverb, the sweat of one person has significance only when it serves everybody. We need to mentor each other more and nurture each other. But also, we need to work on dismantling the patriarchal structures that oppress us. We also need to work on changing attitudes that are a part of the structures. We can work on the structures, such as providing gender policies, providing avenues for redress in cases of discrimination, monitoring admissions and hiring, mainstreaming gender issues, affirmative action policies, but in addition, we need to work on attitudes. Every decade, women like us have to write this paper. Our vision is that we should come to a situation where women in the academy no longer need to write papers like this. Our vision is also that at our university we should never again have a calendar that contains pictures of only men. We envision a time when we see women working alongside men in all areas of academic life.

References

Acker, S., 1994, *Gendered Education: Sociological Reflections on Women, Teaching and Feminism*. London: Open University Press

Ake, C., 1994, "Academic Freedom and Material Base", in M. Diouf and M. Mamdani (eds), *Academic Freedom in Africa*. Dakar: CODESRIA.

Ali, A., 1994, "Donors' Wisdom Versus African Folly: What Academic Freedom and Which High Moral Standing?", in M. Diouf and M. Mamdani (eds), *Academic Freedom in Africa*. Dakar: CODESRIA.

Amin, S., 1976, *Unequal Development: An Essay on the Social Formations of Peripheral Capitalism*. Trans. By Brian Pearce. New York: Monthly Review Press.

Belenky, M.F., B.M Clinchy, N.R. Goldberger and J.M. Tarule, 1997, *Women's ways of knowing: The development of self, voice and mind. Tenth anniversary edition*. New York: Basic Books.

Bennett, J., 2002, "Exploration of a 'Gap': Strategising Gender Equity in African Universities", *Feminist Africa* 1:34–63.

Boafo, S. and E. Aryeetey (eds.), 1990, "Practical Constraints in Social Field Research in Ghana, in Narula and Pearce, *Cultures, Politics and Research Programs:* An Assessment of Practical Problems in Field Research. New Jersey: Lawrence Erlbaum, Assoc.

Bortei-Doku, E. and E. Aryeetey, 2000, "A Southern Lens on Poverty Research: Setting the Agenda". Report on the First National Conference on Norwegian Poverty Researcn in the Third World. Oslo: Crop, Bergen and Norges Forskningsrad.

Boserup, E., 1970, *Women's Role in Economic Development*, London: George Allen and Unwin Ltd.

Diouf, M., 1994, "Intellectuals and the State in Senegal: The Search for a Paradigm" in M. Diouf and M. Mamdani (eds), *Academic Freedom in Africa*. Dakar: CODESRIA.

Fanon, F., 1967, *Black Skin, White Masks*. New York: W.W. Norton.

Frank, A.G.,1978, *Dependent Accumulation and Underdevelopment*. London: MacMillan Press, Ltd.

Friere, P., 1972, *Pedagogy of the Oppressed*. Trans. by Myra Bergman Ramos. Harmondsworth: Penguin.

Gramsci, A., 1971, *Prison Notebooks*. New York: International Publishers.

Hagan, G.P., 1994, "Academic Freedom and National Responsibility in an African State: Ghana", in M. Diouf and M. Mamdani (eds), *Academic Freedom in Africa*. Dakar: CODESRIA.

hooks, B., 1994, *Teaching to Transgress: Education as the Practice of Freedom*, New York: Routledge.

Imam, A., 1990, "Gender Analysis and African Social Sciences in the 1990's, *Africa and Development* Vol. XV, nos. 3&4.

Imam, A. and A. Mama, 1994, "The Role of Academics in Limiting and Expanding Academic Freedom", in M. Diouf and M. Mamdani (eds), *Academic Freedom in Africa*. Dakar: CODESRIA.

Lorde, A., 1984, "The Master's Tools Will Never Dismantle the Master's House", in A. Lorde, *Sister Outsider*. New York: Crossing Press.

Mafeje, A., 1994, African Intellectuals: An Inquiry into their Genesis and Social Options in Academic Freedom in Africa, in M. Diouf and M. Mamdani (eds), *Academic Freedom in Africa*. Dakar: CODESRIA.

Magubane, B., 1979, *The Political Economy of Race and Class in South Africa* New York: Monthly Review Press.

Mama, Amina, 1996, "Women's Studies and Studies of Women in Africa during the 1990s", available at www.gwsafrica.org.

—, 2002, "Gains and Challenges: Linking Theory and Practice", keynote address at Women's World Congress, Makerere University, July 2002.

Manuh, T., 2002, "Higher Education, Condition of Scholars and the Future of Development in Africa", *CODESRIA Bulletin* Nos. 3&4.

Marcuse, H., 1964, *One-Dimensional Man: Studies in the Ideology of Advanced Industrial Society*. Boston: Beacon Press.

Mies, M., 1999, *Patriarchy and Accumulation on a World Scale: Women in the International Division of Labour*. London: Zed Press.

Mikell, G., 1989, *Cocoa and Chaos in Ghana*. New York: Paragon House.

Pereira, C., 2002, "Between Knowing and Imagining: What Space for Feminism in Scholarship on Africa", *Feminist Africa* 1:9–33.

Prah, M., 2002, "Gender Issues in Ghanaian Tertiary Institutions: Women Academics and Administrators at the University of Cape Coast", *Ghana Studies* 5:83–122.

Rodney, W., 1981, *How Europe Underdeveloped Africa*. Washington: Howard University Press.

Tamale, S. and J. Oloka-Onyango, 1997, "Bitches at the Academy: Gender and Academic Freedom at the African University", *Africa Development* Vol. XXII, No. 1.

Wallerstein, I., 1980, *The Modern World System II*. New York: Academic Press.

Zeleza, P., 2002, "African Universities and Globalisation", *Feminist Africa* 1:64–85.

CHAPTER SEVEN

Doing Women's Studies
Problems and Prospects for Researchers and Activists in Nigeria

Nkoli N. Ezumah

Introduction

The emergence of women's studies as a field of research, teaching and study since the 1970s in Western countries has been associated with the impact of the international women's movement. In Nigeria, an early publication on women was Ogunsheye's "The Role and Status of Women in Nigeria" published in 1960. However, it was really from the mid-1970s that many Nigerian women, like women in other African countries, started developing an interest in doing women's studies and gender research. The United Nations's Decade for Women (1975-85) and subsequent forums that focused on the adverse effects of development on women, contributed immensely to the evolution of Women's Studies in Nigeria. The production of such knowledge is not limited to researchers in academia. The endeavours of activists in non-governmental organisations (NGOs) who work at the grassroots level are invaluable in producing vital knowledge that can be used by academics for teaching and research in Women's Studies.

This chapter focuses on the importance of linkages between research and activism in women's studies in Nigeria. It also addresses some of the challenges confronting academics and activists engaged in women's studies in that country. The chapter is divided into three parts. The first part focuses on the development of women's studies in Nigeria. The second examines the phenomenon of the national machinery. The third part deals with the challenges facing researchers doing work in the area of gender. In the concluding section, I discuss local resistance to global agendas.

The Development of Women's Studies in Nigeria

Various definitions have been given for what constitutes 'women's studies'. Gloria Thomas-Emeagwali (1988:48) noted that:

> ... women's studies is not merely the study of a particular sex, but rather it is a study of women in society and gender relations – a field which goes beyond structural functionalism and modernisation theory and which is integrally related to studies on the national question, ethnicity and even colonialism in so far as these are concerned with varied forms of chauvinisms. It is a field, which must also focus on the question of resource distribution and societal transformation.

A.K. Omideyi (1988:80) defined women's studies as: "... work done on women in their different spheres of life. It includes reports and analyses of research work carried out on women of all ages, professional, ethnic background, religious beliefs, social organization etc. It would also include narrative experiences and observations of day-to-day activities of women in their domestic life, among their kin and in the community at large." More recently, Charmaine Pereira (1999:111), has defined women's studies as "... studies of women as a social group, motivated by the exclusion of women from mainstream scholarship and understanding of social realities ..."

In this, chapter women's studies is conceptualised as the study of women, which is geared towards reflecting women's realities in various spheres of life by addressing the socio-cultural, economic and political constraints that have been engendered by gender inequality in the society. The basic assumption is that issues affecting women's lives, which have long been overlooked, underreported and inadequately accounted for, are areas of intellectual inquiry.

Scholars and the Development of Women's Studies

Interest in women's studies in Nigeria was boosted by the events that followed the declaration of the UN's Decade for Women. The momentum has been sustained through publications, workshops and conferences, research and teaching in different universities, as well as through activism by NGOs and through government initiatives. Many of the earlier publications, which appeared during the colonial period and soon after independence, were mostly anthropological texts produced by Western researchers. These authors (Basden 1921; Galletti et al. 1956; Hill 1969; Leith-Ross 1965; Lloyd 1965; Paulme 1971; Ottenberg 1959; Smith 1954; and Berry 1975 to mention a few) took for granted the subordinate position of women and did not adopt a critical gender lens in their analyses of women's and men's work. For example, Galletti et al. (1956), writing on cocoa farmers in Western Nigeria, perceived only men as cocoa farmers, while their wives were regarded as farm hands. However, a more gender-conscious documentation of women's work, especially in the informal sector, started emerging with the writings of Niara Sudarkasa (1973), Bolanle Awe (1974), Kamene Okonjo (1976) and Nina Mba (1982). Okonjo's (1976) paper, "The Dual Sex Political System: Igbo Women and Community Politics in Mid-Western Nigeria" discussed the role of women in governance in the traditional political system and the impact of colonial encounters on women's status. Awe's (1974) paper on the *Iyalode* also provided excellent documentation of the position of prominent women in the traditional Yoruba political system in Nigeria, and Mba's (1982) book, *Nigerian Women Mobilized,* highlighted the effects of historical changes on the political position of women in Southern Nigeria.

In 1975, the first seminar on women and national development was held at the University of Ibadan to mark the beginning of the UN's Decade for Women. In 1980, the Centre for Social, Cultural and Environmental Research (cenSECER) at the University of Benin organised a national conference on Integrated Rural Development and Women's Research in Nigeria. The papers presented at that conference included Pauline Makinwa-Adebusoye's "The Role of Women in Nigeria's Socio-Economic Development"; Reuben Ogbudinkpa's "Constraints on Women's Labour Force Participation in Nigeria's Development Process"; and D.H. Afejuku's paper on "Equal Opportunity and Infringement of the Contractual Rights of the Nigerian Woman". Makinwa-Adebusoye specifically highlighted the fact that a lot of women's work was not adequately accounted for. She also identified the constraints females experienced in their pursuit of education and in their roles as food processors and distributors. Makinwa-Adebusoye further emphasised the need for women to be integrated into mainstream development processes. Ogbudinkpa's paper identified the physiological, demographic, cultural, socioeconomic and political factors that constitute impediments to women's participation in the labour force. Afejuku's paper highlighted the fact that gender equity can only be achieved if there are equal opportunities for men and women in their access to education. With respect to discriminatory practices existing in the workplace on the basis of marital status, she advocated that married and unmarried women should have equal access to job opportunities as well as to payment of fringe benefits.

In 1985, the Institute of African Studies at the University of Ibadan organised a national seminar on Nigerian Women and National Development in order to assess the impact of the UN's Decade for Women. My colleague, Fumi Oluyomi, and I coordinated that seminar. The themes covered included Women and Agriculture, Women and Labour Force Participation,

Women and Education and the Women's Movement. The communiqué issued at the end of that seminar urged the government to set up women's studies programmes in institutions of higher learning as a way of ensuring that women's issues were incorporated in school curricula. In 1987, the Institute of African Studies, University of Ibadan, also organised a national conference entitled Women's Studies: The State of the Art in Nigeria. The establishment of a Women's Research and Documentation Centre (WORDOC) followed that conference. The goal of the centre was "to provide a focus for women's studies in Nigeria through the coordination of research projects on women's issues in Nigeria and the promotion of new methodologies in the study of Nigerian women" (WORDOC *Newsletter* 1987).

From the inception of WORDOC in 1987 until 1990, I served as the coordinating secretary of the centre and at the same time was a Research Fellow at the Institute of African Studies, University of Ibadan. Because of the multidisciplinary orientation of WORDOC, its members were drawn from various faculties and research institutes within the University of Ibadan. Links were also forged with researchers in other universities in the country and abroad. A linkage programme on women's studies was established between WORDOC, two Canadian universities, namely Mount Saint Vincent's University and Dalhousie University, as well as with Obafemi Awolowo University (OAU) Ile-Ife, Nigeria, with funding from the Canadian International Development Agency (CIDA). In 1988, a joint workshop involving participants from these four universities marked the inauguration of the link programme. This workshop provided a comparison of the theoretical and methodological issues in women's studies in Nigeria and Canada. The funding from CIDA contributed immensely to capacity development in women's studies in the two participating Nigerian universities through a staff development programme, which was an integral component of the link programme. Twelve fellowship opportunities were provided under the programme (six for Obafemi Awolowo University, Ile-Ife, and six for WORDOC). I was the first beneficiary of the fellowship from WORDOC. It provided me the opportunity to spend three months at Mount Saint Vincent's University, which has a well-established women's studies programme. The exposure I received, and the excellent human and material resources available at both Canadian universities were of tremendous benefit to me intellectually. I had several opportunities to network with academics and students through seminars, workshops and personal interactions. Those experiences contributed immensely towards enabling me to grapple with critical issues and concerns in women's studies in relation to the subject matter, practical difficulties in institutionalising the discipline and undertaking research. Moreover, while at Mount Saint Vincent's University, I had the time and space to produce a draft of my doctoral dissertation without being encumbered with the regular academic schedule and other domestic obligations that were serious constraints for me in my normal working environment at the Institute of African Studies at home in Nigeria.

Since the 1990s, concerted efforts have been made and are still continuing to institutionalise women's studies in institutions of higher learning. A few women's studies centres in addition to WORDOC have been established. These include the Women's Studies Unit at the University of Nigeria, Nsukka; the Centre for Gender and Policy Studies, Obafemi Awolowo University, Ile-Ife; and the Documentation and Gender Studies Unit at Nnamdi Azikiwe University, Awka. Some social science, agriculture and humanities faculties offer courses in women's studies, and many long essays and theses are written on women and gender issues at Ahmadu Bello University, Zaria, and at the University of Lagos, University of Calabar, University of Jos, University of Ibadan and University of Nigeria, Nsukka.

In recognition of the need to establish a sustained network of scholars and activists interested in and working in women's studies, a Network for Women's Studies in Nigeria (NWSN) was formed in 1996 during a national workshop on Setting an Agenda for Gender and Women's Studies in Nigeria in Kaduna. The objective of that forum was for teachers and researchers to review the history and state of women's studies in Nigeria. Amina Mama, the convenor at the time, put it this way, "We felt we could better chart our own course if we could collectively come together to reflect on the social, cultural and political conditions under which we work, and decide what we would like a national agenda for gender and women's studies in Nigeria to comprise" (Mama 1997:1–2). Consequently, that workshop emphasised the need for the definition of basic concepts and terms for women's and gender studies. The importance of developing 'home grown expertise' was also highlighted. A committee was consequently set up to propose a core curriculum for women's studies. A second workshop held later in the year focused on the development of concepts and methods for women's studies. In 1997, during the third workshop of NWSN, participants examined how to embark on curriculum development and the requirements for institutionalising women's and gender studies in Nigerian universities. The criteria for membership in NWSN are involvement in and commitment to the development of gender and women's studies in Nigeria (see also Charmaine Pereira's discussion of the objectives of NWSN, now ISWN, in this volume).

NWSN has produced three reports of its activities, namely *Setting an Agenda for Gender and Women's Studies in Nigeria*, *Concepts and Methods for Gender and Women's Studies in Nigeria* and *Curriculum Workshop for Gender and Women's Studies in Nigeria*. In October 2003, in response to the need to provide accurate data on gender-based violence in Nigeria, NWSN embarked on a pilot study of sexual harassment at three Nigerian universities, namely Usman Dan Fodio University, Sokoto; Ahmadu Bello University, Zaria; and University of Nigeria, Nsukka. I was happy to be one of the researchers who took part in this study, which we expect will make an important contribution towards highlighting the hidden but pervasive phenomenon of harassment and its adverse consequences in our institutions of higher learning.

Contributions of Activists within NGOs in the Development of Women's Studies in Nigeria

It is important to note that activism in women's issues in Nigeria is not limited to researchers in academia. Various NGOs and, in particular, women's organisations have been involved in activism to improve the status and conditions of women. As early as 1929, the now famous Aba Women's War was a protest against the introduction of taxation unleashed by Igbo women's associations against the British colonial authority. Also, the Nigerian Women's Union and the Federation of Women's Societies were organisations which tried to achieve better conditions for women by fighting for women's concerns through their involvement in nationalist struggles (Mba 1982). One of the oldest NGOs that has been involved in activism to protect the interests of women in the social, economic and political spheres is the National Council of Women's Societies (NCWS). NCWS was inaugurated in 1959. It has branches across Nigeria. Its aims are to "… promote the welfare and progress of women, especially in education, and to ensure that women were given every opportunity to play an important part in social and community affairs …" (Mba 1982:189). From its inception, NCWS has, through its activism, tried to influence government policies on issues affecting women. Its members include elite women and working class women, professionals, teachers, market women, rural women and representatives from many religious groups. Past national presidents have included Ifeyinwa Nzeako, a lawyer; Hilda Adefarasin, a nurse; Emily Imokhuede, who owned an art gallery; and Hajiya Dogonyaro, a politician (Iweriebor 1998). Some of its founding members were involved in nationalist activities prior to Nigerian independence in 1960. In 1961, during its annual conference, members of the NCWS branch in Eastern Nigeria indicated their opposition to the civil service regulation which encouraged the transfer of wives to posts away from their families. In a similar vein, the 1962 conference of the Western union branch of the NCWS passed a resolution urging the government to ensure that women were appointed as ministers as well as to top positions in the civil service (Mba 1982).

The NCWS has assumed the role of the recognised umbrella for other women's organisations. In 1986, the organisation protested against the marginalisation of women in governance through the policy of tokenism in the appointment of political office holders. Subsequently, NCWS demanded the implementation of a quota system, which would make it possible for women to occupy 30-40 per cent of positions in the cabinet and legislature. In 1992, the president of the NCWS vehemently accused "most of the governors of appointing all male cabinet, director generals and heads of parastatals without as much as giving thought to the role women would play in the third republic" (*National Concord* 25 February 1992:13). Although its activities are not carried out in a radical manner, NCWS has not relented in its efforts to protect the social and political interests of women.

The year 1982 witnessed the formation of a movement known as Women in Nigeria (WIN). Its members comprise men and women who are committed to the liberation of women from all forms of oppression in the socioeconomic and political spheres. Hence, WIN's activities have been geared towards sensitising women to organise and seek the realisation of social, economic and political rights in the family, the workplace and in the general society. WIN's work is carried out through research, conferences and publications. It organises an annual conference in its various branches, which provide fora for members of WIN as well as invited non-members, including intellectuals as well as market women, to discuss their research findings. Some of the conferences have dealt with topical issues including Women and the Family, Child Abuse, Women and Health, Women and Violence and Women in the Transition to Democracy.

The development of women's studies in Nigeria has also been significantly influenced by the publications and activism of WIN. Some of its publications include *Women in Nigeria Today*, *The WIN Document: Policy Recommendations towards the Year 2000 AD*; *Women and the Family* and *WIN's Position on Women in Politics*. These publications have been invaluable in providing an understanding of the socioeconomic and political predicaments women experience in Nigeria. Despite its laudable efforts at advocacy and activism, WIN'S membership has been dwindling. Part of the reason is that some of its leaders have formed their own NGOs and therefore no longer participate in WIN's activities. Such a development has serious implications for the sustainability of the organisation. A major consequence is that its stature and effectiveness have become diffused (Pereira 2002).

Several other NGOs with qualified professional members emerged in the 1990s and many have distinguished themselves in activism. I list here a few of the NGOs that have been involved in activism, but this list is in no way meant to be exhaustive, just illustrative. The Legal Research and Resource and Development Centre organises seminars and workshops on human rights, democracy and development discourse and also publishes them. Women's Health and Action Research Centre (WHARC) focuses on reproductive health issues that constrain women's health status. Women's Centre for Peace and Development (WOPED) serves as an information and advocacy centre for the pursuit of the rights of women, youth and children. Women Aid Collective (WACOL) and The Civil Resource and Documentation Centre (CIRDOC) have organised national tribunals on reproductive health and violence against women and also focus on human rights issues and provide legal aid to poor women, including widows.

I would like to dilate a bit on the work of BAOBAB as an illustration of what I consider to be best practices in NGO activism. The organisation was formed in 1996 with a vision to defend, promote and develop women's human rights in customary, secular and religious law, and to undertake research to identify rights or constraints that exist in laws, the implementation of these laws and in social practice. BAOBAB also disseminates information on these issues and educates people on how to access those rights. In recognition of the difficulty women face in accessing their rights under Muslim laws, particularly because they are ignorant of those laws, BAOBAB provides legal literacy classes for women (and men), produces leaflets on these topics, carries out training workshops (for example, for paralegals in leadership skills for women) and campaigns for a more feminist interpretation and implementation of Muslim laws. BAOBAB has produced reports on women's rights and laws in Nigeria and draws public attention to women's rights issues. Since 2002, BAOBAB as well as other similar NGOs have been providing support to women convicted under Sharia laws in Northern Nigeria. In particular, in conjunction with Civil Liberties Organisation (CLO), BAOBAB initiated a defence, which successfully stopped the death sentence on Amina Lawal from being carried out. Lawal had been condemned to be stoned to death in 2002 for adultery by a Sharia court.[1] In fact, on 9 December 2002, BAOBAB and Ayesha Iman, a BAOBAB board member, received the John Humphry Freedom Award from the International Centre for Human Rights and Democratic Development, a Canadian-based organisation, in recognition of their work in defending and developing women's human rights in secular, customary and Muslim religious law in Nigeria.

A challenge exists, however, in strengthening linkages between researchers and activists. This linkage is of paramount importance for the growth and development of the discipline, as well as for the effective articulation of issues covered. It has been pointed out that the emergence of women's studies in North America or Europe was largely influenced by the feminist women's movement. The interest in women's studies in Nigeria is no longer restricted to researchers in the academy. NGO activists are involved in producing data, which can, and should be infused into women's studies. It remains important, in Amina Mama's words "to strengthen the links that do exist between African women's studies and the African Women's movement, and so ensure that African women's studies emanate from the collective concerns and interests of African Women" (1996:22). In the next section, I examine the ambiguous contributions of National Machineries and First Ladies in promoting women's issues in Nigeria.

National Machineries, First Ladies and Women's Issues in Nigeria

As an aftermath to the UN's Decade for Women, the Nigerian government began to initiate the establishment of structures and activities to address women's issues. In 1982, it established The National Committee on Women and Development within the Federal Ministry of Social Development, Youths and Sports. Officially, the task of the committee was to advise the government on all issues affecting women. However, that committee was rendered ineffective due to lack of adequate subvention from the government (Mama 2000). In 1987, Maryam Babangida, the wife of the then president of Nigeria, introduced the Better Life for Rural Women Pro-

---

1. Amina Lawal was originally convicted of adultery by an Upper Area sharia court in Katsina State, Northern Nigeria. With the assistance of legal representation from BAOBAB and other Nigerian women's organisations, she successfully appealed the death penalty in the Katsina State Sharia Court of Appeal.

gramme (BLP) and controlled the programme with the assistance of the wives of military governors. Although the programme contributed in some way to creating awareness about women's issues in Nigeria, the public seriously criticised the BLP for its urban bias. Its activities were also perceived to have benefited mostly elite women and those with some connection to the military. Other criticisms of BLP were that it lacked accountability and transparency with regard to the large sums of money it received from the state and donors, since the organisation was largely under the single control of the First Lady (Mama 2000).

In 1996, the Ministry of Women's Affairs was established. In addition, a Women's Documentation Centre was established at Abuja and in 1989 the National Commission for Women (NCW) was inaugurated. Regrettably, First Lady Maryam Babangida and the military regime controlled the policies and programmes of the NCW. Operatives in NCW experienced financial and bureaucratic constraints, which hindered the execution of some of its laudable projects. Its first chairperson, Professor Bolanle Awe, reported in an interview that the commission depended on government subvention, which did not come readily or freely. Consequently, the commission was cash strapped and unable to undertake some viable projects (*The News* 4 October 1993:21). Elsewhere it was also reported that Awe "lamented that well-meaning people, who have tried to make positive changes by taking part in government organs designed for women's development, have been disappointed" (Mama 1996:32).[2]

This situation was not peculiar to Nigeria. As Tsikata (2000) pointed out, governments that established women's bureaus in Africa from the 1970s were not democratic regimes. Most of them adopted authoritarian and dictatorial governance strategies. Hence, "it was not quite clear to what extent the government structures were effective vehicles for the articulation and defense of women's collective concerns and interest" (Mama 1996:25). Due to the lack of funding from the state, most of the National Machineries in Africa, including Nigeria's, depended, ironically, on foreign donors to support their activities (Tsikata 2000). Moreover, a major criticism of Nigeria's NCW by women's organisations was that it did not adequately represent the interests of women.

---

2. Bolanle Awe subsequently resigned her position as chairperson of the National Commission on Women due to the bureaucratic and financial constraints she experienced.

Challenges Confronting Researchers

Challenges facing researchers doing work on women include, inter alia, the following: a) problems faced in the institutionalisation of women's studies; b) the nature of intellectual, material and financial resources available for women's studies, including difficulties in finding publication outlets; and c) problems of linkages between knowledge generation and external funding.

Problems of Institutionalisation of Women's Studies

It is important to begin by noting that researchers in Nigeria are still confronted with the problem of setting up institutionalised structures for women's studies. In some of the institutions of higher learning, there is an ongoing debate about the need to create formal structures for imparting knowledge and teaching in women's studies. One of the constraints in this regard is the problem of acceptability of women's studies as a discipline by university administrations. At a joint workshop on women's studies organised by WORDOC, University of Ibadan and Obafemi Awolowo University, Ile-Ife, in 1988, one of the misgivings raised by some of the participants about institutionalising women's studies was the fear about employment prospects for graduates of women's studies, especially since the unemployment rate is high. So far, efforts have been made in some institutions such as Ahmadu Bello University, University of Lagos, University of Calabar and University of Nigeria, Nsukka to integrate women's studies into existing disciplines such as political science, education, sociology and in the humanities. In the Department of Sociology/Anthropology at the University of Nigeria, Nsukka, where I teach, we offer a major in women's studies at the graduate level. Graduate courses offered include Gender Roles and Human Sexuality, Women and Health, Women in Development and Women in African Culture. However, since the mid-1990s, when I joined the Department of Sociology/Anthropology, only three of my own students have graduated with Master's degrees in Women's Studies and two have applied to pursue their PhD programmes in Women's Studies. Many others take courses in Women's Studies as electives. The department also offers a course in Women in Society at the undergraduate level in the second year. However, I still experience difficulties incorporating new curricula into the discipline. In 2000, I proposed three new courses, two at the undergraduate level to provide some grounding, as well as a new course at the graduate level. Unfortunately, only one of the courses was put forward by the male head of department to the senate committee. It is not uncommon for male colleagues to manifest resistance to the development of women's studies courses.

Intellectual and Material Resources Available for Women's Studies

Another problem scholars in the area of Women's and Gender Studies in Nigeria face is in publishing and disseminating their work. Although many African women and men are now involved in the generation of knowledge in women's studies, due to the difficulties associated with publication their work remains largely invisible to an international readership.

Closely connected to the scarcity of publishing outlets is the scarcity of intellectual resources available for women's studies. Many of the scholars working on women's studies in Nigeria have been involved in integrating knowledge from their related disciplines into the field of women's studies. Consequently there are no set curricula for the teaching of women's studies.

However, although this situation is problematic to some extent, it could also be a source of strength and advantage for scholars in the evolving discipline. In 2002, the African Gender Institute (AGI) at the University of Cape Town initiated a programme to enhance transformative teaching of Gender and Women's Studies in Africa. Workshops were held at which curricula were shared and developed, and a website on Teaching Resources /Feminist Thought in African Contexts on Gender and Women's Studies was set up to provide resources for curriculum development. The teaching resource group (TRG) identified some strategic areas of focus, namely Sexuality; Culture and Identity; Law and Politics; and Feminist Theories and Practice. One of the central arguments of the TRG is that there should be no 'ideal curriculum'. The idea is to encourage flexibility and ensure that people utilise their experiences and ingenuity in developing curricula that not only reflect their peculiar circumstances but would also be internationally valuable. The need for African experiences to be incorporated in the development of concepts and theories used in gender and women's studies is also emphasised. This means that where there is no set curriculum, we can design one, and we can include materials that speak to the African experience. Other useful reviews for teaching are emerging. Adomako Ampofo et al. (2004) have provided a review essay of major themes covered in women's studies in English-speaking sub-Saharan Africa by scholars on the continent.

Linkages Between Research Funding and Knowledge Generation

A major challenge for women's studies in Nigeria, and in Africa generally, is related to the issue of whose research agenda is pursued, which in turn is often tied to the issue of research funding. More than two decades ago, Kisekka (1983) found that many research topics and their methodologies are determined by donor agencies. In some cases, donor funds may be earmarked for research agendas that may not be the priority need of the country in which the research takes place. Especially with dwindling resources of the universities in Nigeria, the problem of donor-driven research persists. Participants at the meeting on setting the Agenda for Gender and Women's Studies in Nigeria held in 1996 expressed concern about external donor agencies having excessive influence on the direction of women's studies. They felt that people's motives for embarking on women's studies should not be in response to external funding or because a particular topic is in vogue. Hence, dependence of researchers and activists on donor funding raises the issue of whose agenda is being pursued and whose 'knowledge' is generated.

On the other hand, it is also the case – despite these misgivings about funding sources – that external funding has been instrumental in building the capacity of many scholars working in gender and women's studies in Nigeria. I will cite a few examples from my own experience. It was with funding from the Ford Foundation that I was able to undertake my PhD programme at the University of Ibadan, which focused on the Role of Igbo Rural Women in Agricultural Production. Funding from CIDA enabled me have my first opportunity to network with scholars working in women's studies in Canada through the linkage programme with WORDOC. As a recipient of the John D. and Catherine T. MacArthur Foundation's grant for Leadership Development in Nigeria, I was able to undertake a baseline study and subsequent advocacy and activism on reproductive health among adolescents and adults in some sections of Anambra and Enugu States of Nigeria. I am feeding those experiences into my research and teaching at the University of Nigeria, Nsukka. Further, consultancy work, in addition to providing me with the resources I need for personal survival, has also broadened my expertise in the area of Gender and Women's Studies.

Yet another challenge confronting scholars in Women's and Gender Studies is the issue of maintaining ethical standards. I recall a question that was posed during a presentation of my research findings on "Perception of sexuality and gender relations and implications for the reproductive health of men and women: Selected findings from Awka and Agulu, Anambra State Nigeria" at the University of Cape Town, South Africa where I was an Associate at the African Gender Institute in 2000 (Ezumah 2000). My presentation identified some of the reproductive heath problems women encounter in their bid to fulfil their gender roles of child bearing and wifehood, roles which are still very important in defining women's status in Nigeria. One of the other scholars present asked me what efforts I had made to identify the women's views about sexual pleasure. Obviously, that scholar failed to put into perspective the situations and concerns of the Igbo women who were the subject of my case study. The study clearly indicated that because of the stigma associated with wives who are childless, women who suspect that their husbands are infertile resort to clandestine sexual relationships purely for the purposes of procreation, a practice referred to as 'taking shelter'. Another problem mentioned by the women in my study, especially those from low socioeconomic backgrounds, was the inability of women to refuse sex with their husbands /partners, even if they suspected it might not be safe. They feared the repercussions. Given these scenarios, I found it grossly out of place for a scholar who should be interested in addressing the reality of the women's situation in different settings to be questioning why the issue of sexual pleasure was not foregrounded. For me, it was particularly problematic because it did not appear that she was herself concerned about the women's context and circumstances.

Global Agendas Imposed on Women and Local Resistances

Activists often experience harassment and threats from agencies of the state. For example, during the 1985 UN Decade conference in Nairobi, WIN members presented their findings about oppression and discrimination against women in Nigeria. Right there, some women who attended the meeting as government delegates challenged them. One of them upbraided the WIN members, calling them "irresponsible girls" who came to Nairobi to wash their dirty linen in public, while they themselves insisted that Nigerian women were not experiencing discriminatory practices. It was a South African woman at the meeting who aptly reminded the 'warring' Nigerians that that if they as women could not identify and discuss their problems, the men were not going to do it for them (personal observation during the forum). On their return to Nigeria, security forces questioned some of the leaders of WIN (Mama 2000). Such harassment and threats constitute serious impediments to activists.

Research on certain issues, such as reproductive health, women's work and women's participation in politics, tend to be favourite areas for donor support. Although foreign support has been useful, one of the problems associated with this is that the researchers end up producing technical reports, which are submitted to the donors, but often the findings are not made available to colleagues in the academy. In order to have synergy between research and activism, it is of paramount importance that NGOs and researchers undertaking such projects feed their findings to researchers in the academy. As more university researchers serve as resource persons or consultants for NGOs, such processes of creating synergies may begin to evolve.

Conclusions

This chapter has examined the development of women's studies in Nigeria. I have focused on the contributions of scholars in the academy and activists in NGOs as well as those working within state structures. The importance of collaboration between research and activism in the evolution of women's studies in Nigeria has been highlighted, and I have identified major challenges confronting researchers and activists in women's studies. These include difficulties scholars experience in institutionalising women's studies, concerns about the intellectual and material resources to build the discipline and researchers' problems with publication and dissemination of materials they produce. The issue of research agendas being directed by funding agencies has been discussed, and I have pointed out the need for linkages to be established between researchers and activists in order to strengthen the development of women's studies in Nigeria.

References

Adomako A.A., J. Beoku-Betts, N.W. Ngaruiya and M. Osirim, 2004, "Women's and Gender Studies in English-Speaking Sub-Saharan Africa: A Review of Research in the Social Sciences", *Gender & Society,* Vol. 18, No. 6, December 2004, pp 685–714.

Afejuku, D.H., 1980, "Right of the Nigerian Woman", in A.O. Omu, P.K. Makinwa and A.O. Ozo (eds), *Proceedings of the National Conference on Integrated Rural Development and Women in Development.* Center for Social, Cultural and Environmental Research (CenSECER), University of Benin, pp. 723–748.

Awe, B., 1974, " Notes on the Institution of the Iyalode within the traditional Yoruba political system". Unpublished paper.

BAOBAB. Http//: www.baobabwomen.org/events.htm accessed June 30, 2005

BAOBAB. Http//: www.baobabwomen.org/publications_b.htm accessed June 30, 2005

Basden, G.T., 1921, *Among the Ibos of Nigeria*. London: Frank Cass & Co Ltd.

Berry, S., 1975, *Cocoa Custom and Socio- Economic Change in Rural Western Nigeria*. Oxford: Clarendon Press.

Odejide, B. and I. Isiugo-Abanihe (eds), 1999, *Curriculum Workshop for Gender and Women's Studies in Nigeria*. Report of the Network for Women's Studies in Nigeria. Ibadan: Mosuro Publishers, No 3.

Ezumah, N.N., 1999, "Integrating Feminist Perspectives in Sociological Research", in *Reflections on 50 Years of Social Science Education in Nigeria*. Proceedings of the 11th General Assembly of the Social Science Academy of Nigeria, held at the National Women Development Centre, Abuja, Nigeria, July 5–7,1999.

—, 2000, "Perceptions of Sexuality and Gender Relations Among the Igbo and Implications for Reproductive Health of Men and Women: Selected Findings from Awka and Agulu, Anambra State Nigeria", in E. Salo and H. Moffett (eds), *African Gender Institute Associate Publications 2000*. African Gender Institute, University of Cape, pp. 30–62.

Galletti, R., K.D.S. Baldwin and I.O. Dina, 1956, *Nigerian Cocoa Farmers*. Published on behalf of the Nigerian Cocoa Marketing Board, London. Oxford: Oxford University Press.

Gender and women's Studies Teaching Resources, available at http://www.gwsafrica.org/teaching/index.html

Hill, P., 1969, "Hidden Trade in Hausa Land", *Man* 4, (3):392–409.

Iweriebor, I., 1998, "Carrying the Baton: Personal Perspectives on the Modern Women's Movement in Nigeria", in O. Nnaemeka (ed.), *Sisterhood, Feminisms and Power: From Africa to the Diaspora*. Trenton NJ: Africa World Press, pp. 297–321.

Kisekka, M.,1983, "Association of African women For Research and Development: Achievements, Problems and Prospects". Mimeo for AAWORD General Assembly.

Leith-Ross, S., 1965, *African Women: A Study of the Ibo of Nigeria*. London: Routledge & Kegan Paul.

Lloyd, P.C., 1965, *The Yorubas of Nigeria*, in J. Gibbs (ed.), *Peoples of Africa*. New York: Holt, Reinhart and Winston.

Makinwa-Adebusoye, P., 1980, "The Role of Women in Nigeria's Socio-Economic Development", in A.O. Omu, P.K. Makinwa and A.O. Ozo (eds), *Proceedings of the National Conference on Integrated Rural Development and Women in Development*. Center for Social, Cultural and Environmental Research (CenSECER),University of Benin, pp. 638–657.

Mama, A., 1996, "Gender Research and Women's Studies in Africa", in A. Mama (ed.), *Setting An Agenda for Gender and Women's Studies in Nigeria*. Zaria: Tamaza Publishing Company Limited, pp.19–31.

—, 1997, "Defining Terms and Concepts for Ourselves", in C. Pereira (ed.), *Concepts and Methods for Gender and Women's Studies in Nigeria*. Report of a Workshop held at Kongo Conference Hotel, Zaria, 4th-8th November, 1996. Zaria: Tamaza. Network for Women's Studies in Nigeria. Report #2.

—, 2000, *Feminism and the State in Nigeria: The National Machinery for Women*. Third World Network-Africa, National Machinery series No. 4. Accra-North, Ghana.

Mba, N. 1982 *Nigerian Women Mobilised: Women's Political Activity in Southern Nigeria 1900–1965* Institute of International Studies, University of California Berkeley.

McFadden, P., 2003, "Sexual Pleasure as Feminist Choice", *Feminist Africa* 2:50–60.

National Concord,1992, February 25, pp. 13.

Ogbudinkpa, R.N., 1980, "Constraints on Women's Labour Force Participation in Nigeria's Development Process", in A.O. Omu, P.K. Makinwa and A.O. Ozo (eds), *Proceedings of the National Conference on Integrated Rural Development and Women in Development*. Center for Social, Cultural and Environmental Research (CenSECER),University of Benin, pp. 658–670.

Ogunsheye, F.A., 1960, "The Role and Status of Women Nigeria", *Presence Africaine* (Paris) 4:33–49.

Okonjo, K., 1996, "The Dual-Sex Political System in Operation: Igbo Women and Community Politics in Midwestern Nigeria", in N.J. Hafkin and E.G. Bay (eds), *Women in Africa. Studies in Social and Economic Change*. Stanford University Press, pp. 45–59.

Omideyi, A.K., 1988, "Problems and Prospects of Research and Teaching", in *Women's Studies In Nigeria and Canada: A Comparative Approach*. Proceedings of the initial Workshop for the Canadian – Nigerian Linkage in Women's Studies. Published by the Institute for the Study of Women, Mount Saint Vincent University, Halifax, pp 80—85.

Ottenberg , P., 1959, "The Changing Economic Position of Women Among the Afikpo Ibo", in W.R. Bascom and M.J. Herskovits (eds), *Continuity and Change in African Cultures*. University of Chicago Press.

Paulme, D., 1971, *Women of Tropical Africa*. Berkeley and Los Angeles: University of California Press.

Pereira, C., 1999, "Feminist Knowledge- Alternative Visions, New Questions for the Social Sciences in Nigeria", in *Reflections on 50 Years of Social Science Education in Nigeria*. Proceedings of the 11th General Assembly of the Social Science Academy of Nigeria held at the National Women Development Centre, Abuja, Nigeria, July 5-7,1999, pp. 111–120.

—, 2002, "Locating gender and women's studies in Nigeria: What trajectories for the future", available at http//: www.gwsafrica.org/knowledge/index.html

—, 2003, "Where Angels Fear to Tread?" Some Thoughts on Patricia McFadden's "Sexual Pleasure as Feminist Choice", *Feminist Africa Changing Cultures* Issue 2, pp. 61–65.

Robson, E. (ed.), 1993, *Women in Nigeria: The First Ten Years.* Zaria: Women in Nigeria WIN).

Smith, M.F., 1954, *Baba of Karo: A Woman of the Muslim Hausa.* London: Faber and Faber.

Sudarkasa, N., 1973, *Where Women Work: A Study of Yoruba Women in the Marketplace and in the Home.* Anthropological Papers No. 53. Ann Arbor: University of Michigan.

Thomas-Emeagwali, G., 1988, "Methodological Considerations in Women's Studies in Nigeria", in *Women's' Studies In Nigeria and Canada: A Comparative Approach.* Proceedings of the initial Workshop for the Canadian –Nigerian Linkage in Women's Studies. Published by the Institute For the Study of Women Mount Saint Vincent University, Halifax, pp. 43–51.

WORDOC (Women's Research and Documentation Centre), 1987, *Newsletter* Vol. 1 No. 1, May 1987, p. 1, Institute of African Study, University of Ibadan, Nigeria.

CHAPTER EIGHT

Discursive Challenges for African Feminisms
Desiree Lewis

Introduction

It is sometimes assumed that the 'indulgence' of deconstructing discourses is undertaken mainly in Northern contexts and that 'practical' and 'material' struggles are paramount in the South. The fallaciousness of this assumption is revealed in Nawaal el Saadawi's comments on the universal use of language against oppressed peoples. "We need", she writes, "to unveil the words used by global and local governments, by their media and education" (2004:5-6). Describing one of the most potent weapons in the attack on women's rights, she argues:

> Language is often used against women and the poor in every country, especially in our countries, the so-called 'South'. Today, the word 'liberation' means military and economic occupation in Iraq and Afghanistan. The word 'peace' means war, and 'terror' means the massacre of Palestinian women and children under Israeli occupation. The word 'development' means neo-colonialism, robbing people's economic and intellectual riches in Africa, Asia and Latin America. (2004:5)

Our present context of limitless information, globalised power relations, transnational media oligarchies and commoditised academic knowledge mystifies patriarchal and neo-imperial injustice through the rhetoric of 'liberalisation' and 'legitimate' paternalist protection and patriotism. Radical struggles have become increasingly challenging because the exercise of domination has become progressively more overwhelming. The deluge of information that routinely bombards us has contributed to and ensured this. Those who wield power in the present age also wield control over and access to knowledge: knowledge circulated via the World Wide Web; information – promulgated in institutions of higher learning – that often only *appears* progressive; 'public' information ostensibly aimed at marginalised groups, yet concerned least with their interests and most with profit-making.

Critiques of neoliberal challenges to African gender struggles have increased in recent years. Ruth Meena (1992) and Marjorie Mblinyi (1992) writing on Tanzania, Pat McFadden (2001) dealing with Zimbabwe and Dodzi Tsikata (1997) focusing on Ghana have all critically examined ways in which 'good governance', structural adjustment, patriarchal state building and elite consolidation have led to neo-imperial states acting in collusion with the donor community and international capital to orchestrate token policy-making for gender transformation. Such manoeuvring addresses the proviso made by donor communities that Third World countries should liberalise in order to obtain foreign funding. They also seek to placate women's movements in countries where such movements have battled for substantive gender transformation.

But a relatively neglected facet of the neoliberal environment is the upsurge of what could be termed *a gender industry* on the continent, and the extent to which this, ultimately, has been shaped by the developmentalist paradigms that entrenched neo-imperialism and economic dependency. Ranging from the growth of duplicitous discourses on rights to the mushrooming of technocratic and conservative trends in tertiary education, the industry has set in place technologies of gender designed to reconstitute what is substantively transformative and to institutionalise a bureaucratic ethos of top-down engineering and politically correct rhetoric.

The neoliberal cooption of feminist demands is not, of course, unique to Third World contexts. It is an overwhelming feature of contemporary ostensibly 'post-feminist' liberal-democratic societies. The hegemony of global imperialism is increasingly eroding feminism and radical cultural expression and discourses in civil society at an international level. What takes the place of these are industries of information and knowledge production that often work to consolidate elite interests, exploitative patterns of consumption and distribution and long-established global economic and political inequalities.

In what follows, I draw attention to the necessity for connecting national and continental feminist challenges to those that confront feminisms globally. Two main discursive manifestations of the neoliberal cooption of feminism are explored: first the growth of moderate rights-based discourses; and secondly, the cooption and adulteration of gender research and teaching. While there are important differences in the way that these trends have evolved and currently function in different parts of the world, I stress that they are politically connected. In the third and final section, I focus on ways in which some feminist commentators are invigorating the language and practice of feminism to contest our present context of hegemonised knowledge and information.

Ambiguities of Gender Equality/Mainstreaming Language

In analysing the politics of contemporary women's rights discourses, it is instructive to examine the development of gender discourses in South Africa. This is because South Africa during the last decade exemplifies the way mainstreaming progressively dilutes gender activism and discourses. This trend has been a rapid one: in the space of a decade, South Africa has come to be viewed as one of the most 'gender sensitive' countries in the world because of the centrality of women's rights and gender equity to an official narrative of nation-building. The ambiguity of this language of gender equality is the focus of the first half of this section. In the second half, I discuss some implications of the language of gender mainstreaming.

The 1980s marked a high point for integrating gender into public and political discourses on human rights in South Africa. Various community, regional and national organisations[1] provided structures for working women, students and activists to play dynamic roles in anti-apartheid politics. From the early 1990s, by the time of the release of political prisoners and the national preparations for dismantling apartheid, the ground had been laid for systematically confronting both gender and racial injustices, since women's organisations and civil society activism had effectively prioritised feminist demands in the struggle for South African democracy.

A crucial event marking the shift away from the articulation of gender struggles in civil society activism was the formation of a Women's National Coalition (WNC) four years before the first democratic election. As the culmination of years of activism, lobbying and organisation, the coalition's primary objective was to ensure women's equality in the constitutional dispensation being negotiated by different parties and organisations at the time. Its role has been described in the following way: "In creating the WNC, all of the major women's organisations allowed something larger and more representative to command an authority that none of them could achieve alone, making the WNC something that they could not avoid affiliating to as well as something that could not be controlled by any one organization" (Kemp, Madala, Moodley and Salo 1995:151).

The Coalition, of course, was distinctive not only because it drew together different groupings, but also because this amalgamation marked a process of sidelining political differences to achieve consensus around nation-building

---

1. These included the Natal Organisation of Women, the United Women's Congress, the Federation of Transvaal Women and other organisations aligned with the United Democratic Front.

and 'democracy'. It indicated how the 'mainstreaming' of gender concerns into the national democratising agenda entailed compromise, arbitration and regulation as myriad organisations and individuals focused on negotiated legal and formal rights. The taking up of gender into the nation-building agenda, or what Shireen Hassim has identified as the "gender pact" (2003), entailed an arbitration process through which particular gender concerns were identified as those that should be institutionalised in the discursive construction of democracy. It could be argued, then, that the Coalition signalled the displacement of the nature of gender activism, as earlier preoccupations with women's agency and interests were jettisoned in favour of pursuing consensual rights-oriented lobbying and policy-making that postulated common rights and entitlements monitored or granted by the state.

The transformation of the nature of gender activism was accompanied by a concomitant displacement of the *locus* of gender struggles – away from civil society and into the state bureaucracy. This was associated, for example, with the committee work of a caucus of parliamentarians; the Women's Budget in 1996, which focused on policy areas specifically concerning the needs of women; the Office of the Status of Women in the office of the president, regional gender desks and a national Gender Commission.

It is indisputable that women's movements and radical currents within civil society prompted mainstreaming in the first place. It is also clear that gender mainstreaming is a desirable goal when defined as a systematic and holistic process for introducing policy implementation, institutional restructuring, educational transformation and planning in ways that rectify persistent gender inequalities. In fact, the belief in this structural change motivated the concerted involvement of radical organisations and individuals in mainstreaming processes during the 1990s. In recent years, however, there has been growing scepticism about the effectiveness of state structures. In particular, many feminist writers and activists have raised questions about the disparity between policy and practice.

Generally, the argument is that blueprints for gender transformation in South Africa are in place, but there has been a failure on the part of policy-makers, actors within the state or existing structures and institutions to realise the goals of policies. A special issue of South Africa's leading feminist journal, *Agenda*, entitled "Realising Rights", made this argument very clearly in 2001, with the editorial stating:

> While our Constitution is regarded as one of the most progressive in the world, 'Realising Rights?' questions the extent to which women are able to

> realise the rights enshrined therein. The passing of a number of progressive laws and the amendment of certain pieces of legislation, theoretically implies the improvement of women's positions in society – yet the reality is that the majority of women continue to face marginalisation and discrimination in their homes, workplaces and communities. (Moolman 2001:2)

A persuasive explanation of the gap between South Africa's gender-oriented theory and practice is provided by Amanda Gouws (2004, 2005). Gouws draws attention to how different voices are always already inscribed in legislation, and to "different discursive inputs being made within different sites" (2004:43). Her discussion is suggestive in its Foucauldian attention to the way that power is played out through a "multiplicity of discursive elements that can come into play in various strategies" (2004:43). The analysis of policy-making can be taken further if we bear in mind how much discursive power is unequally distributed. Negotiation processes in South Africa have not simply entailed various voices in dialogue with each other. They have involved domination, covert censorship and hegemonisation, with different voices having hugely disparate access to sites for articulating knowledge, information and goals.

The uneven allocation of discursive authority has led to the evolution of a levelled, mediated and compromised notion of what the interests and goals of a generalised group of women are, and to the circumscribing of terms around who is included and who is excluded in discussions about justice. The emphasis in public discourses of gender transformation has therefore shifted dramatically from a bottom-up articulation of the interests of women's organisations to the top-down codification of negotiated rights and entitlements that are believed to have national relevance.

From 'Justice' to 'Rights'

The discursive terrain has changed in remarkably swift ways. Where the language of gender transformation was formerly marked by a climate in which the class, regional and racial political interests of particular women drove them to struggle for distinct agendas for social transformation, our current rights-based discourse assumes that melioristic and state-engineered transformation can grant rights and entitlements in terms of generalised notions of what 'women' of South Africa need and want. These abrupt changes in the first decade of democracy have gone hand in glove with a veering away from the notion of 'justice' towards a veneration of 'rights'. 'Rights' have levelling and universalised legal meaning. 'Justice', on the other hand, is far broader, and implies a holistic understanding of ways in which certain groups and institutions can prevent others from realising their different liberties. Speaking for 'rights' can occur within the framework of formal procedures that ensure the nominal access of all to certain platforms or resources, without comprehensively considering whether all relationships and structures in society actually guarantee this access.

The emphasis on women's rights in policy-making, legislation and the language of transformation has generated a very distinctive national mythology about gender transformation in post-apartheid South Africa. A rhetorical climate shaped by circumstances including the constitutional emphasis on gender equality, policies on sexual harassment and employment equity in the workplace, and legislation such as the Domestic Violence Act of 1998, has set in place a persuasive rhetoric, and has charged certain words and expressions with a sense of their reflecting a new reality. Phrases such as 'gender equality', 'women's empowerment' and 'gender transformation' therefore permeate public discourses in ways that are both remarkably authoritative and also deeply superficial and complacent. First, it is as though rhetorical force were being substituted for any real reflection on actual gender relations and agendas for change. Secondly, the terminology in place consistently stresses the technical and formal dimensions of social dynamics, rather than their political and socially transformative repercussions.

The persuasiveness of the current language revolves considerably around the fact that it often refers to conditions or situations that are fundamentally in accord with neoliberal development and patriarchal anxieties around changing the gendered status quo. It is noteworthy, for example, that 'women's empowerment', 'women's equality', 'gender parity' or 'gender equity' are often used in policy documents or public discourses, rather than phrases such as 'women's freedoms' or 'feminist liberation'. The former expressions point fairly straightforwardly to the idea of power within the status quo, to women's aspirations to the status and privileges that men have, while the latter complicatedly opens up the possibility of situations and conditions that may lie beyond existing class and gender models of material achievement and public success.

From 'Women' to 'Gender'

Many other terms that have become current underline the gradual shift towards moderacy. The term 'gender' in itself has acquired growing influence in defining interest groups, social change and political goals. Consequently, where it used to be legitimate to argue that the voices and interests of *women* were paramount in identifying how patriarchal domination marginalised a group on the basis of gender, the current ascendancy of 'gender' neutralises power relations and almost implies that the social categorisation and identity of women as women and of men as men is not of key importance. Revealing too is the way that 'gender activism' has successively displaced the term 'feminism'. It as though the radicalism signalled by the latter term was being anaestheticised and patriarchal anxieties about change were being appeased. Ostensibly, the jettisoning of 'feminism' is made in relation to claims about its being Western-centric. But this argument disguises a deep-seated conservativism thinly masquerading as a healthy populism. The avoidance of 'feminism' placates the unease of patriarchal nationalism, which routinely invokes the charge of spiralling 'Westernisation' to attack African women's radicalism.

The need to placate anxieties about change is well-illustrated in the consistent avoidance of 'patriarchy' and its substitution by phrases such as 'male dominance' or 'gender inequality'. Repeatedly, the tendency is to underplay politics and power relations and to construct a view of hierarchies and inequalities which turns them into 'anomalies' easily corrected through moderate, melioristic and formal rights-oriented strategies for change.

Cooption and Compromise through Language

As the rapid transformation of the political terrain around gender struggles in South Africa reveals, mainstreaming has been born out of a process of negotiation in which the language of rights both reflects and regulates the accommodative incorporation of political agendas into the state bureaucracy and official narratives of nation-building. The effects of mainstreaming in an environment characterised by the unequal distribution of discursive power must lead us to ask hard questions about how and why ostensibly progressive agendas can so easily be watered down. By turning to the ways in which cooption and compromise occur through language, we can become more vigilant about the ways in which double standards and duplicity deflect progressive action. Rather than simply positing a gap between language and goals or action, it may be more useful to explore as well the ambiguities and paradoxes embedded in discourse itself, as well as the range of institutions, texts and discourses that rewrite messages of freedom.

The impetus behind mainstreaming in South Africa has been the women's movement and progressive forces in society, although the discursive and political context in which gender activism is now located dilutes its political focus. A similar situation prevails globally. Internationally, what became known as 'gender mainstreaming' peaked from the early 1990s, and, through the Beijing Platform in 1995 was identified as a *radical* strategy for guaranteeing state, intersectoral and international collaboration in alleviating women's structural subordination (see True and Mintrom 2001).

Rights Discourse and Victimisation

The visibility of this global diffusion, however, needs to be considered in the light of how international instruments and policies function as discourses. Transnational instruments set in place a language of rights which targets universal and transhistorical subjects as clients or beneficiaries who 'receive' what has been conceptualised as just mainly by others. Apart from the projection of individuals as supplicants, the main problem here is that rights discourse assumes the universality of social subjects. In other words, rights discourses privilege certain forms of freedom and justice over others: they fallaciously assume generalised access to measures and mechanisms that are set in place to safeguard individuals. There are related practical problems associated with the universalistic model. When we consider the Convention on the Elimination of All Forms of Discrimination against Women (CEDAW), for example, it is clear that there are no actual mechanisms by which states can be held accountable to the United Nations. While the UN may insist on certain measures to protect women's freedoms across the world, legislation and policy-making that directly affect women is undertaken and regulated at the level of the nation state. Through rights discourses, gender mainstreaming consequently constructs universal subjects as passive recipients, impedes their agency in driving change, thereby foreclosing possibilities for them to drive alternative gender transformation in society and privileges the subject positions of globally and regionally dominant subjects. The language of rights is firmly entrenched in lobbying, planning and policy-making around gender justice, while the radical activism that formerly drove feminist transformation is now, according to popular wisdom, dismissed as passé, outmoded or obsolete. By a deft sleight of hand, the discourse of rights, which so evidently sets in place passive, de-historicised and politically disempowered subjects, has achieved ascendancy as the language of social transformation.

It is noteworthy how the language of rights has set in place a model for 'dealing with gender' which mirrors the model that over the last decade has been entrenched in South Africa. It is small wonder, then, that the idea that many women in the North today live in a 'post-feminist' age, namely, an age where feminist struggle has become obsolete, has gained currency. When paradigms of progress and freedom are shaped by a language that identifies universally agreed upon and measurable success and achievement, and when such models are instituted by states or through international agreements, it is difficult to insist that there is a need to struggle for change within civil society or through women's actions: change appears to be guaranteed both by the 'gender-sensitive' paradigms that exist and by the language inscribed in these models. Naomi Wolf's (1993) writings have gone some way towards critiquing this situation. By condemning the salience of what she terms "victim feminism", she accurately describes the present mood of gender awareness in the North: "... over the last twenty years, the old belief in a tolerant assertiveness, a claim to human participation and human rights – power feminism – was embattled by the rise of a set of beliefs that cast women as beleaguered, fragile, intuitive angels: victim feminism" (1993:147). Wolf identifies the construct of women as supplicants in relation to the state and policy-makers, of women positioned as recipients rather than agents; of generalised notions about women's universal needs and entitlements. And as Elizabeth Schneider (1991) has argued, the pre-eminence of rights discourse turns women into passive targets and victims who become dependent on the state and other instruments and sources of power both for articulating and granting their freedoms.

Gender Teaching and Technocratisation

The manoeuvring around language in relation to popular myth-making and public discourses is reflected in gender teaching and research. This has been the case nationally and globally. In South Africa, 1994 marked a stage when the state and state-recognised sectors within civil society created a new mood around gender research, new patterns of funding and support for it and also a new public awareness of its relevance to emerging agendas for democratisation. One effect of this galvanising of governmental support for 'gender' was a trend towards technocratic and functionalist developmentalism. This was buttressed by the shift towards market-driven and career-oriented teaching in South African higher educational institutions.

Nationally, over five women's and gender studies units offering postgraduate programmes in gender studies were launched in different provinces. And the climate of institutionalised gender research quickly encouraged technocratisation. Teaching increasingly became less concerned with feminism in the academy, with students' political and personal growth or with making women visible in research and writing, and progressively more preoccupied with how gender analysis should equip students with applied or analytical skills.

I am referring here mainly to the packaging of courses within universities, which have become more and more concerned with marketing degree programmes. Whether or not individual lecturers and researchers have resisted the depoliticisation of gender, teaching courses within the broader framework of university policies are marketed and defined according to the logic of their practical usefulness for the job market. The effect of this has often been to underplay the humanities and arts and privilege disciplines like psychology and the social sciences.[2]

The mid-1990s ushered in a phase of consolidation and marketisation around women's and gender studies, with this 'mainstreaming' being geared towards teaching gender 'expertise' and 'skills' to promote the efficiency of state structures, policy-making and commerce. Bureaucracy, professionalisation and technocracy spiral in this context, alongside a prominent group of 'experts' whose analytical tools, methodologies and concepts often directly shape planning and policy-making. Pat McFadden astutely points to this trend at a continental level in her polemical "Why Feminist Autonomy Now?"

> Our staid matrons (the continent's 'experts' on gender training and mainstreaming) also serve as the link between the women's movement and the state in almost every country on the continent. They control the flow of resources between the state and donor communities ... They carefully tread the thin lines drawn by Northern donors on issues of reproductive health and sexuality, cautiously referring to difficult issues like abortion and sexual orientation only in moderate tones, and rarely, if ever, rocking the national or international boat. (McFadden 2004)

Spaces and discourses that seem progressive have been coopted into national efforts to mainstream and market technologies of gender, and to situate gender concerns within neoliberal state building and 'good governance'. This is starkly reflected in the painstaking efforts to market women's studies courses as being of 'use' to students in the demand for skilled human

---

2 For a further discussion of this, see Lewis 2002, especially Appendix: Institutional Review.

resource persons in government and the workplace. Higher education has increasingly become a commodity. No longer is there an assumption that women's studies matters because it prompts the broad personal and political transformation of human beings. Gender studies is seen as serviceable because it is securely written into a moderate template for state consolidation and neoliberal development under the aegis of 'mainstreaming'.

Pros and Cons of 'Gender Studies'

A mainstreaming trend that has been growing increasingly prominent in Africa is one in which 'women's studies', as the title of a discipline or of departments, is being viewed with greater awkwardness and anxiety. 'Women's studies' is rapidly giving way to 'gender studies', and the new term is embraced for its inclusiveness and its rejection of ghettoisation. Many courses have been revamped, course outlines rewritten and the general culture of departments altered to turn them from supportive spaces aimed primarily at empowering women students into spaces where men and women are believed to grapple collaboratively with issues to do with gender.

The intellectual usefulness of 'gender' is indisputable: 'gender studies' correctly captures the extent to which feminists need to engage with identities and processes that mould relations between men and women, in other words, gender dynamics. Clearly too, 'gender studies' captures the fact that the subject of study cannot be 'women' in isolation, but women in relation to men, as well as processes and relationships that are gendered. What remains revealing, however, is the way in which the new labelling of a field of study has modified the *politics* of the field of study, and in many ways buttressed a broader climate around mainstreaming.

The emphasis on opening up the field and making it inclusive for women and men occurs alongside the underplaying of long-entrenched power relationships, a neglect, for example, of the fact that today there is still an absurdly preponderant focus in knowledge production on men as subjects. The question that this situation therefore begs is why there should be a concern within women's studies with 'balancing out', when this is one of the few spaces where the privileging of men's knowledge production is directly contested. Overall, therefore, I have huge problems with the 'commonsensical' idea that mainstreaming gender studies corrects a passé emphasis on the compensatory and atomistic focus on women. Distinct institutional needs and contexts (for example, the fact that rape is a regular occurrence in many universities in South Africa and more generally throughout Africa) make separate women's studies departments important and strategic. Separate women's studies departments have the potential to provide invaluably supportive cultural pockets of focused feminist support, research and teaching within institutions which remain, overall, extremely fraught spaces for women academics and students to negotiate.

Commoditisation and Professionalisation

The skewing of feminist research and education has also occurred in the North. In a powerful critique focusing on the meanings and fate of 'theory', Barbara Christian (1990) identifies the two connected trends of commoditisation and professionalisation that over the years have worked to depoliticise feminist scholarship. In the 1970s and 1980s, a collective identity of women in academia – supported and influenced by the resurgence of feminism in the 1960s – formed caucuses and associations, or engaged in lobbying, or spearheaded disciplinary innovations in contesting the exclusiveness of the patriarchal academy. Their interventions were deeply political and radical, and they struggled to challenge injustice, silencing and domination on various fronts.

By the 1990s, as Christian notes, much left-wing academic theory had "become a commodity which help[ed] to determine whether we are hired or promoted in academic institutions" (1990:37-8). Professionalism, through which feminist academics and discourses are absorbed into the canon by echoing its exclusivist and monolithic language and procedures, became the goal of many feminist academics. As Joan Scott (1991) therefore concludes, the elevation of 'professionalism' firmly replaced the preoccupation with 'politics' as many feminist academics capitulated to notions of mastery and excellence, and so sanctioned the exclusion and silencing that an earlier generation of feminists had squarely denounced.

In the North, the 'success story' of feminist scholarship revolves largely around its progressive shift away from a defiant 'marginality' towards a mastering of the theoretical tools and strategies of the mainstream. Women's studies, as the site in which a language for speaking about women's agendas was inaugurated, can be seen to have moved from the disparaged margins to the triumphant centre. The centrist destination has been linked to a fixation with high theoretical rigour and a recuperation of the idea, formerly anathema for many feminists, of knowledge as science, of knowledge as that which can 'stand up firmly by itself'. The professionalisation of gender research and education in Africa has revolved mainly around the growing complicity between a gender industry and the state's ideological apparatus, creating a situation in which much gender education and research tends to service mainstreaming and neoliberal development. In the North, such professionalisation has mainly involved the commoditisation of research and the elevation of knowledge as cultural capital. This has led to the growing alienation of academics and knowledge production from civil society activism and women's organisations.

Post-structuralism: Pitfalls and Possibilities

This trend is clearly reflected in the turn towards an uncritical post-structuralist deftness. Here there has been a growing depoliticisation of language as the site of revolutionary practice, towards a preoccupation with language as that which must capture the 'complexity of things'. The consequence of this has been astutely explained by Jacqui Alexander:

> Postmodernist theory, in its haste to disassociate itself from all forms of essentialism, has generated a series of epistemological confusions regarding the interconnections between location, identity and the construction of knowledge ... Postmodernist discourse attempts to move beyond essentialism by pluralizing and dissolving the stability and analytic unity of the categories of race, class, gender, and sexuality. This strategy often forecloses any valid recuperation of these categories or the social relations through which they are constituted. (1997:XVII)

On the intellectual left, therefore, discourses have spawned such deft phrases as 'negotiating identity' or 'negotiating freedom', which often foreclose any systematic attention to power.

Many post-structuralist concepts are aimed at destabilising fixed notions of struggle and drawing attention to the multiplicity of agencies and social identities. They seek to stress how social actors make sense of their experiences from their point of view and to emphasise their agency in the face of those who presume to speak and act for them. These concepts have been invaluable in dislodging doctrinaire notions of struggle associated with leftist orthodoxy. This includes the leftist orthodoxy of Marxism and Westerncentric feminism. Post-structuralism intervenes here because it allows one to think about processes, consciousness and agency beyond hegemonic notions of what impossibly 'universalised' persons must want. In particular, they allow us to take into account the extent to which certain social actors are circumscribed by particular relations and practices. They also encourage us to consider how certain women's struggles make sense on their terms and to respect the fact that particular groups have distinctive legacies of resistance.

But the concepts and methods of post-structuralism also hold out the possibility of disarticulating relations of power. In short, they can provide ideological cover for proliferating divisions and injustices in the contemporary world, and especially for shifting attention away from identifying power and its effects. Bell hooks, among many other feminist commentators, shows how this language has developed as certain academics seek legitimation and access to academic and intellectual canons. She writes:

> While academic legitimation was crucial to the advancement of feminist thought, it created a new set of difficulties. Suddenly the feminist thinking that had emerged directly from theory and practice received less attention than theory that was metalinguistic, creating exclusive jargon; it was written solely for an academic audience. It was as if a large body of feminist thinkers banded together to form an elite group writing theory that could be understood only by an 'in' crowd. (hooks 2000:22)

What should be stressed here is not – as I hope my preceding discussion has demonstrated – the belief that African and other Third World and socially engaged feminists should concern themselves only with 'bread-and-butter' issues rather than with theory, with discourses and with deconstructive and postmodern theories. The language and practice of deconstruction can contribute enormously to shaping radical and revolutionary social and intellectual activism and struggles for gender justice. What I am concerned about here is the extent to which certain applications of postmodern feminism can feed into existing relations of power and function purely or mainly as symbolic capital for individuals and groups who use intellectual currency to gain access to the centre.

Imagination and the Public Sphere

Today, an unprecedented circulation of information is guaranteed by apparently limitless knowledge production, the massive growth of print technologies, global flows of information and knowledge, cyberspace and the Internet. At the same time, intellectual knowledge production is uniquely registering the intricacy of social identities, the complexity of individual and social behaviour, the nuances of institutional and social processes. The deluge of information, knowledge and language that persistently over-determines the political has led Manuel Castells to coin the term "information politics" (1997:310). Although Castells is referring mainly to the burgeoning electronic media as the new "privileged space of politics", it is important to acknowledge the complicity of pervasive professionalisation and commoditisation within the academy, and the steady process through which ostensibly subversive knowledge has been adulterated and depoliticised. At the same time, the language of 'rights from above' dominates public debates about gender transformation at the communal, national and international level, and seriously constrains civil society activism and independent debates. The result of this hegemony has been silencing. When we consider the evolution of discussion and debate in the public sphere, and the current apathy within civil society, we must ask what all these apparently liberating and democratising discursive processes really mean. Somehow, the promise of lively public discourses and civil society activism has rapidly diminished in recent years.

This stasis should encourage us to reassess what the new forms of wielding power in our current information age are. Specifically, they must lead us also to reconsider, for example, what 'censorship' means in our present age. To what extent can we think about radical feminist knowledge as being 'censored' despite the fact that it is allowed, formally, to exist. To what extent do the procedures and value systems for elevating certain kinds of expert knowledge function as forms of repression, surveillance and silencing? And how do current forms of gate keeping curtail the circulation of radical knowledge even in spaces that seem amenable to the free flow of information and ideas?

It is no coincidence that many radical feminist writers today are searching restlessly for terms that powerfully invoke transgression, the quest for new ways of thinking and speaking and the pursuit for what is 'visionary' and 'imaginative' (see, for example, McFadden 2004, hooks 2000 and Pereira 2002). Posing a challenge to African feminists to transcend neo-imperial and patriarchal frontiers, Charmaine Pereira raises imperatives that have both cognitive and practical implications:

> There is no way of creating knowledge that is not circumscribed by the oppressions of our times if we cannot imagine a better future ... Without imagination, we cannot search for the kind of knowledge that allows us to fully understand our divided realities in order to transcend them. It is the imagination that allows us to move from where we are to where we would like to be even before we get there. We must learn to liberate the imagination, to unleash the energy that so many of us dissipate, often without realising, in

upholding the intellectual barriers that divide us not only from one another, but also from ourselves and from other ways of knowing. (Pereira 2002)

One of the primary challenges facing feminists today is the challenge of re-imagining our goals, of insisting on the powers of the imagination to articulate our desires in ways that transcend the limiting visions bequeathed by neoliberal globalisation. In an argument that the struggle for democracy needs to take new forms, Alan Touraine identified the slipperiness of discursive control in neoliberal democracy and called for the need to rethink 'activism':

> Power used to be in the hands of princes, oligarchies and ruling elites; it was defined as the capacity to impose one's will on others, modifying their behaviour. This image of power does not fit with our reality any longer. Power is everywhere and nowhere; it is in mass production, in financial flows, in lifestyles, in the hospital, in the school, in television, in images, in messages, in technologies ...The fundamental matter is not seizing power, but to recreate society, to invent politics anew, to avoid the blind conflict between open markets and closed communities, to overcome the breaking down of societies where the distance increases between the included and the excluded, those in and those out. (Quoted in Castells 1997:309)

Touraine describes our present age of globalised neo-imperial domination, a phase following the independence of many African countries, the disintegration of Soviet societies and the attack on left-wing movements in the North. These processes occur against the backdrop of a global diffusion of coercive control and 'manufactured consent'. The situation that currently faces feminists is far more insidious and multifaceted. And as we confront our current discursive landscape, we must squarely face the need 'to recreate society, to invent politics anew'.

References

Alexander, J. and C. Mohanty, 1997, "Introduction: Genealogies, Legacies, Movements", in J. Alexander and C. Mohanty, *Feminist Genealogies, Colonial Legacies*. London and New York: Routledge.

Castells, M., 1997, *The Power of Identity*. Massachusetts and Oxford: Blackwell.

Christian, B., 1990, "The Race for Theory", in A. JanMohamed and D. Lloyd (eds), *The Nature and context of Minority Discourse*. Oxford and New York: Oxford University Press.

El Sadaawi, N., 2004, "Foreward", in N. Van der Gaag, *The No-Nonsense Guide to Women's Rights*. London: New Internationalist in assoc. with Verso.

Gouws, A., 2004, "The Politics of State Structures: Citizenship and the National Machinery for Women in South Africa", *Feminist Africa*, Issue 3.

—, 2005, "Shaping Women's Citizenship. Contesting the Boundaries of State and Discourse", in A. Gouws (ed.), *(Un)thinking Citizenship. Feminist Debates in Contemporary South Africa*. Cape Town and Aldershot: UCT Press and Ashgate

Hassim, S., 2003, "The Gender Pact and Democratic Consolidation: Institutionalizing Gender Equality in the South African State", *Feminist Studies*, 29:3.

hooks, B., 2000, *Feminism is for Everybody: Passionate Politics*. Cambridge, MA: South End Press.

Kemp, A., N. Madala, A. Moodley and E. Salo, 1995, "The Dawn of a New Day: Redefining South African Feminisms", in A. Basa (ed.), *The Challenge of Local Feminisms: Women's Movements in Global Perspective*. Boulder: Westview Press.

Lewis, D., 2002, "Gender and Women's Studies in South Africa: A Review Report", http://www.gwsafrica.org/knowledge/index.html.

Mbilinyi, M., 1992, "Research Methodologies in Gender Issues", in R. Meena (ed.), *Gender in Southern Africa: Conceptual and Theoretical Issues*. Harare: SAPES.

McFadden, P., 2001, "Cultural Practice as Gendered Exclusion: Experiences from Southern Africa", in *Discussion of Women's Empowerment: Theory and Practice*. SIDA Studies, 3. Stockholm: SIDA.

—, 2004, "Why Feminist Autonomy Now?" *fito*, www.fito.co.za

Meena, R. (ed.), 1992, *Gender in Southern Africa: Conceptual and Theoretical Issues*. Harare: SAPES Books.

Moolman, J., 2001, "Editorial", *Agenda Realising Rights*, No. 47.

Pereira, C., 2002, "Between Knowing and Imagining – What Space for Feminism in Scholarship on Africa", *Feminist Africa* 1, October. www.feministafrica.org/fa%201/2level.html

Scott, J., 1991, "Women's History", in P. Burke (ed.), *New Perspectives on Historical Writing*. Cambridge: Polity Press.

Schneider, E., 1991, "The Dialectic of Rights and Politics: Perspectives from the Women's Movement", in B. Sullivan and G. Whitehouse (eds), *Gender Politics and citizenship in the 1990s*. Sydney: University of New South Wales.

True, J. and M. Mintrom, 2001, "Transnational Networks and Policy Diffusion: The Case of Gender Mainstreaming", *International Studies Quarterly* No. 45.

Tsikata, D., 1997, "Gender Equality and the State in Ghana", in A. Imam et al., *Engendering African Social Science*. Dakar: CODESRIA.

Contributors

Akosua Adomako Ampofo is an associate professor and Director of the Institute of African Studies at the University of Ghana, Legon. She was, until recently, the first Head of the Centre for Gender Studies and Advocacy (CEGENSA) at the same institution. She is also a member of several networks including the Network for Women's Rights, Ghana (Netright); the Ghana Domestic Violence Coalition; and the Women's Caucus of the African Studies Association. Her current research and civil interests include: race and identity politics; gender and violence on university campuses; masculinities; and representations of women in popular music. Among her recent publications are: "Phallic Competence: Fatherhood and the Making of Men in Ghana", *Culture, Societies and Masculinities* (with Michael P.K. Okyerefo and Michael Perverah, 2009); "Collective Activism: The Domestic Violence Bill becoming Law in Ghana", *African and Asian Studies*; and "Race, Gender and Global Love: Non-Ghanaian Wives, Insiders or Outsiders in Ghana?", *International Journal of the Family* (with Akosua Darkwah, 2008).

Ximena Andrade, a feminist geographer, graduated from the prestigious Universidad de Chile, to which she is still attached. Since 1978, Andrade has been associate professor in the Department of Geography, Faculty of Humanities and Social Sciences, at the Eduardo Mondlane University, Maputo, Mozambique. Andrade is a founding member of WLSA Mozambique, the Mozambique branch of the Women and Law in Southern Africa research trust. She has also conducted and participated in a series of studies regarding women's human rights, especially sexual and reproductive rights in the context of the HIV/AIDS pandemic.

Signe Arnfred is an associate professor at the Institute for Society and Globalisation (ISG) at Roskilde University, Denmark. From 2000–06, she worked at the Nordic Africa Institute in Uppsala as coordinator of the Sexuality, Gender and Society in Africa research programme. One focus of her research is critical studies of sexuality in Africa, while another (partly overlapping) is on African feminist research. A long-term research project investigates sexuality and power in northern Mozambique. Other work focuses on post-colonial feminist theory and on areas of convergence between social science, feminism and art. Notable recent publications include the edited volume *Re-thinking Sexualities in Africa* (2004), "African Feminists on Sexualities", *Canadian Journal of African Studies* (2009) and a guest-edited issue of *NORA:* "Sex & Politics – Case Africa" (2009).

Jane Bennett is an associate professor at the African Gender Institute at the University of Cape Town, South Africa. She has worked as a researcher, teacher and activist for two decades in the fields of gender, violence, sexuality and feminist philosophies. She has published academic works in these areas, and has also published works of fiction.

Isabel Maria Casimiro is a feminist scholar and activist who has been based at the Centre of African Studies, Eduardo Mondlane University, Maputo, Mozambique since 1980. She is a co-founder of Women and Law in Southern Africa (WLSA) Regional (1988) and WLSA Mozambique (1990) and founder of the Department of Women and Gender Studies at the Centre of African Studies (1990). She is also a member of various feminist organizations in Mozambique, including Fórum Mulher (Woman's Forum), a network of about 80 organizations concerned with women's human rights. She is also co-founder of Cruzeiro do Sul – Instituto de Investigação para o Desenvolvimento José Negrão (Southern Cross – José Negrão Research Institute for Develoment, 1998). In 2004, she wrote "'Peace on Earth and War at Home'. Feminism and Women Organizations in Mozambique" and in 2009 "African Women's Movements. Changing Political Landscapes" (with Aili Mari Tripp, Joy Kwesiga and Alice Mungwa).

Nkoli N. Ezumah is a professor of sociology in the Department of Sociology/Anthropology, University of Nigeria, Nsukka. Her teaching and research work focuses on women's gender roles and human sexuality in African societies, women's reproductive health and rights and HIV/AIDs in Nigeria and feminism in Africa. Other areas of focus include women's roles in agriculture and paid employment; access to justice; health policy and malaria treatment services in Nigeria. She is a contributor to the feminist publication *Women Writing Africa: West Africa and the Sahel* (2005) and co-ordinator of the research project, Challenges of University Accommodation and Implications for Sexual Harassment and Sexual Violence at University of Nigeria, Nsukka, under the auspices of the Initiative for Women's Studies in Nigeria (IWSN). She was a visiting associate at the African Gender Institute, University of Cape Town, South Africa in 2000 and a visiting fellow at Mario Einaudi Center for International Studies and the Institute for African Development, Cornell University, Ithaca, New York, September 1990-June 1991.

Adetoun Ilumoka, a lawyer by training, has been very active in the international women's movement over the past two decades, and has participated in pioneering research and advocacy on issues of women's health and human rights in Nigeria since 1989. She taught in the Faculty of Law at the University of Jos in Nigeria between 1984 and 1990 and from 1992-2004 was the executive director of the Empowerment and Action Research Centre (EMPARC), a social justice advocacy organization based in Lagos. She has also worked as a legal practitioner and consultant at various times. Ms Ilumoka's research interests are in the area of critical legal theory with a focus on historical and contextual understandings of law and human rights and their implications for local and global social regulation in the 21st century. Much of her recent research and writing is on women's struggles for health and land rights in Africa. She is currently the Daryl T.Been Professor in Women's Studies and Feminist Research and Law at the University of Western Ontario in Canada.

Desiree Lewis is associate professor in the Department of Women's and Gender Studies at the University of the Western Cape, South Africa. She has taught courses on feminism in Zimbabwe and the United Sates, and participates in civil society movements and non-governmental organizations focusing on gender transformation and sexual rights in South Africa. Lewis has published on gender and visual culture, constructions of gender and sexuality, African feminist knowledge production and literary studies. The guest editor of special issues of the African-based feminist journals, *Feminist Africa* and *Agenda*, she is also the author of *Bessie Head and the Politics of Imagining* (2007).

Nancy Lundgren is an associate professor in the Department of Sociology and Anthropology at the University of Cape Coast (UCC), Ghana. Currently she is applying her expertise in anthropology, political economy, child development and systems of inequality, in a follow-up ethnography of the peoples and cultures of the southern region of Ghana. In addition, she has been working for some years on gender and inequality among Fra Fra-speaking peoples of the northern part of Ghana. Her research has also taken her into a long-term, ongoing ethnographic commodity chain analysis of cement. An early women's scholar and activist in universities in the US, she has been active in the women's organization at UCC and is one of the architects of the university's sexual harassment policy. She now serves on the committee to develop a gender centre on the UCC campus.

Charmaine Pereira is a feminist scholar-activist who has worked extensively on the themes of feminist thought and practice, sexuality, gender and university education, and civil society and the state. Based in Abuja, Nigeria, she coordinates the Initiative for Women's Studies in Nigeria (IWSN), which strengthens teaching and research capacity in gender and women's studies. As IWSN national coordinator, she oversees programmes on the politics of sexual harassment and sexual violence in universities, gender justice and women's citizenship and women's empowerment. She is the author of *Gender in the Making of the Nigerian University System* (2007).

Mansah Prah is an associate professor in the Department of Sociology and Anthropology and the immediate past dean of the Faculty of Social Sciences, University of Cape Coast (UCC), Ghana. She was a key player in the introduction of a sexual harassment policy at UCC. Her research interests are in gender and education, gender and sexuality and popular culture. Her current interest is in exploring pedagogies suitable for teaching gender and sexuality. Her paper "Help! I Do Not Love my Husband: Advice Columns as a Teaching Resource for Gender and Sexuality: Experiences from the University of Cape Coast" appeared in, *SIGADA, Studies in Gender and Development in Africa*, September 2008.

INDEX

Note: *n* after a page number denotes footnote, with number where appropriate

AAWORD/AFARD (Association of African Women for Research and Development), 9, 11
abortion, 113–18, 124–5
academic freedom, 175–6, 179–81, 183
academics *see* universities; women academics
activism
 civil society activism, 46, 219
 in the classroom, 47
 Mozambique, 147–8, 149
 Nigeria, 192–5
 and research, 17–18, 86, 201
 state harassment, 200
 see also advocacy
Adefarasin, Hilda, 192
adolescents, 39–40
advocacy, 17–18, 45–7, 49, 68, 128
 see also activism
AFARD (Association of African Women for Research and Development), 9, 11
Afejuku, D.H., 189
African Gender Institute, 47, 58–9, 74, 75*n*3, 76, 198
Ahmadu Bello University, 86, 92, 105–6
AIDS/HIV, 48–9, 145–6
Ake, Claude, 177, 178, 182
Alexander, Jacqui, 217
Arnfred, Signe, 147
Association of African Women for Research and Development (AAWORD/AFARD), 9, 11
autonomy, 18–20, 89, 94–5
 see also academic freedom
Awe, Bolanle, 189, 196

Babangida, Maryam, 195–6
BAOBAB, 194–5
Beoku-Betts, Josephine, 42–3
Better Life for Rural Women Programme, 195–6
British Council, 19–20, 24–5, 92, 105–6

Canada, university linkage programme, 190–1
Canadian International Development Agency (CIDA), 190, 199
CEDAW (Convention on the Elimination of All Forms of Discrimination against Women), 212
CEGENSA (Centre for Gender Studies and Advocacy), 20, 24, 40–1, 47, 48–9
Christian, Barbara, 216
Christianity, 32–3
church, 46–7
CIDA (Canadian International Development Agency), 190, 199
civil society, 46, 207–8, 219
CODESRIA (Council of Social Science Research in Africa), 88
consultancy work
 attractions and benefits, 21–2, 35, 44–5, 48–9, 87, 199
 ethical dilemmas, 22
 geographical location of consultant, 181–2
 intellectual piece-work, 87–8
 Kulhuvuka Project, 145–6
 political agendas of funders, 173
 time-bounded nature of, 44, 87, 106
 to supplement university pay, 34–5
Contexts of Gender in Africa 2002 meeting, 8–10, 28–9
contraception, 118–20

Index

Convention on the Elimination of All Forms of Discrimination against Women (CEDAW), 212
Corrêa, Sonea, 146
Council of Social Science Research in Africa (CODESRIA), 88
culture, 39

Danida (Danish International Development Agency), 20
Datta, Ansu, 65–7
DAWS (Development and Women's Studies Programme), 19–20, 24–5
debt, 24n
Decade for Women (UN), 187, 189
DEMEG (Department of Women and Gender Studies), 142–8
development projects
 cause of Third World underdevelopment, 182–3
 and knowledge, 12–14
 mainstreaming, 90–1, 207–9, 211–12
 marginalisation of women, 178
development studies, 10–12
Development and Women's Studies Programme (DAWS), 19–20, 24–5
Diouf, Mamadou, 171
discrimination, 37, 166–8, 171, 212
 see also sexual discrimination
Dogonyaro, Hajiya, 192
domestic violence, 49
 see also rape; sexual harassment
Domestic Violence Coalition (Ghana), 46
donor organisations
 conditions for obtaining funding, 206
 impact of funding, 20
 influence on research agenda, 15, 23, 100–1, 127, 135, 174, 177–8
 and research autonomy, 94–5, 179–81, 183

economic discrimination, 171
el Saadawi, Nawaal, 205

family planning, 33–4, 118–20
feminism
 definition, 32$n8$
 postmodern feminism, 217–18
 professionalism in the North, 216
 term replaced by gender activism, 210–11
 theories, 54–5
 victim feminism, 213
feminist research, 6–7, 55–6, 151–4
fertility, 33–4
Ford Foundation, 143, 199
funding
 discrimination against women, 37
 and donor agendas, 15, 23, 127, 135, 174, 177–8
 impact measurement, 20
 influence on research, 96–100, 144, 199
 of national women's bodies, 196
 positive impact on scholarship, 199
 and researcher autonomy, 18–20, 94–5, 179–81, 183
 self-determination of need, 100–1
 see also consultancy work

gender, 139–41, 210–11
Gender and Development (GAD), 10, 13
gender identities, 69–70
gender mainstreaming, 90–1, 207–9, 211–12
gender research, 38–43, 158–9
gender studies, 151–4, 215–16
 see also women's studies
gender teaching, 46-47, 146, 213–15
gender violence, 48–9
 see also rape; sexual harassment
Ghana
 Akan people, 8
 Domestic Violence Coalition, 46
 Ministry of Women's Affairs and Children (MOWAC), 46

see also University of Cape Coast; University of Ghana
Gouws, Amanda, 209
government
   Ghana, women's issues, 46
   Mozambique, women's issues, 140, 148
   Nigeria, women's issues, 195–6
   South Africa, women's issues, 208
   structural adjustment programmes (SAPs), 85
   women in, 193
   women's bureaus, 196

health, 33–4, 39–40, 112–13, 126–7, 131–2, 199–200
Higher Education Links programme, 19–20, 24–5, 92, 105–6
HIV/AIDS, 48–9, 145–6
hooks, bell (author), 218
human rights, 122–3, 194–5
   see also reproductive rights; rights discourse

identity
   and feminist research, 6–7, 27, 151–4
   gender identities, 69–70
   racial groupings in Nigeria, 83–4
Imam, Ayesha, 174, 195
Imokhuede, Emily, 192
information
   disparity in access, 37
   dissemination, 41–2, 198

Jesus Christ, 32*n*9
Johnson, Bernadette, 59*n*, 62
Jubilee 2000, 24

knowledge
   and activism, 26, 34
   androcentricity of, 138–9
   and censorship, 219
   and development projects, 12–14
   and emancipation from oppression, 174–5
   and imagination, 218–20
   limited by patriarchal values, 158
   scientific vs. social science, 174
Kulhuvuka Project, 145–6
Kwenaite, Nozipho, 67

language
   chain of equivalence, 14
   development concepts, 12–14
   invisibility of females, 36
   meaning of words, 205, 207, 209–12
   in Mozambique, 150
Lawal, Amina, 194–5
Letsie, Lebohang, 60, 62, 65, 75–6
Lies, Secrets and Silences (Rich), 55
Liverpool University, 92, 105–6

McFadden, Patricia, 16–17, 66–7, 68, 214
Machel, Graça, 145, 147
mainstreaming, 90–1, 207–9, 211–12
Makinwa-Adebusoye, Pauline, 189
Mama, Amina, 19, 70, 90, 195
Manuh, Takyiwaa, 44
masculinities, 69–71, 78
Mate, Rekopantswe, 75–6
Mba, Nina, *Nigerian Women Mobilized*, 189
Millett, Kate, *Sexual Politics*, 55
Mkandawire, Thandika, 44
Mount Saint Vincent's University, 190–1
Mozambique
   Community Development Foundation (FDC), 145–6
   electoral process project, 143–4
   Family Law, 148
   gender policies in government, 140
   languages, 150
   liberation struggle, 137–8, 149–50
   NGOs, 147–8, 149
   WLSA project, 148–50

see also Universidade Eduardo Mondlane (UEM)
Muslim laws, 102–4, 194–5
Muthien, Bernedette, 75*n*32, 79

National Council of Women's Societies (NCWS), 192–3
neoliberalism, 205–6
NETSH (Network of Southern African Higher Education Institutions Challenging Sexual Harassment/Sexual Violence)
 Coordinating Committee, 64–5, 72–7
 evaluation, 75*n*32
 funding, 79
 membership, 72–4
 organisational history, 57, 62–71
 role, 72*n*, 77–8
 subjective narratives of rape, 18
networks, 18–20, 88–9, 179
 see also NETSH (Network of Southern African Higher Education Institutions Challenging Sexual Harassment/Sexual Violence); NWSN (Network for Women's Studies in Nigeria)
NGOs
 and local agendas, 15, 132–4
 Mozambique, 147–8, 149
 Nigeria, 192–5
 not necessarily altruistic, 43*n*
Nigeria
 Aba Women's War, 192
 abortion, 113–18
 BAOBAB, 194–5
 Better Life for Rural Women Programme (BLP), 195–6
 contraception, 118–20
 government machineries for women, 195–6
 National Commission for Women (NCW), 196

National Committee on Women and Development, 195
National Council of Women's Societies (NCWS), 192–3
NGOs and women's issues, 192–5
racial groupings, 83–4
university linkage programme, 190–1
university system, 84–6
Women in Nigeria (WIN), 131–2, 193–4, 200
women's healthcare, 14–15, 112–13, 126–7, 128–9, 131–2
women's studies, 187, 188–92
see also Ahmadu Bello University; NWSN (Network for Women's Studies in Nigeria)
Nigerian Women Mobilized (Mba), 189
NORAD (Norwegian Agency for Development Cooperation), 143–4
Nordic Africa Institute, 100
NWSN (Network for Women's Studies in Nigeria)
 aims, 89–90, 191
 funding, 24–5, 93–5
 lack of institutional base, 92–4
 membership, 91–2
 sexual harassment research proposal, 96–100, 192
 workshops and activities, 92, 93, 191–2
Nzeako, Ifeyinwa, 192

Ogbudinkpa, Reuben, 189
Okonjo, Kamene, 189
Oloka-Onyango, Joseph, 176, 177
Omideyi, A.K., 188
Osirim, Mary, 42–3, 45, 47

patriarchy, 158, 211
Pereira, Charmaine, 17, 25, 173, 174–5, 177, 188, 219–20
population control, 119
Population Council, 25

Population and Development Conference (1994), 14, 120–1
postmodern feminism, 217–18
poverty, 42*n*
Prah, Mansah, 36
psychosocial problems, women academics, 159, 171–2, 175–7
publication, 41–2, 54, 198

racism, 55–6, 61*n17*
Ramphele, Mamphela, 63, 71, 99
rape, 18, 59–60, 62
Rape Crisis Centre, 52–3
religion
  and women's rights, 15–16
  see also Christianity; Jesus Christ
reproductive rights, 14–15, 115–17, 124–5, 128–9
research
  and activism, 17–18, 86, 201
  feminist research, 6–7, 34-36, 55–6, 151–4
  importance of, 35–6
  need for African emphasis, 30
  North-South collaboration, 40–3
  policy-oriented, 39
  see also consultancy work; women academics
research funding *see* funding
Rich, Adrienne, *Lies, Secrets and Silences*, 55
rights discourse, 14–16, 121–5, 209–10, 212–13

Saadawi, Nawaal el, 205
Sadza, Hope, 69
Sardien, Tony, 69–70
Save the Children Fund, 44–5
Sen, Gita, 13–14
sexism, and sexual harassment, 66
sexual discrimination, 183–4
  Ghana, 160–5, 179–80
  United States, 166–8

sexual harassment
  link to sexism, 66
  NWSN pilot study, 192
  personal experiences, 64
  seen as normal in universities, 95, 176
  in universities, 60–2, 66, 79, 95–9, 168–9
  women not destroyed by, 80
  see also NETSH (Network of Southern African Higher Education Institutions Challenging Sexual Harassment/Sexual Violence); rape
sexual pleasure, 16–17, 199–200
Sexual Politics (Millett), 55
sexual violence *see* rape; sexual harassment
Sharia laws, 194–5
  see also Muslim laws
Solomon, Collette, 59–60
South Africa
  gender mainstreaming, 207–9, 211–12
  Women's National Coalition (WNC), 207–8
  women's rights, 209–10
  women's studies, 213–14
  see also University of Cape Town (UCT)
Swiss Research Fund, 145

Tamale, Sylvia, 176, 177
Tlou, Sheila, 60, 62
Touraine, Alan, 220
Tsikata, Dzodzi, 40

UEM *see* Universidade Eduardo Mondlane (UEM)
United Nations
  Convention on the Elimination of All Forms of Discrimination against Women (CEDAW), 212
  Decade for Women, 187, 189
  and feminist agendas, 13

Population and Development Conference (1994), 14, 120–1
United States, universities, 166–9
Universidade Eduardo Mondlane (UEM)
 Centre of African Studies (CEA), 137–8, 142
 Department of Women and Gender Studies (DEMEG), 142–8
 Nucleus for Women's Studies (NEM), 142
 research on women, 141–2
 seminars, 146–7
universities
 corporatisation of, 175
 gender teaching, 146, 213–15
 linkage programmes, 19–20, 24–5, 92, 105–6, 190–1
 low work ethic of staff, 86
 problems, 171
 sexual harassment in, 60–2, 66, 79, 95–9, 168–9
 women in administration, 36–8, 159–60, 176
University of Benin, 189
University of Botswana
 1997 Gaborone Conference, 65–8
 sexual harassment in, 60, 62
University of Cape Coast, 36, 160–5, 179–80
University of Cape Town (UCT)
 1994 Conference, 62–4
 African Gender Institute, 47, 58–9, 74, 75*n*3, 76, 198
 sexual harassment in, 60–2
 student base, 61*n*17
University of Ghana
 Centre for Gender Studies and Advocacy (CEGENSA), 20, 24, 40–1, 47, 48–9
 female academic staff, 36–8
University of Ibadan
 Institute of African Studies, 189–90
 Women's Research and Documentation Centre (WORDOC), 190

University of the Western Cape (UWC), sexual harassment, 59–60, 62
University of Zimbabwe, 2000 Conference, 68–71

WIN (Women in Nigeria), 131–2, 193–4, 200
WLSA (Women and Law in Southern Africa), 20–1, 144–5, 148–50
WLUML (Women Living Under Muslim Laws), 102–4
Wolf, Naomi, 213
women
 and Christianity, 32–3
 employment constraints, 189–90
 invisibility of work, 44
 marginalised in development projects, 178
 maternal mortality, 112–13
 and political office, 193
 victim feminism, 213
women academics
 'chilly climate', 170, 173–4
 collaborative encounters, 40–1
 as dodos, 157*n*, 170
 invisibility, 36, 167
 low pay, 34–5, 171
 multiple roles, 31, 37, 158, 172
 psychosocial and intellectual problems, 159, 171–2, 175–7
 self-awareness, 29–30, 56, 102–4
 support structures, 37–8, 165
 see also universities
Women and Development (WAD), 10
Women in Development (WID), 10, 178
Women and Law in Southern Africa (WLSA), 20–1, 144–5, 148–50
Women Living Under Muslim Laws (WLUML), 102–4
Women in Nigeria (WIN), 131–2, 193–4, 200
women's rights
 Nigeria, 193–5
 and religion, 15–16

reproductive, 14–15, 115–17, 128–9
South Africa, 209–10
women's studies
  considered frivolous, 172
  curricula, 178, 197–8
  definition, 187–8
  dissemination and publication, 41–2, 54, 198
  and employment prospects, 197, 214
  institutional structures, 90–1, 197–8
  professionalisation of, 216–17
  replaced by gender studies, 215–16
  successes, 179
WORDOC (Women's Research and Documentation Centre), 190
World Bank, 23

Yeboa, Kweku, 44–5

Zeleza, Paul, 175, 178
Zimbabwe, NETSH Conference, 68–71

www.ingramcontent.com/pod-product-compliance
Lightning Source LLC
Chambersburg PA
CBHW050205230526
45470CB00001B/242